Praise for Roger Cohen's

The Girl from Human Street

"Exquisite. . . . [Cohen] writes with a poetic fragility . . . always striving for moral clarity, even when his own inner contradictions and complexities impede him."　　—*The Jerusalem Post*

"Brave, honorable and enlightened."
　　　　　　　　　　—*The Daily Telegraph* (London)

"I am moved by this book. I find fascinating the fusion of the private, even intimate family story with the history of European Jews in the twentieth century, the marriage of a subtle memoir with an essay on Jewish identity, tradition, and assimilation, various diasporas and Israel, Israelis and Palestinians, humanism vs. fanaticism."　　　　　　　　　　—Amos Oz

"Impressive. . . . [Cohen's] moving, beautifully written book may be a 'story of the twentieth century,' but it also explores how Jewish identity might evolve in the twenty-first."
　　　　　　—Ian Critchley, *The Sunday Times* (London)

"A moving, complex story that traces a family's century of migration."　　　　　　　　　　—*Financial Times*

"By tracing where his mother came from, Cohen, the Jewish runaway, speaks universally in this disarmingly raw narrative, and his lovely but haunted mother even more so—not least in her refusal to give up trying to love." —*The Guardian* (London)

Roger Cohen

The Girl from Human Street

Roger Cohen is a columnist for *The New York Times*, where he has worked since 1990, first as a correspondent in Paris and Berlin, then as bureau chief in the Balkans, covering the Bosnian War (for which he received an Overseas Press Club Award). He was named a columnist in 2009. He became foreign editor on 9/11, overseeing Pulitzer Prize–winning coverage in the aftermath of the attack. His columns appear twice a week, on Tuesdays and Fridays. His previous books include *Soldiers and Slaves* and *Hearts Grown Brutal*. He lives in New York City.

The Girl from Human Street

The Girl from Human Street

A JEWISH FAMILY ODYSSEY

Roger Cohen

Vintage Books
A Division of Penguin Random House LLC
New York

FIRST VINTAGE BOOKS EDITION, DECEMBER 2015

The Library of Congress has catalogued the Knopf edition as follows:
Cohen, Roger.
The girl from Human Street : a Jewish family odyssey / Roger Cohen.
— First edition.
pages cm
Includes bibliographical references and index.
1. Cohen, Roger—Family.   2. Jews—Lithuania—Biography.
3. Holocaust, Jewish (1939–1945)—Lithuania—Biography.   I. Title.
DS135.L53 C54 2015   940.53'18092757'91aB 757'912 23   2014017900

Vintage Books Trade Paperback ISBN: 978-0-307-74141-7
eBook ISBN: 978-0-385-35313-7

Author photograph © Rebecca Ring
Book design by Maggie Hinders

www.vintagebooks.com

For my father, Sydney Cohen
And to the memory of my mother, June

"It's a poor sort of memory that only works backwards."

—LEWIS CARROLL, *Through the Looking Glass*

Set your flag at half mast,
memory.
At half mast
today and for ever.

—PAUL CELAN, *Shibboleth*

"When people go to Johannesburg, they do not come back."

—ALAN PATON, *Cry, the Beloved Country*

Contents

Family Tree

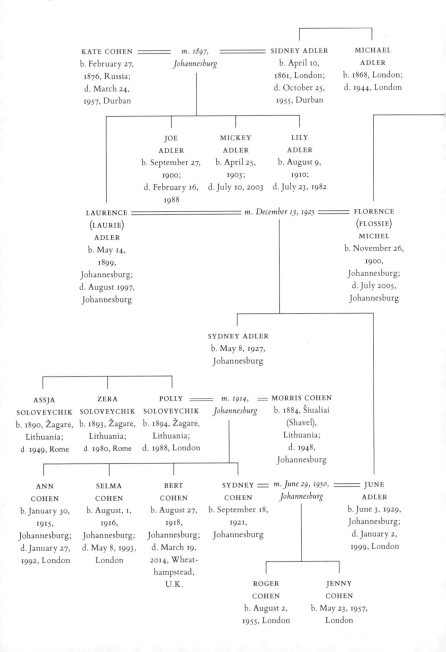

KATE COHEN
b. February 27,
1876, Russia;
d. March 24,
1957, Durban

═══ *m. 1897,*
Johannesburg ═══

SIDNEY ADLER
b. April 10,
1861, London;
d. October 25,
1955, Durban

**MICHAEL
ADLER**
b. 1868, London;
d. 1944, London

**JOE
ADLER**
b. September 27,
1900;
d. February 16,
1988

**MICKEY
ADLER**
b. April 25,
1903;
d. July 10, 2003

**LILY
ADLER**
b. August 9,
1910;
d. July 23, 1982

**LAURENCE
(LAURIE)
ADLER**
b. May 14,
1899,
Johannesburg;
d. August 1997,
Johannesburg

═══ *m. December 13, 1925* ═══

**FLORENCE
(FLOSSIE)
MICHEL**
b. November 26,
1900,
Johannesburg;
d. July 2005,
Johannesburg

SYDNEY ADLER
b. May 8, 1927,
Johannesburg

**ASSJA
SOLOVEYCHIK**
b. 1890, Žagarė,
Lithuania;
d. 1949, Rome

**ZERA
SOLOVEYCHIK**
b. 1893, Žagarė,
Lithuania;
d. 1980, Rome

**POLLY
SOLOVEYCHIK**
b. 1894, Žagarė,
Lithuania;
d. 1988, London

═══ *m. 1914,*
Johannesburg ═══

MORRIS COHEN
b. 1884, Šiualiai
(Shavel),
Lithuania;
d. 1948,
Johannesburg

**ANN
COHEN**
b. January 30,
1915,
Johannesburg;
d. January 27,
1992, London

**SELMA
COHEN**
b. August, 1,
1916,
Johannesburg;
d. May 8, 1993,
London

**BERT
COHEN**
b. August 27,
1918,
Johannesburg;
d. March 19,
2014, Wheat-
hampstead,
U.K.

**SYDNEY
COHEN**
b. September 18,
1921,
Johannesburg

═══ *m. June 29, 1950,*
Johannesburg ═══

**JUNE
ADLER**
b. June 3, 1929,
Johannesburg;
d. January 2,
1999, London

**ROGER
COHEN**
b. August 2,
1955, London

**JENNY
COHEN**
b. May 23, 1957,
London

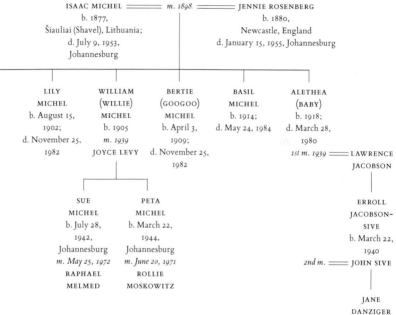

ISAAC MICHEL ══════ *m. 1898.* ══════ JENNIE ROSENBERG
b. 1877,   b. 1880,
Šiauliai (Shavel), Lithuania;   Newcastle, England
d. July 9, 1953,   d. January 15, 1955, Johannesburg
Johannesburg

LILY   WILLIAM   BERTIE   BASIL   ALETHEA
MICHEL   (WILLIE)   (GOOGOO)   MICHEL   (BABY)
b. August 15,   MICHEL   MICHEL   b. 1914;   b. 1918;
1902;   b. 1905   b. April 3,   d. May 24, 1984 d. March 28,
d. November 25,   *m. 1939*   1909;   1980
1982   JOYCE LEVY   d. November 25,   *1st m. 1939* ══ LAWRENCE
                                   1982   JACOBSON

         SUE   PETA   ERROLL
       MICHEL   MICHEL   JACOBSON-
     b. July 28,   b. March 22,   SIVE
        1942,   1944,   b. March 22,
    Johannesburg   Johannesburg   1940
  m. May 25, 1972   *m. June 20, 1971*   *2nd m.* ══ JOHN SIVE
     RAPHAEL   ROLLIE
     MELMED   MOSKOWITZ   JANE
                                                                          DANZIGER
                                                                        b. February 26,
                                                                             1944

The Girl from Human Street

CHAPTER I

Circle of Disquiet

The promontory of Bellagio tapers to the Punta Spartivento, the point where the wind divides. I stand at its tip watching bright cumulus clouds puff over the ridges into a still blue Italian sky. Ferries of unromantic doggedness plow their zigzag white furrows across the water. Cypresses, aligned like sentries, cast their shade over shuttered villas of pale pink and ocher. I look north to Dongo, where Mussolini was captured, and beyond to the snowcapped peaks where Italians by the tens of thousands starved above the tree line during World War I. To the southeast lies Lecco, and to the southwest, Como. The water is clear and the peace abundant at the confluence of the three-limbed lake. Europe has long since quieted itself after its suicidal convulsions. Not a breath of wind stirs at the division of the winds.

Yet I find myself uneasy. Calm surrounds me but eludes me. A journalist's life is agitation. What brings me of a sleepy afternoon to a place where the bells of Bellagio toll the hours and the half hours is a whispered admonition: "Stop!" I have grown suspicious that all the running in my peripatetic life might not have been toward something but *away* from something. Stillness feels like the most dangerous state of all.

My life has been spent crossing lines, gazing at the same picture from different angles in order to evoke it. The journalist moves in the opposite direction from the crowd, toward danger, often leaving the settled majority perplexed. Why, people ask, do you do that? In search of a fair understanding, you say, and they shake their heads. There is nothing to understand, they insist, just write the truth!

But truths are many, and that is the problem. Memory is treacherous, as distinct from history as emotion from form. Every war is fought over memory. Violent nationalism is revived memory manipulated as revealed truth.

Conflict is incubated in the contested "truths" the past bequeaths. Questions swirl: Who came first to the land? Who planted the millennial olive trees? Who killed whom first? Does the church predate the mosque? What of the synagogue that may precede them both? The slaughter on that dusty plain where skulls were piled has never been avenged nor set on the scales of justice. As for the rape of the daughters of the house, it will not be forgiven until the last tree withers.

Identities are assembled piece by piece. Each drop of blood shed, each shrapnel scar on a wall, each land grab, is annotated in the Book of Unforgiving. In the Middle East, the events of a thousand years past can seem as vivid as yesterday's, their poison undiluted. The enemy imperatives of Arab and Jew demand that memory, like the fuse for a bomb, be shaped for maximum explosive effect. Truces last no longer than a cheap umbrella in a storm.

The river of discord runs on. Its tributaries are fed by the fashioning of myth. So, with reluctance, I have concluded that the only truth I can know is my own. However small, it is mine. Being a Jewish story of the twentieth century, it bears upon migration and displacement and suicide and persecution and assimilation. It also recounts bravery, a passionate quest for learning, obstinate love, and the pursuit of beauty. From Lithuania and then South Africa, the family path winds on through Britain to Israel and the United States. Joseph Brodsky wrote: "If there is any substitute for love, it's memory. To memorize, then, is to restore intimacy." The restoration of intimacy is more than an act of love; it is an attempt, by writing down a lost world before it dissolves, to bring memory closer to truth.

It has taken me a long time to piece all this together. Memories come not like heavy rain but like the drops falling from leaves after it. There were elements missing. At last I knew I would not be whole until I found them.

On May 7, 1945, my uncle, Capt. Bert Cohen of the Dental Unit of the Sixth South African Armored Division, Nineteenth Field Ambulance, made the following entry in his war diary:

> After lunch Hilton Barber lent me his jeep and I scudded away on a delightful jaunt. We traveled through twisting country byways until the town of Monza. There we followed route 36 northward to Lecco. As we bypassed the town we got our first view of the famous Alpine lakes . . . an azure strip of unbelievable blue flanked by great mountains. . . . We passed through several icy tunnels and the beauty of the scene grew more breathtaking as we neared Bella-gio, a wonderful village nestling in the fork of the lake beneath the majestic mountains. . . . A drove of little boys clambered onto the jeep, an incredible number appeared from all over the place. At one stage Wilson counted 21 of them on the jeep. Bellagio was indeed delightful. It was while there that we heard that the war was over, a report that was subsequently verified as we drove on down Lake Como to Como. . . . All along the road from Bellagio throngs had lined each village street and flowers in profusion had been tossed into the jeep.

So, in Bellagio, right here, feted by children and flowers, my uncle's war ended. "GUERRA FINITA!!!"—"WAR OVER!!!"—he exulted in his diary. He was twenty-six and far from home. As a young dentistry graduate from the University of the Witwatersrand, he had enlisted in Johannesburg on January 15, 1943. After training, he flew by stages to Egypt to join the Allies' North African campaign. From there, in April 1944, he embarked for Italy, on the lowest deck, landing in Taranto, near the heel of Italy's boot. Churchill had called Italy "the soft underbelly of the Axis," but resistance to the Allied assault was stern. Bert's progress northward through Naples, Rome, and Florence to Bellagio was no sunlit Italian *passeggiata*. The winter of 1944 was spent encamped high in the freezing Apennines facing a German line stretching across the country from Pisa to Rimini. He filled teeth in freezing, improvised dental surgeries.

I spent a busy morning. After lunch H.B. very kindly lent me his jeep & I scudded away on a delightful jaunt with Arthur, Norris & Wilson. We travelled through terrific country always until the town of Monza we are followed Route 36 northwards to Lecco. As we bypassed this town we got our first view of the famous Alpine Lakes. Lake Lecco stretched before us, a square strip of unbelievable blue flanked by great mountains & tapering to the foot of a snow mottled monarch. The road wound along the lower slopes of the verdant mountain about 100 feet above the limpid water. We passed thro' several tiny tunnels & the beauty of the scene grew more breathtaking as we neared Bellagio, a wonderful village nestling in the fork of Lake Lecco & Lake Como beneath the majestic mountains. We walked thro' the scrupulously clean cobbled streets of the village & visited some of its little shops there. I bought some quaint paper knives for my collection. In Bellagio a droll of the boys clambered on to jeep. An incredible number of people from all over the place shrieking with joy! At one stage Wilson counted 21 of them on the jeep! Bellagio was indeed delightful. It was here that we heard that the war was over, a report that was subsequently verified. We drove on down Lake Como to Como. The magnificence of the scenery along this drive had to be seen to be believed. In Como we found crowded streets, excited townsfolk, German soldiers. All along the road from

My uncle Bert's exultant entry in his war diary for May 7, 1945:
"GUERRA FINITA!!!"—"WAR OVER!!!"

Bert had to battle through the German lines. At Finale Emilia, north of Modena, on April 24, 1945, he was ordered into a bend in the Penaro River where a Nazi column was trapped. *Skiet gemors*— Shoot the garbage—was a rough guide to his Afrikaner commander's battle code. An artillery battery pulverized the enclave. Wrecked vehicles smoldered. Wounded horses, nostrils flared in gasping horror, bayed—a terrible sound. In the carnage, ammunition exploded and tires burst. The stench of roasted flesh and putrefaction pervaded the air. Intestines of gutted animals ballooned from their carcasses. A squad of South African infantry marched through the ruins, bringing a bullet of mercy to animals that still agonized. One dead German in particular caught Bert's eye: a blond, square-jawed young man with a long straight nose, hair flecked with blood and smoke, legs twisted grotesquely, abdomen ripped open, coils of gut spilling through a ragged gash into the dust, sightless blue eyes gazing at infinity. Beside the corpse lay scattered letters from the soldier's mother in Hamburg. She wrote about *Der Angriff,* the Allied bombardment of the city that killed more than 42,000 people. Uncertain what to do, Bert returned the letters to the dead man's pocket before grabbing a few ampoules of morphine found in an abandoned, ammunition-filled German ambulance.

That single German corpse among the more than 600,000 casualties of the Italian campaign haunted my uncle for the rest of his life. Bert dwelt on him as if this death were his responsibility, or as if he, a Jew from South Africa, might somehow have brought this handsome young man, Hitler's model Aryan, back to the life denied him. The dead man inhabited his dreams. Bert thought that he should have kept the letters, for some reason, perhaps to return them to a bereaved mother in Hamburg. He was a link in a circle that never closed.

Bellagio also marked him. He returned four days after his first visit, on May 11, 1945, and was billeted for a week in the magnificent Villa Gerly, on the banks of the lake. His diary records a lunch that day at Silvio's restaurant. "We lunched sumptuously on fresh trout and fresh butter," Bert wrote. "Such food was so novel and so exciting to our palates long jaded by M and V that I for one ate far too much." Canned meat and vegetables (M and V), tasting of neither, were the staple military diet. After lunch Bert dozed off on the grass, a siesta troubled only by ants. In the late afternoon he decided to go for a swim:

> We rowed out into the middle of the lake and there I plunged in. The water was icy cold a few feet below the surface. About halfway I realized I had overestimated my swimming ability and underestimated the distance. The swim turned into a horrifying ordeal. I was fighting panic, not with complete success. It is one thing to be able to take a grip if you can stop and weigh up the situation but quite another if you can't stop to collect your calm. I couldn't stop. It would have been better to have doggy paddled and relaxed but driving panic made my haste frantic. I was exhausted when I reached the shore. My heart was pounding and my head was bursting with pain. It was quite the most unnerving and terrifying experience I have had since I left home.

In this way, four days after the end of the war, Captain Cohen almost lost his life in Bellagio. He would have gone out in a sumptuous manner, after a lunch of delicious fish, in the midst of a beautiful lake, beneath the mountains, a few hundred yards from the Punta Spartivento. It is a good thing, however, that he did not encounter a watery North Italian grave. What a waste, people would have said, to die when the war was over. As if the war being over made any difference to the waste and the grief. The thing about life's chains, and the lines of memory that eddy along them, is you never know when they may get broken—in a mountainous trench, on a bend in the river, or three hundred meters down in a sunlit lake after a good lunch celebrating peace.

———

Europe was a return journey. My paternal family had left the imperial Russian province of Kovno, in what is now Lithuania, a half century earlier. From faraway South Africa had filtered accounts of sunlight and ostrich feathers, diamonds and gold, space and opportunity on the high veld. Set against the drab Russian winter and the anti-Semitic tribulations of the Pale of Settlement, this prospect was enticing.

The decision to leave proved prescient. Shavli, or Shavel, now the

Lithuanian town of Šiauliai, was home to almost ten thousand Jews, or 75 percent of the population, when, in 1896, my grandfather Morris Cohen departed for South Africa. About eight thousand Jews were still there in 1939 at the outbreak of World War II, active in the leather and shoe industries, working as laborers and craftsmen, attending several synagogues. They, and thousands of others who came there as refugees from points farther west during the first two years of the war, would be wiped out. Starting on July 18, 1941, the Jews were herded into a ghetto. Many thousands did not get that far: they were driven into the forests and shot at the mouths of pits they had been made to dig themselves. The Nazi *Einsatzgruppen,* abetted by Lithuanian collaborators, massacred them in droves. The Jews of Lithuania were killed fast and killed locally.

A handful of survivors of the ghetto, closed down on July 24, 1944, were driven westward by the retreating Germans. The men were thrown into the Dachau concentration camp, where, already weakened by years of confinement and the long death march into Hitler's heartland, most of them met a skeletal end.

A photograph of Jews in the Šiauliai ghetto shows a dozen men standing to attention against a concrete wall in front of two Nazi soldiers with their backs to the camera. The Jews have their jackets buttoned, a straining for some scrap of dignity. There is defiance in certain eyes, resignation in others, fear, bewilderment. The faceless menace of the Nazis has a gleam about it. A helmet gleams; leather belts gleam; a rifle gleams; the knee-high black boots into which their breeches are tucked gleam. This is the brilliant surface of an ideology whose murderous progress has extinguished every human stain.

That might have been the end of the line, nameless in a nameless ditch in the depths of a birch forest, dispatched by the Reich's executioners and their Lithuanian accomplices. It is possible to die without a trace.

Matters took much the same course in the village of Žagarė (Zhager in Yiddish), twenty-nine miles north of Šiauliai, close to the present Latvian border. My grandmother Pauline ("Polly") Soloveychik left Žagarė for South Africa in 1906, a decade after Morris Cohen. A massacre of at least 2,250 Jews in the Žagarė market square and surrounding woods would take place in October 1941.

Nazi soldiers terrorizing Jews in the wartime ghetto at Šiauliai, my grandfather's birthplace   THE GHETTO FIGHTERS' HOUSE MUSEUM/ISRAEL/THE PHOTO ARCHIVE

By the end of that month—well before the Nazis' Wannsee Conference in January 1942, when the "Final Solution" was formalized—the centennial Jewish presence in Lithuania had been shattered. Of a population of a little over 200,000 at the start of World War II, the majority had been slaughtered, many of them in villages and the surrounding woods with the help of zealous locals. The gas chambers relieved the emotional strain on Nazi executioners who had cut down tens of thousands of women and children at the edge of pits or in village squares.

Soloveychik, in Russian, means "nightingale." When asked his mother's maiden name, my father would always respond: "Nightingale." The nightingale had flown the nest.

She alighted in Johannesburg. Polly and Morris were married there in 1914. Four children, two girls and two boys, followed in seven years.

The last of them was my father, Sydney Cohen, born on September 18, 1921. He wrote these "fragmented memories" of his first home on the gold ridge running east to west through the nascent city:

> Our house at 88 Honey Street, Berea, was commissioned by my Dad shortly before he married Mum. Johannesburg at that time was a burgeoning town, younger than most of its inhabitants, arisen from a hectic mining camp and set among flat-topped, yellowing mine dumps. The main gold reef of the Witwatersrand had been discovered in 1884 and two years later the township of Johannesburg, which boasted a thrusting population of four thousand, was proclaimed. Carts and wagons from Barberton, Kimberley and even further afield lumbered along convergent dusty roads loaded with building materials and elementary mining machinery. By 1914 the original shantytown had acquired the trappings of urban order and a population close to 100,000. The most desirable suburb, originally Doornfontein, had edged progressively over Hospital Hill to Hillbrow and Berea and spread to the commanding ridge of Parktown.

Please sit for a moment, will you, in the middle of the yard at 88 Honey Street, in the shade of the peppercorn tree with a gnarled old trunk, under the pendulous olive-green leaves hiding white flowers that, in every season, produced a succession of peppercorns, small and green at first, turning to bright red. Sit on the sturdy wooden seat of the swing suspended from metal arms that might, in spasms of excitement, propel you as high as the top of the red water tank, or lull you, in moments of contemplation, with a rhythmic swaying. Listen to the sounds: the crowing of the cock as the dawn breaks; the frequent afternoon thunderstorms in summer; the rain beating against the red corrugated iron roof of the one-story house and rushing from the gutters into that mysterious tank; the clucking of two dozen hens lorded over by the cock in the wire-fronted henhouse against the neighbors' fence, pecking and scraping in pursuit of scatterings of corn, or squawking in terror if picked for the Sunday roast; pickaxes rising and falling in unison in the street outside to a haunting Zulu chorus as a trench the length of the block is laid by a phalanx of black convicts and filled with brown earthenware sewage pipes whose arrival marks the demise of the bucket privy in the yard; the resounding clatter of coal being unloaded from sacks into the store next to the garage; the sizzling of the kosher sausages for Saturday lunch; the creaking of wooden wagons drawn by blazing-eyed mules with nostrils flared, the cries of street vendors, and the churn and thud of construction as the great, restive mining city spreads over the hill onto the high plateau.

Watch from that seat in the shade of the peppercorn tree as Mac and Daisy, the black staff, go about their domestic duties, he compact and lithe and bare-chested, she ample in a bright floral cotton dress with a head scarf wound tight and knotted at her neck where beads of sweat form. Mac clamps the chosen hen under a garbage can lid, head and neck protruding. Knife in hand, he proceeds with a swift decapitation. Once in a while a bird escapes and manages a brief weaving, headless sprint. Mac plucks the bird. He kindles a wood fire in the yard to burn away feathery remnants. The smoke mixes with the waft of Morris's Loyalist cigarettes, oval-shaped in cross section and made from Turkish tobacco.

Follow Daisy inside as she dusts and cleans. She prepares the chicken. She moves with a lively grace across the *stoep,* or veranda, where flowers tended by Polly cascade. Mystery accompanies Daisy, a smile that hides something. Wander, as my father was occasionally allowed to do, into Mac's concrete-floored, low-roofed, single-windowed sleeping quarters in the yard, an enclave of faint menace. Mac has a sideline as the local medicine man. My father contemplates the throwing of the bones. First they are shaken in a rough linen bag. Then, to the accompaniment of Mac's rhythmic chant, they are spilled onto the bare floor. Mac, a hunched figure, assumes an air of such intensity that the child sees the bones tremble. Mac snaps the long forefingers of his clasped black hands. What message the trembling bones convey remains an enigma. The child, trembling himself, learns to snap his forefingers but not to decipher meaning in the fragments. That is Mac's ancient shamanic secret, a mystery to the city's ingenuous white prospectors.

Morris works with little respite. Cohen & Sons, established in Johannesburg by his father, Shmuel, as the twentieth century dawned, opened its doors at 103 Pritchard Street, a downtown wholesale grocery selling local produce and goods imported from England. Anything from Britain had my grandfather's approval. It was the home of liberty and liberal thought. Opposite was a motor accessories shop owned by a Barry Cohen, who changed his name to Colne.

Business gets done item by item, guinea by guinea. Orders are delivered on a trolley, or wagon, pulled by six mules kept behind the store and tended by Elias, hat always perched on the back of his head. Morris is busy. When he and Polly have something to hide, they speak in Yiddish: *Red nich vor die Kinder*—Don't talk in front of the children. The code conceals secrets. It is freighted with something, a topic in the background, the European past. In this past lurks anxiety, something carried over. It is a good life but a worried life on Honey Street. Precariousness lingers. It is about more than money. It is the puzzle of belonging, a quandary borne around the globe.

Deep within the earth a vibration stirs. Tremors follow a rockfall. What is the unceasing throbbing in the soil? Thousands of feet beneath the ground, frenzied activity underwrites the growth of Johannesburg. The city spreads on the surface because of the rich seams below it. The heart, arteries, and ligaments of the metropolis reside at the bottom of shafts. Drills and scrapers and hammering and falling ore fuse in the cacophony of an underground labyrinth with its murky sumps. Black workers flock to the city the Zulus call eGoli—City of Gold. They provide much of the labor force at the white-owned mines, crawling along narrow gullies to extract gold from the reef that keeps giving. This is no land without a people waiting for a people without a land, as Lord Shaftesbury suggested in 1853—with equal heedlessness and onerous consequence—of Palestine and the Jews. Out of Africa's immense horizons come Africans in search of a living wage.

At night the workers are housed in hostels and squatters' camps on the outskirts of the city. They sleep ten to a room on concrete bunks in bleak dormitories far from Honey Street and still farther from the mansions of the gold barons and the British colonial administrators. Denied the right to form unions, they come as contract labor. It is this separation and exploitation that will be codified after World War II by the Afrikaner-dominated National Party into the system of white domination and racial segregation called apartheid. Racist hatred, defeated in 1945 in the ruins of Berlin, found new expression in the "Bantustans" created in South Africa in 1948. Blacks, shorn of dignity, were to be the human raw material of South African growth.

Two months after his Bellagio sojourn, Capt. Bert Cohen found himself in Padua, in the Po Valley. It was August 24, 1945. A Rabbi Podashnik, attached to South African forces, invited him to visit a refugee camp. Bert's diary records the following:

> Among the many thousands there were 950 Jews. These were the people we visited. They lived in a large room, sleeping side by side on the stone floor. No beds, few blankets. Their possessions were wrapped in small bundles. Many struck me as being less human than animal. My companion took out his cigarette case and the scramble that ensued appalled me. Many of these people are starved and stunted. Why do they cling so preciously to life? Is it so important to stay alive that one should surrender everything, succumb to any humiliation, in order to preserve the precious spark? I looked at their eyes and sometimes I saw ugliness. Sorrow elicits sympathy, but I saw more than sorrow. I saw cunning and slyness and hatred too, for was I not well dressed and well fed? I did not feel drawn to these unfortunate people. Instead I was repelled. I could not feel that they were kith and kin of mine. This worried me and I felt ashamed.

Extreme suffering engenders revulsion. Bert felt what Saul Bellow would call the "sense of personal contamination and aversion" engendered by the "disintegrating bodies" of the survivors of the Nazi camps. He hated himself for it. He felt shame but could summon no sympathy. The humiliated Jew was a pathetic figure, his humanity shredded. As Joseph Roth observed, "No one loves victims, not even their fellow victims." Israel arose to consign that figure to the past.

Podashnik told Bert these survivors of the Holocaust had come from Dachau. Bert could not have known to what degree the bedraggled Jews scrambling on that Italian concrete floor were indeed "kith and kin of mine." He could not have known then that the few Jewish ghetto survivors of his father's Lithuanian hometown, Šiauliai, had been marched by the Nazis to Dachau in 1944. A circle had been closed.

Life consists of what is but also of what might have been. What happens only just happens; then inevitability is conferred upon it. Sometimes the hypothetical meets reality in the mirror, and the confrontation is intolerable. Those Jews on an Italian concrete floor in 1945 might have included my grandfather. Dreams complete pictures the conscious mind will only half-acknowledge.

It was Jean-Luc Godard who remarked that a movie should have a beginning, a middle, and an end but not necessarily in that order. So it has been with my family. Like Chagall's fiddlers, we have been looking in various directions at once.

My parents were South African immigrants in postwar Britain, part of the great transcontinental reflux from retreating empire. Their priority was assimilation in a country of shrinking ambitions but enduring pretensions. Jewishness was the minor key of their identity. They were not about to change their name, a move urged on my father by a concerned relative back in Johannesburg and met with the retort that the only alternative to Cohen that he would entertain was "Einstein"! Nor, however, were they about to rock the boat.

Dispatched to learn Hebrew at Johannesburg's Yeoville synagogue in 1933, in preparation for his bar mitzvah, and having retained from that experience only a couple of Hebrew phrases, my father reached England with scant inclination to inflict such instruction on me. To the quest for assimilation was added distaste for the Jewish experience insofar as he had lived it. He was inclined toward the silence, or at least discretion, shared by many Jews—whether Holocaust survivors or not—in the postwar years. There was after Auschwitz something shameful about survival that no Jew could abjure. The horror went latent for a long period after Nuremberg. Better to look forward, work hard, say little, and confine protest to shunning German cars.

A cultural and spiritual vacuum resulted from this attempt to begin again with the mark and scar of each generational upheaval effaced. England was embraced as if we had always had it. We lived as if we had always taken tea and Jaffa Cakes at four o'clock in the afternoon and always bought the chicken for our Sunday roast at the supermarket. We came from South Africa and nowhere. Industrious and circum-

The synagogue in the Yeoville district of Johannesburg where my father
had his bar mitzvah in 1934. All he recalled from long study was the Hebrew for
"Go down from your bed and run to the House of the Book."

THE ARCHIVES—SOUTH AFRICA JEWISH BOARD OF DEPUTIES

spect, we adopted habits of silence that cloaked the fortuitousness of our deliverance. There were no screams in my garden suburb other than those issuing from my imagination.

The London house stood halfway up a hill, a solid redbrick affair with a large back garden steadily embellished by my father's deft hand. It was acquired when I was six. A cable, dated December 21, 1961, to family in South Africa expressed joy and gratitude at its purchase: "Greenaway finalized. Everyone thrilled. Many thanks." Here was an anchor at last in the English fog. Ice-blue hydrangea and luxuriant rhododendron spread along one wall. Along another, red, pink, and vanilla-yellow roses grew in bright abundance. My father mowed the lawn in straight up-and-down swaths, with the grass in one swath at the opposite angle to the adjacent one and so a different tone of green, one dill-pickle light, one pool-table dark. He would pause to detach the receptacle at the front of the mower and dispose of the cut grass on a compost heap in the far corner of the garden. The lawn, soft where it had been prickly in South Africa, was smooth enough to putt on. An ivy-clad stone birdhouse shaped like a small tower stood watch over this flourishing patch of London suburbia like a gray sentinel. Spring brought daffodils and tulips to the garden's wilder depths. A large bay tree of perennial green shaded a corner where caged hamsters and rabbits lived and died, usually rather fast. Beyond the flowers, against the picket fence, lay a ditch into which stray soccer and tennis balls would fall. In fear, knee-deep in the weeds and nettles, I would forage for them, swatting away the gnats. I played for hours, happy in the summer sunlight, shooting balls across the length of the grass into a goal constituted by the wooden legs of a bench. The only question in my mind then was which form of sporting glory would be mine.

We lived on the ground floor. Upstairs there was a tenant, an American Jew with a Mark Twain moustache and an elaborate aquarium that held pride of place. It was full of colorful, pouting fish and a jellyfish detonating silky orbs of light. He would be killed in an auto accident during the annus horribilis of 1978. An L-shaped corridor formed the axis of our floor, with my parents' bedroom at the tip of the long stem and my sister's and mine at the other end. It was impossible within that space to be farther apart. At the elbow of the hallway, tethered by a hook, was a heavy, fire-resistant door of ominous thickness. I would imagine it swinging shut and wonder where I would find the strength to reopen it. Between that door and my bedroom was the cellar, accessible by a staircase and housing a clangorous boiler, piles of suitcases, and assorted bric-a-brac. The cellar afforded, through rectangular breaches in the wall, glimpses into the tenebrous foundations of the house, recesses easily peopled with ghouls. These dark hideouts held a powerful fascination.

The house was proper. The red tiles at the entrance shone. The umbrella stand was always in its place. My father's snack, kosher salami on rye and a sliced gherkin, awaited him every evening on a dresser in the hall. Opposite the dresser was an alcove where the telephone sat on a shelf beneath net-curtained windows. "Hampstead-double-one-nine-five": my mother never modulated her greeting when she picked up.

The closet beside the phone contained a safe hidden behind a wooden panel with a hook on it. There was a "lounge," containing the best settees (not sofas) and rugs and bibelots, the silver Ronson table lighter (a de rigueur wedding gift in my parents' time), and a vintage soda siphon bottle. It was sealed at all times other than in the presence of guests, often friends of my mother who would come for tea. The door to my father's study was usually closed, penetrable only with trepidation. Immersed in his papers and his Brahms concertos, he was impatient with interruption, increasingly so with the years as frustration hardened him.

Family life was centered on the kitchen, where my mother's braised tongue sat in the pantry and we always had a good roast for Sunday lunch, and on the "playroom," where the furnishings were functional and the black-and-white television set did not give way to color until my late teens. In the lounge, over the fireplace, hung a good Dutch painting of a field of haystacks stretching away toward a small village with a church. The scene was bathed in a golden light. Its summer air shimmered with life. Everything in that flat, ordered Dutch countryside glowed. The earth was bountiful; surely the churchgoing folk who worked it were, too. I could not take my eyes off the scene. There was so little of that light where I lived. After South Africa, my mother never got used to London's dirty-bathwater skies and the dullness seeping from them. The sun might never have set on the British Empire, but it set early on Britain, and it rose late.

Her soft hands were cool. She craved heat. She would breathe heat in as voraciously as the smoke from her Rothmans cigarettes, their toffee-colored filters stained with her bright red lipstick. From the small pale blue cushions that she would rest her head on while reading in bed emanated the bittersweet scent of tobacco and Chanel. She was an avid reader. She was often in bed.

My mother wanted everything just so. She needed insurance against disorder. My father added a conservatory abutting the garage from which the garden he had created could be admired. He would sit there with a gin and tonic and admire it. There was no peppercorn tree, no clucking chickens in a coop, no tropical storms, and no Mac reading the bones of Africa in an outbuilding. No avocados dropped from trees. Things were tamer in the Northern Hemisphere. Twilights were longer, impossibly long. The day lingered, where it died in Africa like a guillotine dropping.

Colors muted themselves; the horizon closed in. But there was freedom. Apartheid corroded the soul. My father had arrived in London for the first time on May 18, 1945, a just-qualified doctor come to treat the war victims of a victorious nation at the brink of rapid imperial decline. He returned to South Africa in 1948, spent almost a decade going back and forth between the two countries, and then settled with my mother in England in 1957, when I was almost two.

In a greenhouse down near the ditch, tucked away in a corner, my father nursed to life cuttings he had brought from scientific trips to Gambia, Kenya, and other African countries. They flourished in big-leafed splendor and rich blooms. Often he gave cuttings to friends. Nothing he touched, nothing in the plant kingdom, ever withered. No graft failed to take. He had a touch inherited from his mother, Polly, who had wandered among the willows of Žagarė. He understood nature's mystery. A sensitive soul, alive to beauty, attuned to nature, resided within the stiffening carapace of his professionalism and what would become an increasingly divided life.

He was busy trying to rid the world of malaria, a demanding task setting human ingenuity against the endless adaptability of the tropical mosquito. I would ask about his efforts as he drove me to school. His responses left me perplexed. My mother tried to be busy—when inertia did not grip her. She hid her fragility as best she could. Children experience things they cannot express. I could never identify the nature of the loss, but I knew elements were missing from the domestic picture, so unblemished on the surface. Our past was a secret, not just the Jewish past of moving on to skirt horror, the transcontinental hopping, but some specific event. All the order was a shield against its recurrence. The locked doors were a bulkhead against the eruption of the uncontrollable.

In my bedroom at night, yellowish streetlights glinted through a mullioned window set high in the wall. Rain beat against the panes. Then it would begin: a high-pitched ringing just within the range of audible sound. The house always seemed vast. The hallway outside my room was too dark and too long to broach, and it ended at a closed door to my parents' bedroom. At most I might get a third of the way down the corridor, to the turning where the heavy door was hooked, before the sight of my parents' closed door and the murky distance to it turned me around.

Now as I shrank in my bed, the spaces grew bigger still. What if the heavy door at the L-shaped corridor's right angle, so like the door to a mental ward, had come off its latch and swung in slowly shrinking parabolas? The ringing rose to envelop me. This is what it feels like to be smothered by blankness. Hands clamped to my ears, limbs immovable, I would awaken and watch the rainwater drip down the windows. An occasional car, changing gears as it strained up the hill, projected shifting lozenges of light onto the ceiling.

My mother, fragrant in her floral dresses, always trim, desired a life as simple and colorful as her embroideries: Make Life a Garden, Friends the Flowers. She was tender. She was a perfectionist. Her South African childhood had been sun-filled, like the Cape watermelons, bright green as sugarcane, opening to yield their vermilion flesh; like the yellow Cape peaches, great firm golden orbs that crunched when bitten into.

She was born on Human Street in 1929. Human Street ran through Krugersdorp, a mining town near Johannesburg, where her father, Laurie Adler, was chief medical officer. Because she was born in June, she was called June. The name suited her. She was bright and full of laughter, small, just over five feet, with lovely pale skin perfect as a pearl, dark, thick bouncy curls, and cool hands. She liked to dance and sing. She was highly strung.

In London she could not have the jacaranda and the frangipani, the mimosa and the palms, the distant horizons and the warm breezes of her youth, but in our house on a hill, she tried to re-create some of that ease. Like those yellow peaches, unavailable in the Northern Hemisphere, she was not made to be lifted out of her environment. Her uprooting had been harsh: from privilege to the austerity of 1950s England, a nation spent by the war. That solid London house, with its familiar feel of the garden suburb, furnished some strand of continuity, a sanctuary. Because of this, she would never forgive herself for precipitating its loss.

June was the granddaughter of another Lithuanian immigrant, Isaac Michel, who had made good. Michel, like Morris Cohen, hailed from Šiauliai in northern Lithuania. They both left in 1896. My great-grandfather was one of the tens of thousands of Jews who streamed from the Pale of Settlement to South Africa between 1880 and 1914—a destination second only to the United States for Lithuanian Jews, or Litvaks. Michel had no formal education, could scarcely read or write, but he knew how to add and subtract. He could see business opportunities in gold-rush Johannesburg. Jews for once were on the right side of things: they were white. To be white was to be invested with automatic privilege. A large buffer against persecution existed: the blacks. Having a plentiful underclass of pariahs constituted protection for a people, the Jews, who were used to playing that role in Europe. Whatever qualms the blacks' troubles might stir—and they did, for they held up a mirror—were weighed against the inversion of roles that afforded Jews newly ushered from the shtetl a fragile sense of security.

Michel worked in retail. He bought land when he could. He traded in stocks. He created South Africa's first unit trusts, a form of investment fund. In 1927 he was one of three founders of the OK Bazaars, South Africa's first large department store. With his pomaded hair, tailored pin-striped suits, and gleaming brogues, Michel grew into the role of tycoon, puffing on his C-to-C (Cape-to-Cairo) cigarettes.

The lavish parties at his sprawling Johannesburg home became legendary. Children—my grandmother Florence ("Flossie") was the first of six—would gather for a Shabbat and be told to "eat up." In time, grandchildren were similarly admonished. My mother was terrified. The property boasted a full-size billiard table of immaculate baize, a stream with a stone bridge, and a gardener known as Old Dad Tomsett who had been brought over from England and liked to amble around the two-acre garden with a shotgun: an English gardener for a shtetl-born Jew on his African manor! It was in this garden that my parents met in 1948. After Michel died in 1953, it would take forty-three years to wind up his will.

My mother was long gone by the time the estate was settled. In 1950, at the age of twenty-one, on graduation from Witwatersrand University, she had married my father, a young doctor of humbler background, wider experience, and sterner temperament.

My mother, June Adler, upon graduation from Witwatersrand University, June 1950

The girl born on Human Street married the boy born on Honey Street. It was love at first sight.

"I loved you after our first night out," she would write to him many years later. "I worshipped you and our children at the brink of death and I'll love you always, always and always." It was, for her, a great love, great also in constancy, even when the marriage became agonizing, a love that did not die just because it came to coexist with a repressed fury that would explode with the suddenness of an African storm.

June went with my father to England in 1954, the last year of postwar food rationing, because he had won a two-year Nuffield Scholarship to pursue studies in immunology. She had had a miscarriage in 1953. Soon after reaching England, she was pregnant again. She was living with my father in a small apartment in Chalk Farm, putting money in the gas meter for hot water and coal in the stove. No black servant hovered to attend to her every whim. In the eighth month of the pregnancy, driving in Primrose Hill, Sydney and June had an auto accident. It propelled her out the door and onto the road. I was born soon after, a long and painful forceps delivery. June's mother, seeing

June and Sydney Cohen, my father, 1948, shortly after they met

my misshapen head, pronounced herself certain I would be a dwarf, a conviction from which she would not be shaken for a long time. By late 1955 we were back in South Africa. A storm-ravaged sea voyage through the Bay of Biscay brought us home. June, the only passenger not seasick, with an infant to nurse, dined alone with the captain.

So, through the skirted menace and the back-and-forth, I might have been born anywhere or not at all. As chance had it, I was born in London, sailed for South Africa as an infant, returned eighteen months later, grew up in England, and in time, after a long odyssey, became an American whose home is New York. For as long as I can remember, I wanted to tell stories. I was watchful, taking mental notes. Journalism was a natural progression. The stories I sought were the small ones that revealed large ones. I looked for history as reflected in a single psyche, the imprint of the past. I chose the profession of the onlooker always waiting to get inside—a closed room, a situation, a mind, or a soul—in order to uncover some truth. It was beautiful when that happened, a resolution.

I am not a religious Jew—I scarcely practice Judaism; but nor, I discovered, is Jewishness something you choose. Acceptance, or not,

My mother and me, shortly after my birth

of the authority of the rabbis is immaterial. Jewishness is chosen for you—history demonstrates that. It is tenacious even in an English vacuum. An old story tells of the Jew who says to the hunchback, as they pass a synagogue, "I used to be a Jew," and is told in response: "Yes, and I used to be a hunchback."

At King Edward VII School in Johannesburg, classes started at 8:25 with prayers. The Jewish boys, including my uncle Bert and my father, were made to stand outside in the courtyard until 8:30. The most violently anti-Semitic kid was Robert Haynes. He was always on about the Jews. Bert asked Haynes why he hated the Jews so much. What had the Jews done wrong?

"When you are born," said Haynes, "you Jew boys have your foreskins cut off. That is why your cock is different. And you keep this skin until your bar mitzvah, when you have a big feast and eat all the foreskins." That's what the Jews did wrong, and Haynes took it out on a scrawny Jewish boy called Mousy Simon—beat him up behind the bicycle shed and made him eat his feces.

The old blood libel, Haynes had imbibed it: Jews with horns, Jews with tails, goats and devils defiling Christian women. Stuff the *foetor Judaicus,* the stink of the Jew vermin, in Simon's face!

What happened to Mousy Simon could always happen to you.

"Yid" was how I was taunted from time to time in my London high school. The settings change; the barriers, subtle or not, endure.

The pressure of assimilation: I recall sitting with my mother in an Italian restaurant in the upscale London neighborhood of St. John's Wood circa 1970 and asking her, after she had pointed to a family in the opposite corner and said they were Jewish, why her voice dropped to a whisper when she said the J word. "I'm not whispering," Mom said, and went on cutting up her spaghetti so it would fit snugly on a fork. That was before the storm returned, before the madness and the loss of the house on the hill, where we had been happy insofar as happiness can be built on false foundations.

My mother *was* whispering in that restaurant, in that subliminal, awkward, half-apologetic way of many Jews in England. To whisper is to conceal, which is a strain.

When a parent dies unhappy, there is something unresolved that keeps nagging. It is irrational to want to save my mother from her torment—and now I cannot anyway. Still, because of her, I have to go back. It took her death for me to realize the strength of her love and how, in the torment, I had loved her back. The void her absence left could be explained only by her refusal to stop believing in love, however compromised by frailty her expression of it was. She left such exhaustion and disarray behind her that after her cremation, nobody paid any attention to the fate of her ashes. They ended in some Dumpster, I suppose.

Doctors, including my father, diagnosed her mental illness as "endogenous"—that is, coming from within. Dr. Silvio Benaim of London's Royal Free Hospital, in a letter of May 10, 1979, wrote: "June Cohen has suffered from a recurrent affective illness for the last two years.

There is a history of a previous similar illness which occurred . . . in 1957 and which was treated with E.C.T."—electroconvulsive therapy. He continued: "Mrs. Cohen is a capable and intelligent woman who has an excellent previous personality, works as a Magistrate, is happily married and has a good relationship with her children. There are no external stresses and I regard her illness as endogenous in type. At the height of her depression, Mrs. Cohen feels totally inefficient, disorganized, sluggish, withdrawn and tends to crawl into bed."

In theory, then, the paralyzing depression, being endogenous, would have happened in any setting, under any circumstances. Happily married or not, enjoying good relations or not with her children (they were often strained), she would have *crawled* into bed. But of course it happened under specific circumstances. I wonder how Dr. Benaim came to write: *There are no external stresses.*

June's first depression overtook her after she was uprooted, bounced back and forth between England and South Africa, set down at last in Mill Hill in the far north of London in 1957, pregnant with my sister, Jenny, in a blustery and gloomy and straitened nation, with a hard-working husband, and obliged to get on with life as best she could as she raised two infants without all the support she had known. It happened as she strained to fit in, to become part of an alien culture, to become English, to drop South Africa and its sunlit ease and its tight-knit Jewish community, to belong again. She wanted to help Sydney, her overriding goal always. And then, with his success in a foreign land assured, the depression returned with a vengeance, and the one anchor she had found, the house on the hill, was lost.

This was not supposed to happen. Immigrants, although that word was never uttered, we were bound to assimilate. The shtetl, pogroms, and penury had been left far behind. They were never mentioned, either. Our gaze was to be forward-looking. June, despite her suffering, made an immense effort to that end. She herself had been raised in a cocoon of new South African wealth so enveloping as to eliminate, almost overnight, the past. I was raised an English boy, as if England were my birthright and its preeminent faith, Christianity, my faith, if I had one at all. So, just as the Lithuanian past was forgotten, the South African past, with its vestiges of Jewish ritual, was to be forgotten in turn.

New opportunity is only one side of the immigrant story, its bright star. The other side, its black sun, is displacement and loss. In each generation on the move, members of my family have been unable to come to terms with the immense struggle involved in burying the past, losing an identity, and embracing a new life—as if the bipolarity from which several suffered were just that, a double existence attempting to bridge the unbridgeable.

The past was as silent as a village at the bottom of a dam. We had lapsed. The question that grew in me was: Into what?

Franz Kafka, in *Letter to His Father,* wrote: "You really had brought some traces of Judaism with you from the ghetto-like village community. It was not much and it dwindled a little more in the city and during your military service; but still, the impressions and memories of your youth did just about suffice for some sort of Jewish life. . . . Even in this there was still Judaism enough, but it was too little to be handed on to the child; it all dribbled away while you were passing it on."

Dribbled away: Our Jewish past had been disappearing since Morris Cohen and Polly Soloveychik and Isaac Michel, Lithuanians all, set foot in South Africa around the turn of the twentieth century. It was a slow process, but it appeared inexorable. Nonetheless, in time I returned to what I was not given, a Jewish identity, because that, simply, is what I felt myself to be, a Jew. Behind that feeling lay an absence, the void behind the calm exterior of our lives. As Hans Meyerhoff has observed, "Previous generations *knew* much less about the past than we do, but perhaps *felt* a much greater sense of identity and continuity with it." I also came to the conviction that the truth of the story of my mother, the girl from Human Street, was not endogenous but exogenous, at least in part. It was not merely a pharmacological issue; it was a psychological issue. It was tied to our odyssey, a Jewish odyssey of the twentieth century, and the tremendous pressure of wandering, adapting, pretending, silencing, and forgetting.

Truth gets displaced. A rheumatologist once told me of a patient who complained that she could not raise her arm above her shoulder. The pain was terrible, she said. Later he discovered that she was suffering because her younger sister had gone off with her lover. There was nothing wrong with her shoulder. But it was there that she had placed the pain.

My uncle Bert in Florence, 1944, "Captain Uccellino"

Before he reached Bellagio at war's end, Captain Cohen was in Florence reconnoitering a site for a casualty clearing station. He found a disused abattoir that seemed suitable. As he was standing there, a bird landed on his shoulder. It did not leave him for five days. He became known as Captain Uccellino, or Captain Little Bird. Some women thought he was a saint. They asked him to bless them. He had forgotten that useful mnemonic—"Spectacles, testicles, wallet, cigar"—for the ports of call in making the sign of the cross. He sketched a rough approximation.

An American soldier approached him on the banks of the Arno. "Say, Captain," he said. "You got a bird on your shoulder."

"Yeah, I know, it's been there for four days."

"You don't say. Mind if I take a picture?"

So there is a photograph of a young South African Jewish officer on the Arno's banks with a bird on his shoulder in 1944. The watchful nightingale has flown onward. The water behind him is still. There is no wind that day. The sky is clear. From the church spire I can almost hear a bell chiming the half hours and the hours—a bell fading, not ceasing, as in Bellagio, where there is a clock on two faces of the tower, one facing the lake and one facing the town.

More than sixty years have gone by. Change comes slowly if at all to Italy. I eat trout at Silvio's. I swim in the chilly lake where my uncle almost drowned beneath the snowcapped mountains. I gaze at the old two-faced clock tower, at the cypresses like green obelisks, at the oozing figs, and at the lazy fronds of the palms in this town set at the tipping point of Alpine chill into Mediterranean languor. Yes, the bird on your shoulder: it comes when least expected to affirm life's miracles, beyond every suffering. Never, my mother liked to say, underestimate the power of hope. Life circles about, its patterns as intricate as the lake water's, as impossible to predict as what a small Florentine bird might say about unlikely springs to come. It is time to retrace things, beginning here at the point where the wind divides.

CHAPTER 2

Bones in the Forest

The River Švėtė divides the town of Žagarė into two halves. They are called the "old" and the "new," but in truth there is not much to distinguish them. The sagging timber homes of the shtetl stand on either bank, emptied of the Jews who built them. On the desolate market square is the green house where the Braude family lived. In a yellow house, the Zagorskis ran a shoe store near the bustling barbershop of the Joffes. One or two prosperous families, the owners of the mill or the slaughterhouse, built in brick or stone rather than wood. Their status, so demonstrated, made no difference to their fate. To stay on in Žagarė was to die.

It is still and silent now in winter. Swift currents cut past patches of gray ice. The streets are empty. Snow imparts its hush. The town is a palimpsest, the present inscribed in too faint a hue to efface a past of which nobody speaks.

The past can be seen in sepia prints: the square filled with horses and wagons laden with flax or hides or maize, the stalls with their produce, the livestock corralled in small enclosures, the chandlers and blacksmiths, the tradesmen placing goods on scales passed from father to son, the merchants offering menorahs and silver goblets and kettles and sewing machines and outsize transistor radios. One can almost hear the tick-tock of old clocks, see the work of the tallith weavers. The hammer blows of small artisans and gravestone cutters reverberate in my mind. The murmurings of the teachers and Torah scribes, their sinuous argumentation with a familiar God, course down the narrow streets of a town once known as a center of Jewish learning and Kabbalah.

The last Jew in Žagarė, Isaac Mendelson, died a couple of months before my arrival in November 2011. So ended a presence that had begun in the sixteenth century. In 1897, three years after my grandmother's birth, there were 5,443 Jews in Žagarė. Mendelson, a community of one, used to stand on the corner of the market square with his dachshund, Chipa. He would recall the times after the war when he was a goalkeeper for the local soccer team. Seldom did he talk about the catastrophe.

Žagarė is a place of echoes and absences, my grandmother's being but one. Like many Lithuanian villages, it hovers over loss, a void that whispers. I have come back to see what might have been. Next to a bridge on the Švėtė a plaque commemorates the death on June 29, 1941, of Jonas Baranauskas, who was "killed defending his homeland." He died a few days after the Nazis invaded Lithuania and embarked on one of the swiftest mass murders of a nation's Jews in the entire European extermination program.

Circumstance was propitious for the slaughter: a local population inclined to blame "Judeo-Bolsheviks" for the Soviet occupation of a year earlier, a nation disoriented by the Soviet deportation eastward of its elites, a Lithuanian nationalist movement bent on the removal of a centennial Jewish presence and given to the naïve belief that Hitler would restore the independence of Lithuania. Purification of the nation meant an end to "Asiatic Bolshevik slavery" and the "long-standing Jewish yoke." By December 1, 1941, of Lithuania's roughly 200,000 Jews, at least 137,346 were dead. The Nazis had broken through the psychological barrier of murdering women and children en masse.

Baranauskas, who merits a plaque, was not a Jew. Yet he alone is identified in Žagarė. He is thereby accorded a presence that feels like more than a dutiful nod to shadows. He lived, he resisted, he died. His name is there, legible. It is there at the center of a town that lies between two disused Jewish cemeteries, one in the "new" and one in the "old" town. In the cemeteries gravestones lurch, lichen advances, and Hebrew inscriptions crumble or fade into mildewed illegibility. Fragments of letters recall Anna Akhmatova's words in *Requiem,* "I should like to call you all by name, but they have lost the lists."

Mendelson was not buried in the Jewish cemeteries; nobody is any longer. His younger son, Vidmantas, tells me he "can't even imagine" how his father "might have been buried in the Jewish cemetery."

None of the people thronging the sepia photographs of the Žagarė market square in the early twentieth century could have envisaged how Jewish life would end. *You, sir, are doomed—and you on the wagon, and you with a hand on your horse's withers.* Deaf to entreaty, they all live and breathe. In every old photograph, as Roland Barthes observed, lurks catastrophe.

Driving across the flat countryside from Šiauliai, I pass Joniškis (where Jews once attended the "white synagogue" in summer and the "red synagogue" in winter) and enter Žagarė through an avenue of oaks and firs that adjoins the former Naryshkin estate. The splendor of the canopy is suggestive of another time, before two twentieth-century totalitarianisms gripped the small town like a vise and excised its raison d'être. The towering trees carry the message that life once had a different scale here, a different tenor. There was commerce, pleasure, a touch of grandeur, before everything faded like vapor trails.

The Naryshkins, a Russian noble family, acquired the property in the nineteenth century, when Lithuania was part of the Russian empire. They decamped every summer with a large retinue, an object of fascination to the shtetl children. My paternal grandmother, Polly, loved to wander in Graf Naryshkin's woods. She spoke often of *spangolių* she picked there. That word, in Johannesburg, was met with great hilarity, a tongue-twisting throwback: *spangolių*! Cranberries were not the town's specialty. Žagarė was renowned for the excellence of its cherries and the quality of its horses. Yet it was the cranberries— *spangolių*—that ushered Polly back from South Africa to a lost world, a memory as comforting as broth.

She grew up in the Pale of Settlement, the large crescent on Russia's western edge, in a time of pogroms. They had flared with the

My grandmother Polly Soloveychik in Žagarė.
She was born in 1894.

assassination in 1881 of Tsar Alexander II—a young Jew named Gessia Gelfman was involved—and intensified after 1903. Polly's older sisters, Assja and Zera, were involved in the revolutionary movement of 1905 against the tsar. That year Cossacks swept into Žagarė, destroyed Jewish houses, shot a tailor named Zemach Essin, and sent several Jews into Siberian exile. The resolve of Assja and Zera hardened.

Polly was still young. Born in 1894, she became a wanderer in the woods, an idler on the banks of the Švėtė, where she would run her fingers along the deep ridges in the trunks of the willows. She would touch the delicate petals of the fragrant sweet peas and gaze at the water eddying through reeds. The busy storks made nests, and when the days grew shorter, they were gone. The river rushed in winter but dwindled to a small stream in summer. You could cross it and scarcely get your ankles wet in the months after the cherry blossoms. She had a love of trees. In South Africa, decades later, she would plant three jacarandas opposite the Houghton golf course. Trees endured. Around the child in Žagarė stirred unrest and uncertainty.

The fate of Assja and Zera has passed into family legend. They were young, they were beautiful, they were arrested by tsarist police, and they ended up in Capri, joining a colony of exiled Russians established on the Italian island in 1906 by the writer Maxim Gorky. This much is known, but not a lot more. In a memoir written in Italian, Assja's daughter Mya Tannenbaum, a concert pianist who became a music critic for the Milan daily *Corriere della Sera,* recalled: "When my mother evoked the events of the revolution, emotion turned her dark almond-shaped eyes a silvery color. At that point I would interrupt her out of fear that the past would sweep me away. And so memory has its lacunae and is full of the question: Why?"

Memory embroiders, facts get lost, and still some fragment of truth remains. My Italian family is in Rome and Capri, the descendants of Assja and Zera. Mya's account has the girls being schooled in Kiev, hundreds of miles from Žagarė. This seems fanciful. But her story of the night of the arrest of Assja and Zera conveys a haunting past that might persuade a child of its power to sweep her away.

Assja and Zera have slipped out at night. They are teaching young, illiterate laborers how to read. One of Assja's students appears, pursued by police. As he races by, he hands her a bound package. She throws it into a well. The package is fished out. It contains subversive documents, manuals of communist agitation. The girls are arrested. They are young and innocent-looking enough to provoke an incredulous outburst from the Russian chief of police: "And these would be the dangerous revolutionaries?" He calls them *deti*—mere children. Still, Assja spends long enough in damp solitary confinement to contract lifelong rheumatic ailments. She hears the cries of fellow prisoners condemned to execution by firing squad: "We will die for freedom!" After a year she and Zera are put in a convoy, to be taken east to a Siberian prison camp. They are saved when an armed revolutionary unit conducts a raid and later engineers their escape westward to Gorky's Mediterranean haven.

Another family account has a letter arriving in Žagarė from Vilnius, today the Lithuanian capital, saying Russian authorities have arrested Polly's sisters for insurrectionary activities. Polly's mother, Sarah, was illiterate; the news was kept from her. Polly invented letters from Assja and Zera to give the impression that all was well. In time her mother saw through her. They went to plead with Graf Naryshkin, who was not himself ill disposed to the Jews, and prevailed upon him to lend a troika and driver for the arduous drive to Vilnius. There contact was made with an organization set up by Gorky to rescue imprisoned young leftists and bring them to Capri, where the author lived between 1906 and 1913. So, in the revolutionary turmoil of 1905, the Italian branch of the family was born. Polly remained in Žagarė until the following year.

Part of the process of getting out, of uprooting, is to shed origins. In Rome, as elsewhere in my family, the past was less a source of fascination than a thing to be overcome. The pride of the Bolshevik revolutionary, confronted with the Soviet terror that spread after 1917 and hardened over decades into Stalin's imprisoning European empire, yielded. This was not the classless paradise of which the young Assja and Zera had dreamed. In time the only trace of communist credo that endured among my Italian family was a dismissal of religion in general and Jewishness in particular.

One of the countries absorbed after 1945 into Moscow's communist realm was, of course, Lithuania. There is a sign now pointing into Polly's woods, where *spangoliu* grew, beneath the snow-clad canopy. It has changed since 1945. A Soviet sign once read, MEMORIAL TO THE VICTIMS OF FASCISM. It now reads, GRAVES OF THE VICTIMS OF THE JEWISH GENOCIDE.

The revised wording reflects the tumult of Lithuanian history and the nation's ongoing struggle with memory. It is not only within families that facts are hard to recall. The Soviet Red Army, driven out by the Nazis in June 1941 as Hitler tore up his pact with Stalin and embarked on the calamitous invasion of Russia, fought its way back into Lithuania in 1944. The country was annexed as a Soviet republic. Lithuania disappeared for forty-six years into the Soviet empire. The liberators were not liberators. They were other occupiers.

When Soviet forces reached Žagarė in 1944, they found a mass grave in the woods. A Soviet special commission examined the remains and determined that there were 2,402 corpses: 530 men, 1,223 women,

625 children, and 24 babies. This accounting showed a small discrepancy from the numbers given by SS *Standartenführer* Karl Jäger, the chief of German security and SD *Einsatzkommando* 3 (EK 3), who in a report dated December 1, 1941, from the Lithuanian town of Kaunas, stated that 2,263 Jews (663 men, 1,107 women, and 496 children) were executed in Žagarė on October 2, 1941.

Jäger, at that time, was in an exultant mood. "Today," he wrote, "I can confirm that our objective, to solve the Jewish problem for Lithuania, has been achieved by EK 3. In Lithuania there are no more Jews apart from Jewish workers and their families." This was a reference to the 45,000 Jews still confined in the ghettos of Vilnius, Kaunas, and my grandfather's Šiauliai. Their labor was required for the German war effort—until the calories the Jews consumed could no longer be justified. Jäger had wanted to shoot them immediately. "I also intended to kill these Jewish workers," he wrote, "but came up against strong protests on the part of the civil administration (the *Reichskommissar*) and the *Wehrmacht*." German bureaucratic wrangling might prolong Lithuanian Jews' lives by a couple of years in the name of extracting their labor. It could not change their fate. The Nazis were meticulous about killing the Jews of Lithuania, as if they were combing out lice.

In Žagarė, there was no stay of execution. Death came as harsh and swift as a hailstorm. On October 2, 1941, the Jewish ghetto in Žagarė—enlarged over the previous months by the herding into it of Jews from the shtetls of nearby villages—was liquidated. So was Jewish life. What remained after that in Žagarė was no more than a coda, a slow drift toward extinction. The corpses were in the 120-meter-long ditch in the trees on the outskirts of town. A shadow had fallen on the fruit-laden woods. Nobody spoke about the mass grave. The slaughter was a nonsubject, even for Mendelson, whose own family lay among the corpses.

The Soviets found the human remains but had scant interest in an accurate identification of them. Stalin spoke once, in 1941, of Hitler's murder of Jews. Otherwise he evaded the issue. His aim was to forge *Homo Sovieticus,* not to reinforce Jewish identity. The Jewish question was delicate and divisive. The Holocaust had to be managed within the Soviet political agenda. A cornerstone of this was that the war had begun in 1941 with Hitler's invasion of the Soviet Union, rather than in 1939 with the Hitler-Stalin pact and the joint Nazi and Soviet invasions of Poland. Over 1.5 million Jews were then killed by the Nazis on territory, including Lithuania, annexed by Stalin in 1939 and 1940. As Timothy Snyder has written, "The murder of the Jews was not only an undesirable memory in and of itself; it called forth other undesirable memories." For Stalin, any manifestation of Jewish separatism was suspect. Religious sentiment was reactionary, and Zionist conviction was seditious.

Hitler had managed to blame the Jews for communism as well as capitalism, one measure of his obsession. Stalin nursed his own hostility to the Jews. They would become the "rootless cosmopolitans," "agents of American intelligence," and "Jewish nationalists" of his postwar propaganda. Jews, rather than victims of Nazism, became agents of an imperial conspiracy against communism. To sustain his victors' history, Stalin had to conflate Jews' particular suffering into the general (read Slavic and Russian) sacrifice of the "Great Patriotic War" against Hitler. So the Jews in the Žagarė ditch and in the Ponary forest near Vilnius, and in countless other pits around Lithuania on the fringes of provincial towns, were identified as "Soviet victims of Fascism." In those days, any mention of the Jews was inadmissible.

In this way, the facts hidden by Nazi propaganda were further entombed by Soviet ideology after the end of the war. That the Jews in the Žagarė death pit should have been identified for decades as "Soviet citizens" killed by fascism, rather than as Lithuanian Jews killed by Nazis and their local Lithuanian henchmen for the crime of their Jewishness, demonstrates how totalitarianism manufactures its own "truth." Once Nazism and Stalinism met in their death dance in Lithuania, the Jews there had to perish, and after death they had to be killed again, airbrushed from history.

Only since Lithuanian independence in 1990 has a memorial detailing the Nazi crime in Žagarė gone up in the woods where my grandmother picked cranberries. It reads: "In this place on October 2, 1941, Nazi killers and their local helpers killed about 3,000 Jewish men, women, and children from the Šiauliai region." The phrase "local helpers" remains controversial. Many Lithuanians would rather see themselves as victims of the Soviets than as accomplices of the Nazis. They do not want to have been both—to have had a double identity in the inferno of triple occupation, first Soviet, then Nazi, then Soviet again. This much at least is clear: if my grandmother Polly had died in the massacre at her hometown, she would have been forty-seven.

—

Žagarė is a town where most homes still have no running water. Wells are shared between neighbors. Roofs sag, masonry is cracked. Even the satellite dishes look battered. Winter is spent keeping warm and summer is spent growing food and gathering kindling and timber for the winter. Young people leave to study or to find jobs in Vilnius or Dublin or Oslo. They do not return. Close to half of the two thousand inhabitants are pensioners.

No more than a mile from Latvia, Žagarė is a border town whose lifeblood was trade in grain and metals before its natural outlet to rich German markets was closed. It paid the price of redrawn European maps. As borders shift or close, a hub may become suddenly isolated. Žagarė's decline has been steady when it was not precipitous. It was a victim of twentieth-century Europe.

Isaac Mendelson returned from the war to Žagarė in 1945, a twenty-three-year-old Red Army soldier who had fought through some of the bloodiest killing fields of the eastern front. He would live in a small apartment on a corner of the Žagarė market square. It was in this square that his mother, two sisters, and a pregnant sister-in-law were gathered on October 2, 1941, before being killed by Lithuanian police units overseen by the Nazis.

Perhaps the massacre of Žagarė Jews, of his own kith and kin, played on Mendelson's mind. The Jews were gone, after all, a vanished community. His mother had disappeared without trace. Still, he was silent. "He never talked about it," says his older son, Mejeris. "The times were like this."

The times were like this. It is not easy to weigh what part the trauma of battle, what part the pressure of Soviet occupation, and what part the isolation or opprobrium of his Jewishness played in Mendelson's silence to his children. There were many such postwar Jewish silences and not only in the Soviet bloc. I lived in one. The shame of survival had many expressions, in Europe and the United States and Israel.

Repressed feelings, forms of wordlessness, inflections of latency were common to all of them. Mendelson was aware that some of the executioners who had taunted and stolen and raped and killed still lived on the streets nearby. They had stripped their victims naked in front of the ditches into which they would be dispatched with a bullet to the back of the head. One man who had helped police the short-lived Žagarė ghetto tried to reconcile with Mendelson. He was rebuffed. At least that is what Mejeris was told by his mother after Lithuanian independence in 1990.

Mendelson had survived by escaping eastward on a bicycle in the mayhem of June 1941. He turned nineteen that month. Soviet forces abandoned Žagarė on June 29. For a Lithuanian Jew, the arrival of the Nazis could only spell doom. For other Lithuanians, it might portend an accommodation with Germany that would restore the country's independence after the Soviet occupation of the previous year. The nation split with devastating consequences.

Jews in Lithuania had been a community still set apart by language—Yiddish—and by ritual, prayer, scripture, and calendar. Integration and emancipation had not gone as far as in neighboring Poland. Some, like my grandmother's sisters, had been Marxists. A few had looked favorably on the Soviet occupation of 1940. But the synthesis of Jew and communist, energetically pursued by Hitler's propagandists, involved the forging of a myth. A significant proportion of the Lithuanians deported to Siberia as enemies of the Soviet Union between June 1940 and June 1941 were in fact Jews. This did not prevent Jews from being paraded in the streets by Hitler's executioners and forced to carry portraits of Lenin and Stalin to demonstrate their supposed communist sympathies.

Nazi hatred of the Jew encountered widespread Lithuanian connivance with that hatred for material or political gain. Mendelson pedaled into Latvia with all the hatred gusting at his back. Other Jews tried to flee on horse-drawn carts. A few found trucks or other vehicles. They were pounded by the Luftwaffe. Mendelson, without his mother and sisters, lost in the screams and turmoil, reached Riga and from there boarded a packed train into Russia, whose vast Asian depths afforded some shelter to Jews.

He worked for a time on a collective farm, almost starving, before joining the Sixteenth Lithuanian Division of the Red Army. Soviet authorities had been suspicious of recruiting Lithuanian refugees, but the need for military manpower overcame mistrust. The division was an unusual unit, including more than five thousand Jews who had fled into Russia and now fought to return. The shtetl Jew, as later in Israel, was transformed into a soldier; Mendelson became an infantryman and machine-gunner. Relations between the three main "nationalities" (as they were termed) of the division—Russians, Lithuanians, and Jews—were sometimes strained, but it held together. Initial combat in February 1943, near Orel, southwest of Moscow, was followed by a long, battle-scarred march westward to the Lithuanian port city of Klaipeda (Memel in German), which was liberated in January 1945. The division numbered more than twelve thousand at its peak in 1942; it took 7,065 dead. Mendelson was injured but battled his way back to Lithuania with his huge two-wheeled, water-cooled Maxima machine gun.

Nothing forges or reinforces identity faster than persecution. In the Sixth Company of the Second Battalion, 167th Brigade, a unit of the Sixteenth Division that was overwhelmingly Jewish, commanders gave orders in Yiddish, and songs were sung in Hebrew. Zionism stirred. There was talk of the Land of Israel and of creating a new Jewish future if the war to go home was ever won.

Home had in fact ceased to exist for the Jews of the Sixteenth Division of the Red Army. In Žagarė, while Mendelson was gone, the danger that had been intuited and experienced by my family decades earlier—that Europe could not and would not assimilate the Jews—reached its logical yet unthinkable culmination. Hell in a small place is an intimate affair of neighbor upon neighbor. The only thing anonymous about death in Žagarė and the other small provincial towns of Lithuania was its nameless aftermath.

As soon as Soviet forces left in 1941, a group of nationalists known as the Žagarė Activists, headed by Stanislovas Kačkys, embarked on retribution against "Bolsheviks" and Jews. On July 25, 1941, the mayor ordered all Jews to wear a yellow Star of David and move into a ghetto adjoining the market square. They were not allowed on the sidewalks. They were forbidden to draw water from wells not belonging to other Jews.

From surrounding towns, Jews were ordered into the Žagarė ghetto. There were 715 Jews in the ghetto on August 25, 1941; a month later that number had grown to 2,402. Many came from nearby villages. Their "Jewish and Bolshevik" property was registered by local authorities and valued at a little over five million rubles. A barbed-wire fence enclosed the ghetto. Local police, headed by Police Chief Juozas Krutulis, formed the guard. Jews were forced to work cutting timber in my grandmother's beloved woods when they were not being selected for humiliation or random execution. Men were made to spit in the face of the rabbi, Israel Reif. If they refused, they were shot. In late August, thirty-eight Jewish men were dragged from the synagogue and executed at the Jewish cemetery in the old district of Žagarė.

On the morning of October 2, 1941, Yom Kippur, all Jews from the Žagarė ghetto were ordered to assemble in the market square. Several *Einsatzkommando* members had arrived from Šiauliai over the previous days, as well as Lithuanian "self-defense" units and the ultranationalists known as White Armband squads. The Nazi commandant appeared on a balcony overlooking the square. He declared that the Jews were to be moved to another location, where they would all be given work. But when he blew a whistle for the Jews to form lines, he saw passivity turn suddenly to violent resistance.

Jäger, the chief of *Einsatzkommando* 3, in his painstaking report on the elimination of Lithuanian Jewry, writes of the 2,263 Jews murdered by his reckoning in Žagarė: "As these Jews were being led away a mutiny arose, which was however immediately put down; 150 Jews were shot." At least seven of Jäger's local henchmen were injured in this brief uprising as Jews, realizing at last the fate awaiting them, used knives or their bare hands to tear at their captors.

Once quelled, the doomed Jews of Žagarė were loaded onto trucks and driven out to the Naryshkin estate, near the stables whose horses commanded local renown. A large pit had been prepared. A survivor of the Žagarė ghetto, Ber Peretzman, described—in testimony taken at the displaced persons' camp in Feldafing, Germany, on March 2, 1949—how the Jews were made to strip naked at the edge of the pit before being shot. To save ammunition, small children had their heads smashed by being swung against trees, or they were buried alive. Isaac Mendelson's sister-in-law, Rochel, went into labor at the edge of the pit. Peretzman writes, "The murderers laid her down on the ground, allowed the child to be born, then killed both mother and child."

This is what it took to end Jewish life in Žagarė. These were the facts of which Mendelson would not or could not speak.

In the depths of Russia, he had known how young men and women bled to death in the snow, heard the cries of the dying, fallen asleep as he walked, collapsed on the bare floors of charred villages, seen how the bones of the starving are etched through their skin, breathed the stench of putrefaction in fields littered with cartridges and corpses, cooked meals from dead horses dragged out of the ice, seen plains before him so wide they broke the spirit, rammed shovels into the frozen earth as he struggled to dig trenches, felt his coat rendered hard as metal by the freezing air, watched those around him fall in a storm of German machine-gun and mortar fire on some forsaken hill. A man might be no more than a black speck in the snow.

Now he was "home," in the town where Nazis and their Lithuanian henchmen had slaughtered Rochel Mendelson and her newborn child, and where Stalin was determined to quash such memories of specific Jewish suffering.

Soon after the war Mendelson married Sonya Swarcbram, a Jewish survivor, in Vilnius. When their son was born in 1947, they gave him the name of Mendelson's late father, Mejeris. He is a quiet, mild man who bears with dignity the wounds of a hard life. Growing up in Žagarė, he felt something was gone but found that thing hard to identify. A mother of a friend once mentioned the former "Jewish presence" and the massacre. He was teased at school as a Jew. But it was taboo to talk.

Locals no longer wanted to call his father "Isaac," for obvious reasons. He was known after the war as "Petras." The Mendelsons divorced; Sonya left for Israel. Mendelson's second wife, Aldona, born in 1927, was Christian. They are buried together beneath a black granite gravestone at the municipal cemetery. On the Day of the Dead, November 1, wreaths of bright chrysanthemums are propped against the graves, lined up neat as shoe boxes. Families pay their respects. Nobody goes to the Jewish cemetery in old Žagarė or to the Jewish cemetery in new Žagarė, where Hebrew inscriptions on listing stones fissure. The Jewish past has no name in Žagarė. It is an enigma. There is no local trace of the Žagarė Soloveychiks, my grandmother's family. Simon Gurevičius, a leader of the small surviving Jewish community in Lithuania, told me almost all records of that period disappeared or were destroyed.

⸺

My paternal grandparents came from two Lithuanian towns twenty miles apart, separated by flat fields and copses. Some Jews from Morris's town, Šiauliai, were taken to Polly's town, Žagarė, to be shot in 1941. Other Šiauliai Jews survived in the town's ghetto long after the Žagarė Jews were liquidated because they were required for labor in a leather factory.

Morris and Polly met far from Lithuania, in downtown Johannesburg, in the general store in which she worked as a teenage girl. A wholesale grocer, Morris would come around on his horse and trap, and she would smile at the familiar exchange with the owner:

"Hello, Joel, how are things?"

"Oh, terrible, business is dead."

"Anything you want?"

"Can't even sell what I got."

"What about some flour?"

"Well, maybe I take a little flour."

"What about soap? I hear soap is going quite well?"

"Okay, maybe I take a little."

Her smile was demure, her dark hair pulled back off her pale face. She had poise beyond her years. He was ten years older than she. They spoke in Yiddish. As they had started life not far from each other in a northern land of dense forests, they had much to talk about. The year they were married, 1914, World War I began in Europe.

The marriage was a happy one. She called him "Meissele"—little Morris. The four children called him "M.J." Polly had once scoffed at a friend with airs who insisted on calling her husband by his initials—"so pretentious," she said. The children seized on this, invented a middle initial "J" for Morris, and that was that.

When the Nazi catastrophe came to Šiauliai and Žagarė, Morris and Polly knew little or nothing of it. They never talked about it to their four children. The two boys, my father Sydney and my uncle Bert, had gone off to join the allies in World War II. My father did not return from Europe in time to see his father again. The year apartheid was enacted, 1948, Morris died at the age of sixty-four. It was also the year that the modern state of Israel came into being and faced the first of many wars. Morris had suffered a heart attack a decade earlier but would not change a diet rich in chicken fat, although he did give up his beloved oval-shaped Loyalist cigarettes. He left these words in a letter to Polly:

> My darling wife, after my illness I feel that my state of health was such that there was some danger that I may leave you suddenly without having the chance of saying goodbye. With heart trouble we must be prepared. This fact worried me. To meet this difficulty I decided to write this letter. I hope that what I tell you will be of some comfort to you. My dear little chum, with the sincerest feeling I want to express my gratitude for the great help and happiness you gave me from the day we were married to the present. I tell you in all honest truth that I found in you the ideal wife and mother. I have lived the happiest married life of anyone I know. My dear Babe, I want you to be brave, carry on for [us] both, see to help our dear children, as far as possible, safely settled and happy, and please my darling try, try very hard to make the best of the remaining days of your life. As you know my pet I have not the popular beliefs after death [sic], but if my spirit will exist, and can do anything for you and our children, be sure it will watch over you and help you even more than in life. I desire to spare you and the children the suffering I went through when I lost my dear parents. If possible, do NOT attend my funeral. I sincerely desire that you and the children should think of me as when you knew me alive. I want no prayers. Avoid it as far as possible. Understand my love, without any boast but in perfect truth, I feel I have lived a clean, moral and honest life. I am prepared to meet whatever there may be beyond without the least fear.

At the Jewish cemetery in the Brixton neighborhood of Johannes-burg, the ground was hard, stones and gravel. When, as demanded by tradition, Morris had been obliged to shovel earth onto the caskets of his mother and father, the sound was harsh and unforgiving. It had haunted him.

Morris went on to talk about his estate, which he reckoned just sufficient to keep Polly and the four children "in fair comfort" and to say that he would like, if there was anything to spare, to "assist those less fortunate" by giving fifty pounds to a needy medical student and fifty pounds to a needy dental student.

In brackets he added a stipulation: "Jew or Gentile."

CHAPTER 3

Gin and Two

South Africa took a grip on my childhood imagination. Perhaps it was the light after the dull skies of England, the brilliance of the air on the high plateau of the Transvaal, the dark-leaved avocado trees, the glistening orange groves, the sun-plunging abruptness of the dusks. Flowers burst into exuberant bloom, bats swooped as night fell, and the horizon was a distant line across the dry veld. I went to live there when I was four months old, crossing the seas from London in my mother's arms. When she had me, she wanted to go home, to the South Africa that would always take her in.

We arrived in the midst of the African summer. I would come to know those Southern Hemisphere summers well: the palms draped in bougainvillea, the canopy of purple-blue jacaranda blossom over the broad avenues of Houghton, the smoke from family *braais* wafting over the bamboo and swimming pools as red meat sizzled. My mother was happy in South Africa. I picture her laughing against a backdrop of golden sand tapering to a faraway point. Love is warmth, heat. Everything seemed untroubled, unless you caught a glimpse of ragged black men in ill-fitting shoes being herded into police vans. Then a cousin might say, "I suppose they don't have their passes. Enjoy the swimming pools—next year they'll be red with blood."

Our return in 1955, the year I was born, to my parents' birthplace coincided with my father's appointment as dean of Douglas Smit House, the residence at Johannesburg's University of the Witwatersrand reserved for black students. A small number could still attend the university at the time, even if they were not allowed to play rugby, that inner sanctum of the white Afrikaner. A decade earlier Sydney had qualified as a doctor at Wits. That was before the victory of the National Party and the imposition of apartheid in 1948. We lived at the residence. My parents employed a black nanny. I enjoyed riding around on her back.

One of the particularities of apartheid was that blacks were kept at a distance except in the most intimate of settings, the home. They cooked and set the table and cleared away; they washed and darned and dusted and beat the rugs and made the beds; and they coddled and cared for white children. Every white household, it seemed, had its Trusted Black Mammy. After the Shabbat meal on Friday night, guests might leave some small token of appreciation on the kitchen counter ("Shame, I don't have much change") or slip a few rand into a calloused black palm. The black women—Betty or Johanna or Doris—who bathed me as an infant touched my skin. Their world was untouchable.

Douglas Smit House was run on the cheap compared to residences for white students, where black waiters provided service. It stood in the midst of white suburbia, and so the black students housed there were subject to a labyrinth of legal restrictions designed to keep Africans out of such areas. Every black South African over the age of sixteen had to carry the *dompas*—the damned passbook—complete with fingerprints and permission from the government to be in a particular area at a particular time for a particular employment or reason. Arrest was arbitrary. An irregularity of some kind could always be found in the *dompas*. University students were given special exemptions, but these were seldom respected. Much of my father's time was spent in police stations negotiating the release of black students from white cops.

He arrived once to hear an Afrikaner policeman taunting a young black woman who was close to qualification: "You think you're some clever student, but really you're just a kaffir." The term *kaffir*, originally an Islamic word for "unbeliever," was picked up by Europeans and deployed in Africa as an insult. Two pillars of apartheid were control of black mobility and prevention of blacks' acquisition of skills. They were to be "hewers of wood and drawers of water." Blacks could carry bricks to the white bricklayer but not lay the bricks themselves or use a trowel because they would then overstep a boundary reserved for a skilled laborer.

The system guaranteed a large supply of cheap, menial labor. South Africa was built on mining fueled by it. White industrialists could pay starvation wages. Apartheid perfected and formalized the system with a host of new rules but did not invent the oppression of the native population. A black woman near qualification as a doctor walking the streets of white suburbia therefore threatened to upend cornerstones of a deep-rooted ethos. My father was outraged at the treatment of his students.

Nelson Mandela had been at Wits a few years earlier. In the late 1940s, Indians and the mulatto South Africans known as Coloreds were allowed on the same trams as whites as long as they sat upstairs in the rear section. Blacks were required to use separate trams that stopped running at night—unless a white passenger accompanied them. One evening Mandela was traveling with three Indian friends on a "white" tram. The conductor tried to eject them: "You coolies are not allowed to bring a Kaffir onto the tram; only whites can do that." Such were the minutiae of South African policing by pigment. If you could whiten yourself, you could elevate yourself. But the barriers were intricate. A popular test of people's blackness was whether a pencil would wedge in their hair.

Later, in a 1978 interview given in London to the *Herald,* my father would reflect on his time at Douglas Smit House: "Men and women of different color got to know each other. It is a tragedy for South Africa that this arrangement was later terminated by the government. In this vital segment of potential leaders, blacks and whites mixed over the fairly lengthy period of their courses, this was a vital human experience and close bonds developed. To have lost that—the higher education of black and white together—has deprived South Africa of potential leaders with genuine understanding of each other."

For many years I was too young to understand. Beauty was abundant, yet a shadow lurked. That is how I absorbed racism, like a twinge, the first hint of a microbe in the blood. Fear, shadowy as the sharks beyond the nets at Durban, was never quite absent from sunlit South African sojourns. The beach at Muizenberg, near Cape Town, was vast and full of white people. The surf leaped. White bathers frolicked. Blacks waded into the filthy harbor at Kalk Bay. They slept in concrete-floored outbuildings whose single small windows resembled baleful eyes.

Duxbury, the house of my maternal grandfather, Laurie Adler, looked out over Main Road and the railway line near Kalk Bay station to the ocean and the Cape of Good Hope. There was the scent of salt and pine and, in certain winds, a pungent waft from the fish-processing plant in Fish Hoek. I would dangle a little net in rock pools and find myself hypnotized by the silky water and the quivering life in it. The heat, not the dry highveld heat of Johannesburg but something denser, pounded by the time we came back from the beach at lunchtime. It reverberated off the stone, angled into every recess. The lunch table was set, and soon enough Betty would appear with fried fish, usually firm-fleshed kingclip, so fresh it seemed to burst from its batter.

At night the lights of Simon's Town glittered, a lovely necklace strung along a promontory. Nobody could tire of that view. A black nanny took me across the road as a small child to the parapet above the rail track beside the sea where the kelp was never still in the tides. She perched me there over a seemingly fathomless precipice. I got the message and can still feel it, although the chasm of my imagination was in reality a drop of no more than a couple of meters.

"Moenie worry nie," Laurie would say as he raised a glass of Scotch or gin and tonic. Don't worry. Everything is fine. Whites are not going to fall off a cliff or over a parapet. Nothing will change. There will always be Sacks deli in Muizenberg, with its salt-cured beef and herring and lox, and there will always be crayfish of finger-licking sweetness. After the second drink—or the "other half," as he put it—Laurie would lick his lips and murmur: "The game is on!" How he loved it, the game of ever-renewed pleasures and chance. He was just manic enough to take the best of life, never get anxious, and not veer out of control, as his daughter, my mother, would.

Laurie lost a fortune on horses but somehow always contrived to come out ahead in the end. He had spent the last three years of World War II overseeing an Allied hospital in Al Qassasin, Egypt. The menu at his farewell dinner on August 26, 1945, comprised hors d'oeuvres, potage St. Germain, Welsh rarebit, fish cakes and tomato sauce, noisettes of lamb Portugaise, fried chicken and potato croquettes, roast beef and Yorkshire pudding, crème flan and caramel flan. He was the kind of man who managed to end a world war that had devastated Europe and destroyed its Jewish population with a meal like that. On his bedside table, under glass, he kept the cards from his one royal straight flush over the course of countless poker games.

"I feel like a new man," he'd say after the "other half" was downed, "and now the new man wants a drink!" He'd clap his hands above his head, and a servant would appear with a refill for the "Baas." *Yes, Master.* "Water never passed my lips," Laurie liked to say. My grandmother Flossie, of cooler temperament, preferred a phrase she learned from her mother: "The things you see when you don't have a gun." Asked how a couple's marriage was doing, she would shoot back, "I don't know—I've never slept under their bed." Flossie said all the women had affairs during World War II while their men were "up north"— several thousand miles up north—in Egypt. The thing was not to flaunt it. That would have been inexcusable. She was a great believer in discretion, charity, a good broker, and the stock of the De Beers mining company.

We would go to Kruger National Park, a favorite haunt of Laurie's. The early mornings were exquisite: lions loping across the road as they made their way to water holes; buck and horned wildebeest springing across the roads; zebra grazing in patterns arrayed across the shimmering grasses; elephants standing and staring and flapping their ears; vultures perched on the branches of dead trees or circling high in the sky over carrion; crocodiles still as logs with a shriek of hideous laughter in their bulging eyes. I watched transfixed as wild dogs tore into the carcass of an impala on the dusty track. The slow passage of a tortoise across the road was no less mesmerizing.

It seemed to me nature was slow, deliberate, with sudden bursts of acceleration. Nothing much moved as the heat of the day rose. Then the air quickened. An eagle soared, elephants charged, a leopard ripped its prey apart. Life then was a question of waiting and timing. It might idle for several years before packing several into a single one.

The living for my family was easy. The staff changed the nappies.

Laurie Adler with my sister, Jenny, and his blossoming watermelon

The houseboys brought the braziers to the right glow for the *braai*. Two gardeners were employed, one for the roses and one for the rest. When dinner ended, the bell was rung, either by hand or by pressure of a foot on a buzzer beneath the carpet. A black servant would appear dressed in a white outfit, perhaps with a red sash across it, often wearing white gloves. Laurie and his friends donned their whites for Sunday lunch, preceded by a cocktail of "gin and two" (one-third gin, one-third Cinzano Bianco, one-third Cinzano Rosso, and "full to the brim with ice"), before ambling off to play bowls. At picnics on Table Mountain, Laurie, a beret on his head, in pressed khaki shorts and white socks pulled almost up to his knees, would plunge a knife into the pale green watermelons, making a series of incisions before, with a flourish, allowing the fruit to fall open in oozing red bloom. We feasted and left a trail of eggshells and bitten-out watermelon rind. As for Sunday breakfast on the patio, there were always fresh scones with whipped cream.

Elsewhere lay the Africa of the Africans—the natives, as they were often called—the distant kaffir townships of dust and dirt and drudgery where water was drawn from a communal spigot, homes consisted of a single room, clothes were patched together from scraps of passed-down fabric, and the alleys were full of the stale stench of urine. I could smell the hardship in the sweat of the houseboys. I saw it in the yellowish tint of their eyes. I felt the separation in the utensils and cups set apart for use by the staff alone. The blacks were always walking as our cars purred past. There were no sidewalks for them to walk on.

A relative told me his first political memory from the early 1950s was of a great tide of black walkers streaming from Alexandra township—"like the Jews leaving Egypt," he said, but of course no liberation awaited. The blacks were protesting against a one-penny hike in bus fares. *Moenie worry nie,* my grandfather Laurie insisted. He had been born in South Africa in 1899, Flossie in 1900. They should know.

South Africa was as good a place as any for a Jew to live through the twentieth century, particularly an oyster-shucking bon vivant like Laurie. A friend of the family let slip a sentiment widely felt but seldom articulated: "Thank God for the blacks. If not for them, it would be us." Jews on the whole kept their heads down; better just to keep *stumm.* Flossie voted for Helen Suzman's anti-apartheid Progressive Party and then prayed the National Party remained in power—or she really might need that gun.

She was far from alone in such genteel hypocrisy. The blacks were a form of protection. If you are busy persecuting tens of millions of blacks, you do not have much left over for tens of thousands of Jews. For South African Jews, aware of the corpse-filled ditches and gas chambers of the Europe they had fled, the knowledge of the sixty-nine blacks cut down at Sharpeville in 1960 or the sight of blacks without passes being bundled into the back of police vans was discomfiting. But this was not genocide, after all. With conspicuous exceptions (more proportionately among Jews than any other white South Africans), Jews preferred to look away.

I tried to bring the picture into focus: my white mother and black nannies; the signs (once I could read them) on public toilets and train compartments, BLANKES WHITES and NIE-BLANKES NON-WHITES; the soothing abundance and the lip-drying fear. I sometimes found myself in the wrong places, a *Blanke* among the *Nie-Blankes,* a "European" among the "non-Europeans," on the wrong bench or at the wrong counter. I pushed on the surface of things, but it seemed to yield like

A beach for whites only not far from Cape Town, January 1, 1970   UN PHOTO/KM

the bark of an old cork tree. Life had two hemispheres, north and south, cool and heat. It was double, two-faced. Its facets did not dovetail. So I absorbed it and learned to cope with it by partitioning. I was a child who kept to the squares and off the lines of the sidewalk, treading carefully. Trust was a stranger to me. Like Janus, I had to look two ways. The family's South African homes overflowed with plenty. Yet their foundations were not deep, their history unclear, their future unsure. Only later did I begin to find out where we had come from and grasp the miracle of my mother's lost South African idyll.

Let us return to the beginning, to June 1895. First sight of Africa: the teeming dock at Cape Town; the bundles and boxes borne all the way from Lithuania; sun beating down on mountains that soar to a clear sky; a sea of people—black and white and brown—moving between the crates and bags piled on the quayside. Table Mountain traces a line so flat, it seems an apparition. Colors have intensified, scale grown. In the shtetl everything was flat and circumscribed. Wonders had to be willed from the trance of religious devotion. Here the very earth is exuberant, and there are peaks that reach to the heavens.

The two-week ocean crossing in steerage, or "third saloon," on a vessel of the Union or Castle Line has been difficult, but arrival on an unknown continent scarcely brings relief from anxiety. I see my paternal great-grandfather, Mateo Soloveychik, in heavy black boots, holding the hand of his eleven-year-old son, Jack (known as "Ponk"), as they make their way through the crowd. Immigration authorities require possession of twenty pounds to approve entry. Perhaps a benevolent *landsman,* or Lithuanian compatriot, is able to offer a little advice in Yiddish.

In the first volume of *Jewish Migration to South Africa: Passenger Lists from the UK 1890–1905,* I found a reference to a Mr. Soloweizik [*sic*], aged thirty-seven, "foreign," a carpenter, accompanied by a "Master Soloweizik," aged eleven, who traveled from London aboard the *Arab* of the Union Steamship line. That would be my paternal forebears, the father and brother of my grandmother Polly from Žagarė. "I. Michel," my mother's grandfather Isaac Michel, from Šiauliai, traveled at age nineteen on the *Doune Castle* on August 16, 1896. He had been born in Lithuania in March 1877 and listed his occupation as "prospector." Some 80 percent of the eastern European Jews making their way to South Africa between the 1880s and 1914 were Litvaks, and at least half of them passed through the Poor Jews' Temporary Shelter at 82 Leman Street in London's East End. The shelter was established in 1885 to ease the passage of Jewish transmigrants from eastern Europe to South Africa.

Rudimentary networks facilitated the journeys of the forty thousand Lithuanian Jews who uprooted themselves to come to South Africa from villages and towns like Žagarė and Šiauliai in the three decades before World War I. Tickets could be bought in advance through agencies in eastern Europe linked to the shipping companies that brought migrants first to London and then on to the African promised land of ostrich feathers and diamonds and gold, where Jews were the right color to have at least an entrée into the privileged caste of an emergent society.

From Žagarė it was not a great distance to the Baltic port of Libau (now Liepāja in the modern state of Latvia). The need to suborn Russian officials could complicate the journey. Bribes were only the first humiliation. The ships departed twice a week with loads of three hundred to five hundred migrants crammed below deck. In London, bedraggled Jews were met and escorted to the Shelter. A large number of them, 41.58 percent, listed no occupation on arrival. The three next-largest occupations were tradesman or dealer (22.48 percent), tailor (6.23 percent), and bootmaker (5.81 percent). The most skilled profession listed was watchmaker (1.06 percent). The learned—the students of the yeshivas—tended to stay back in the *heim.* The New World, whether American or African, was suspect.

The two principal shipping companies—they merged in 1900 to form the Union-Castle Line—paid for accommodation and food at the Shelter for a maximum of fourteen days, before ushering Jews on board at the East India Dock or Southampton. An article in the *Jewish World* of March 9, 1900, under the headline "Southward Ho!," quotes Sir Donald Currie on the quality of the kosher food on his ships and the good behavior of the Jews: "Our officers have never had any reason to complain of the conduct of the third saloon passengers, they are well behaved, and are very grateful for anything that is done for them." The shtetl was not a place that accustomed its inhabitants to even minimal gestures of kindness from men in uniform.

Soloveychik (he would become Solomon in South Africa) has left everything, including his wife, Sarah, and five of his children, and ventured across the world into the unknown. Perhaps it is the arrival in 1894 of Polly, the last of those children, that prompts the gamble, or word filtering back from fellow Litvaks of the opportunities in the Cape and gold-rush Johannesburg, or some humiliation from a Russian official, or just the inability to feed his family—this carpenter with a young son takes the step Jews have taken for millennia on the road from Babylonia to Egypt, and the Land of Israel and North Africa and the Iberian peninsula and, after the expulsion from Christian Spain in 1492, the Polish expanse and eastern Europe. He moves.

Behind him lies a Europe where, even as Jewish life in the eastern shtetl has scarcely shifted in its habits, emancipation for Jews is sweeping the lands west of the Elbe. In postrevolutionary France and in the new nation-state of Germany, Jews are rising in the professions, and some are amassing great fortunes in finance and trade. They have benefited from the elimination of old barriers but will suffer from the rise of new nationalisms—as the Dreyfus Affair of 1894 illustrated in France. Jews alone—unlike Serbs or Italians or Germans or Romanians—are being told that the condition of their emancipation is that they define themselves not as a nation but in exclusively religious terms. Some Jews, led by Theodor Herzl (who covered the Dreyfus Affair as a foreign correspondent based in Paris), are concluding that whatever the Jews' striving for assimilation, Europe will never accept them. The solution to the "Jewish Question" has to be found in a separate independent Jewish state in Palestine, formed through the mass migration of Jews out of Europe. Herzl's book *The Jewish State* (1896) was published just as several of my forebears arrived in South Africa from Europe.

They, too, headed to a state-in-the-making. South Africa was then no more than a patchwork of political units, including the British colonies of the Cape and Natal and two inland Dutch republics, the Orange Free State and the Transvaal. It had been transformed since the late 1860s by the discovery first of diamonds at Kimberley, deep in the interior of the Cape, and then in 1886 of the richest seam of gold in the world on the Witwatersrand ("Ridge of White Water"), so named because Dutch-speaking farmers of the Transvaal had seen streams there on the upland. The Main Reef, a long sheet of ore, was like a rucked-up blanket. It broke the surface at the crest of the Witwatersrand where, at six thousand feet, far from any river, the city of Johannesburg burst into being. To east and west the reef fell away. Initial mining took place where the gold was most accessible, at Johannesburg, but all it took to find gold on either side of the city was to sink a shaft. Countless townships, or *dorps,* including my mother's birthplace of Krugersdorp, grew up along the line of the reef around these so-called deep levels. The quantity of ore was extraordinary. No other goldfield on earth was like it. Word of the discovery reached across the world. It filtered even into the small villages of Lithuania.

My great-grandfathers Michel and Adler and Soloveychik head from Cape Town toward the gold. It is a trek of almost nine hundred miles, but they do not go in a straight line. Opportunity and chance encounters create diversions. All but Adler, who arrives the earliest and has grown up in London's East End, come from Lithuania. Sometimes they can travel a section by railroad, but much of the time the journey is hard. They advance on foot and in mule-drawn wagons or ox wagons. There are few bridges; some rivers have to be waded or swum through. The mules need constant rest. The heat of the day confines travel to the hours after dawn. Native Africans act as guides and sometimes bearers for these white-skinned "Europeans." At night, camped near water, guard is kept against wild animals.

A few Jews like Barney Barnato and David Harris from the East End of London, or Sammy Marks from Lithuania, have already made fortunes in mining, joining the Randlords, but for most life begins as a peddler, or *smous*. Isaac Michel, who would become a retailing tycoon, started out as a *smous*. The origin of the word is unclear—perhaps a corruption of *Moses* or of the German word *Mauschel,* used for the haggling Jewish trader—but there is no doubt about what the *smous* did or how important his activity was in early South Africa. He was a roving peddler with all manner of wares providing the link between scattered *dorps* and far-flung farms. He bought on credit; he bartered and sold. He might start out on foot, graduate to a couple of donkeys laden with goods, and progress to a mule-drawn cart before acquiring horses and a covered wagon. The capital amassed could be used after a few years to acquire a general-goods store. The passage from *smous* to shopkeeper was a natural one.

Michel bases himself for a while in Leeukop (Lion's Head), about sixty miles northwest of Johannesburg, before moving to the city, where his first retail store, on the corner of Commissioner and Eloff Streets, is called C-to-C, like his preferred Cape-to-Cairo cigarette. He was always a man who tailored his ambitions to the size of the African continent. Johannesburg was a natural home for an immigrant on the make.

The city, at first little more than a mining camp with scattered tents and a few huts, grows to the din of the stamp batteries crushing gold ore through the night. The air is tinged with a fine yellow dust. Miners' lamps sway as they walk through shanties where typhoid sometimes rages. The first streets with brick or stone buildings spread from Market Square. Sickly yellow slag heaps, the color of bad school omelets, grow as the town grows. Like the headgear of the mines—the triangular metal structures fitted to lower cages of miners and haul them to the surface again—these viscous mine dumps composed of tailings are visible signs of the hidden riches that propel a new city into being.

Men play dominoes in dark cafés. Bars and brothels and prostitutes multiply to cater to the newcomers, known as *Uitlanders,* or incomers, and to the Boers. In truth, the new city is made up almost entirely of incomers. They are hungry for gold and needy of everything: shelter, water, and food. Meals simmer on braziers, slabs of meat hang on hooks, and from the *kaffir eethuis* (African canteen) wafts the sweet, heavy smell of tripe and other entrails stewing in cauldrons. Burlap sacks of maize and other staples line the walls of general stores. In wooden casks, pickles float in brine.

The city must grow for the reef that keeps giving. Gold production soars. New corporations multiply. Johannesburg from its inception is a commercial town. Its thing is money. It is gaudy and vulgar, a city of English and Boers, Jews and Greeks, Americans and Italians, Chinese and Indians, all of them hustlers at a new frontier. The immigrants are not alone. The townships that sprawl around the city's limits are home to black miners who have been drawn to the Rand in search of money to take back to their families in the East Cape or Basutoland. Tens of thousands of them have already arrived by 1895, living in appalling conditions, vulnerable to moonshine and midday heat.

My maternal great-grandfather from the East End of London, Sidney Adler, was present at Johannesburg's creation. Born on April 10, 1861, he attended the Jews' Free School and was apprenticed as a cabinet-maker before sailing for South Africa on the *Leuton* in 1878. A variety of jobs followed: bookkeeper in Cape Town, diamond digger in Lydenburg, cook and furniture repairer in Kimberley, gold prospector in Barberton, and hydraulic pump operator in a Vereeniging coal mine.

The mine did not fare well. Equipment being transported from Cape Town was lost in the Vaal River after a bridge collapsed. Adler moved on. An account by his daughter Lily describes his arrival in Johannesburg in 1887:

> Sid opened a small liquor business at the corner of Fraser and Commissioner Streets. It was a single storied tin shack with a mud floor. This was one of the first Public saloons and was named "Maggie's Bar" after the buxom blonde barmaid named Maggie. The bar became very popular and miners, very often down on their luck, rubbed shoulders with budding mining magnates who could enjoy a chat and drink together. The Stock Exchange was nearby. It consisted of a chain across Commissioner Street with the brokers on the one side and the public on the other.

Madness gripped the Stock Exchange in 1888, people screaming, fortunes being made and lost in minutes as gold shares rocketed, then collapsed. Sink a shaft, give it a name, incorporate yourself, and trade the paper after a couple of drinks at Maggie's Bar.

In the early days, Johannesburg was sometimes referred to as "Jewburg" or "Judasburg."

With his interest in the liquor business, Sidney Adler would have been labeled a "Peruvian." This was the odd, pejorative term denoting the mass of uneducated, poor Jews pouring into the city and setting up as canteen keepers or peddlers or small tradesmen. The term may have been an acronym for Polish and Russian Union, a Jewish club in Kimberley in the early days; its origin is unclear. The *Johannesburg Times* of 1896 carried this description: "To the ordinary member of the public he presents the apparition of a slovenly, unkempt and generally unwashed edition, in various numbers, of the wandering Jew. As a sort of commercial shield, he carries a basket of eggs on his right arm, while holding his money tightly clenched in his sinister hand."

The Peruvian designation reflected disquiet about the number of Jews arriving in Johannesburg. One correspondent, J. A. Hobson of *The Manchester Guardian,* consulted an early city directory and was disturbed to find "sixty-eight Cohens against twenty-eight Jones and fifty-three Browns." During the Anglo-Boer War of 1899–1902 that would lead to the unification of South Africa, some Jews fled back to the Cape. For Lady Cecil, the wife of the British high commissioner, the worst refugees were "the Jews who had come to South Africa from the ghettos of Eastern Europe . . . a curious people, in rags, with their belongings in untidy bundles and yet it was often found that they were quite well off, and the possessors of valuables."

A prospectus about South Africa published by the Jewish Colonization Association in St. Petersburg in 1905 suggested the extent of the Jewish presence in Johannesburg: "They participate in all areas of industry. . . . Many immigrants are involved in small trade business. Until recently, the alcohol business was very profitable; alcohol was sold to kaffirs; today the law prohibits the alcohol business and punishes it with six months imprisonment, therefore immigrants establish small shops." It estimated the Jewish population of the Transvaal at 25,000, or 20 percent of the "European" population.

Adler moved on from Maggie's to open the Red Lamp Bar and Saloon on Commissioner Street. He then tried his luck with Steyn's Bar in nearby Fordsburg, where, at the age of thirty-six, he met Kate Cohen, who had recently arrived from London to visit her sister. They were married in 1897 in the Park Street synagogue, inaugurated by President Kruger in 1892. Together they opened the Transvaal Hotel on De Villiers Street in Johannesburg, before running The Old Pioneer on the corner of Loveday and Plein Streets. Bedrooms opened out onto a shared veranda. Many of the guests were Cornish miners from England who would hand over their salaries to Adler for room, board, and booze. The couple, by now with four children, sold out in 1915 and moved to the relative peace of Natal, where in Newcastle, on the road from Johannesburg to Durban, they ran the twenty-bedroom Commercial Hotel for many years. It was a popular place to break the journey to the coast. Once a week a bioscope—or movie—was shown in the town hall.

Black-and-white photographs of Sidney Adler all show him as an established family man and proprietor. There are no images of his hustling Red Lamp Bar and Saloon days. He has made his mark in the new country. He is short and stout and well tailored. The gold chain of his pocket watch loops across his buttoned vest, and a handkerchief puffs from his breast pocket. His shoes are shined, stern moustache trimmed, hands clasped behind his back until, in later years, the

My great-grandfather Sidney Adler, a Johannesburg pioneer, 1918

right hand grips a cane. Even on the beach he wears a jacket. He never smiles. By repute, he never swears. He is stoical, a trait inherited by Laurie and by my mother (who was also an immaculate dresser). When gout causes his toes and elbows to swell to the size of tennis balls, he does not complain. His wife, a fraction taller than he, favors bold floral dresses that envelop her matronly form. They are a straight-backed couple. "There are three things in life," she likes to say, "punctuality, cleanliness and honesty." And: "If you can't say anything nice about somebody, don't say anything."

In these images, the incomer's struggle, the dusty past, the uncertain roads, and the long saloon nights have been eclipsed. The pain of uprooting, repeated in my family with each generation for more than a century now, has been concealed. There is a single photograph of me seated on my great-grandmother Kate Adler's lap when we arrived in South Africa in 1955. She was a widow then; Sidney had died earlier

*Four generations: I am seated on the lap of my great-grandmother Kate Adler,
with my grandmother Flossie and mother, June, 1955*

that year at the age of ninety-four. She wears a double string of pearls
around her neck. Her expression is watchful and wise. She had lived
in London before that visit to her sister in 1897. Her life is ending; she
presses her hands to my six-month-old chest; she will be dead within
eighteen months. My twenty-six-year-old mother is seated beside us.
She is radiant with new motherhood and her return to South Africa.

The resemblance between Sidney Adler and Laurie is striking: the
same compact build, clipped moustache, and military bearing. But
Laurie's expression in photos is more carefree. He had not known
the hardscrabble immigrant years. Born at the turn of the century in
Johannesburg, he would be in the second graduating class from the
Witwatersrand Medical School in 1925. That class had seventeen graduates; there were just four graduates the previous year. Some of the
lectures, in botany and zoology, were given in tin huts adjoining the
School of Mines, and early graduates were known as "Tin Templers."

Jewish life, having stood still for centuries in the shtetl, immobilized in devotion and contemplation, was fast-forwarded by Africa.

I went with Laurie to Vereeniging, where his father had operated the hydraulic pump in the coal mine in the late nineteenth century. Laurie was a doctor whose real interest was business. After World War II he had a profitable idea. Tuberculosis was rampant, particularly among the black population. As a young medical officer in 1930, he had written a "Survey of Tuberculosis in the Pretoria, Witwatersrand and Vereeniging Areas." Now he concocted a persuasive interpretation of the labyrinth of apartheid laws that obliged the Afrikaner-led government of the National Party to pay for treatment of "native" tubercular and mental health patients. With partners, Laurie established a corporation that ran the hospitals, often on premises acquired from closed mines, whose vast spartan dormitories with concrete beds could be converted into wards. The company provided all the facilities. The government paid per patient and per day. It was a lucrative business.

The place we went to see in Vereeniging was a mental hospital. We stood in a fenced area, in the middle of a large crowd of blacks with faraway gazes, jerky gestures, and twisted smiles. Laurie handed out shoes and barked orders. His years "up north" in Egypt during the war as a lieutenant colonel with the South African armed forces had ensconced brusque habits of command. One man threw his shoes onto the corrugated-iron roof. He was escorted away. A roll call revealed a missing patient. Sometime before, a patient had wandered out onto the railway line and been killed by a train. The situation seemed combustible. Laurie, unruffled, extolled the care and the food. I looked at him: a stocky, bald white man in a white shirt and pressed khaki shorts and long socks standing in the midst of a horde of troubled blacks with swollen ankles and unfocused eyes. What struck me was his assurance. I don't think Laurie ever allowed doubt to cloud his confidence or dampen his lust for life, even when his own daughter, my mother, became mentally ill. He knew about mental illness but could not acknowledge it within his own family.

My father is not one for family trees. Still, when my mother tried to commit suicide in 1978, he mapped out her antecedents as a scientific exercise. On the genealogical table, he placed a black dot beside those afflicted with mania, manic depression, or depression. Black dots abound. One is inked in next to Laurie's sister Lily, another beside his sister Mickey. On my mother's mother's side, the situation is no happier. Of the six children of Isaac Michel and his wife, Jennie, three suffered from mental instability. Flossie, my grandmother, was spared. Two of her brothers and her youngest sister were not.

My forebears broke with the past, shed it, tried to bury it, losing touch with one another and fanning out across the world. There was the ebb and flow of fortune and the struggles of Jewish identity and assimilation—and all the while they carried within them a gene that formed an unbroken chain with the past, liable to surface in any setting and at any moment. They carried within them something intrinsic to the depressive state: loss. What else, after the adrenaline, is uprooting but loss? In *The Rings of Saturn,* W. G. Sebald writes, "My rational mind is nonetheless unable to lay the ghosts of repetition that haunt me with ever greater frequency." Few escape these *ghosts of repetition.* Life idles and accelerates, as I learned in the quiet and quickening South African dawn of the Kruger Park. It also doubles back.

Human Street runs through the center of Krugersdorp, a modest town thirty miles west of Johannesburg. Hominid fossils dating back more than three million years have been found in the area. The street runs straight, with a line of gnarled plane trees down the middle. It is busiest around the intersection with Market Street, where a cluster of cell phone stores now do business.

The West Rand Consolidated mine used to be located at the end of Market, but the mine is closed. The reef that made South Africa stopped yielding gold here some years ago. Krugersdorp was one of the many settlements strung out along the sixty-mile-long gold gusher of the Witwatersrand. A vast slag heap of yellow cyanide sand, as flat-topped as Table Mountain, testifies to the volume of earth dislodged in pursuit of the most coveted and ductile of metals. Storms would blow in from Randfontein and you would see them split over the dump. Krugersdorp without gold was orphaned.

The town grew in the shadow of Johannesburg and for the same

Human Street in the reef mining town of Krugersdorp,
where my mother was born in 1929   DANIEL LEVY

reason. One of its first residents was Abner Cohen (no relation), who
built the Monument Hotel in 1887—the same year Sidney Adler
opened Maggie's Bar in Johannesburg. By 1894 the Jewish community
in Krugersdorp was large enough to host a minyan; a service was held
that year at Rosh Hashanah. In 1902 the town's first synagogue was
founded, with Cohen as its president.

For many years the Jewish community of Krugersdorp prospered,
active in mining and commerce, outgrowing its original redbrick synagogue on Burger Street. (A Star of David engraved on the facade is
today the only clue to the past of the shuttered building.) A larger synagogue of proud proportions was built on Potgieter Street and opened
in 1966. But soon enough Jews began to dwindle with the town's fortunes. The synagogue, too big for its congregation, was sold to the
Christian Faith Worship Center. A banner at its entrance now says:
"Not all questions can be answered by Google. Follow the word of
God." Inside, the front wall is adorned with a large mosaic in Hebrew
of the Ten Commandments, the back wall with an image of a meno-

My mother at 3 Human Street

rah, and along the side wall in giant lettering run the words JESUS IS KING. June would have hooted with laughter until she had to wipe the tears from her eyes.

My mother was born at 3 Human Street in Krugersdorp on June 3, 1929. Laurie, her father, had established himself there. After qualification at Wits and his marriage to Flossie in 1925, he became mine medical officer to West Rand Consolidated and later medical officer of health for Krugersdorp. He was dapper, like his father, a good boxer, an energetic man, an organizer. In 1924, almost half a century after his cockney father, Sidney, arrived from London in a South Africa that was not yet a Union, he had become president of the student represen-

Laurie with June and brother Sydney, South Africa, 1938

tative council of the University of the Witwatersrand. Laurie had that incalculable asset: a good temperament.

June was a breath-holder as an infant, a condition often linked to frustration or some painful experience. Her father was busy, her elegant mother remote and sparing with physical affection. June was bright, gregarious, intense, and pretty, with side-parted dark hair and skinny knock-kneed legs. Her brother, Sydney (with a different spelling from his grandfather as a nod to the Jewish injunction against naming children after the living), had been born two years earlier. They would ride together along the ridge to Johannesburg in the rumble seat of Laurie's car, the warm air ruffling her curls. She would try to tag along with Sydney when he went out in a gang of Jewish boys to take on the Afrikaners who goaded the Krugersdorp *Jode* (Jews). When a brawl started, she would run away.

Life was placid and predictable in Krugersdorp. The landscape told a single story, of the rush for gold. It was there in the mine dumps and there in the gum trees around the shafts, planted because they grew rapidly and could provide timber to buttress tunnels and low gullies leading to the reef where black miners labored. A thin line tied the whites perched in Africa to the European civilization with which they identified. In such churned-up earth yielding finite wealth, what sort of roots could be planted? This European annex was fragile.

In 1936, when June was seven, upheaval came. Laurie took the family on a return journey to Britain, where he did postgraduate work in public health at Edinburgh University. Little June and Sydney were packed off to English boarding school at Frensham Heights in Surrey. The first children to meet them there in the school's mock-Tudor mansion had a question: If you're really from Africa, how come you're not black?

Life was full of puzzles. Brambles and foxes and berry picking and plummy British accents were not what June had been acquainted with in Krugersdorp. Using a pencil, she wrote a postcard to Laurie in 1936. The image on the card is of a child wearing a crown startled by blackbirds hovering around a pie: *Sing a song of sixpence / A pocket full of Rye / Four and twenty blackbirds / Baked in a pie.* June writes: "Dear Dad, I hope you are very well. Mum came to see us. I hope you are getting on. Lots love, June xx." At seven, in boarding school in a foreign land, you adapt, or at least you try to, and you may want to fly away.

Laurie wrote back from Edinburgh to my mother, now on a school break with Flossie at the Hotel Royale in Bournemouth: "I have been working hard but often think of you my precious one and hope you [are] having a real good time. You must be sweet to mother so that she does not get upset." On May 12, 1937, he sent her a "Coronation Souvenir" postcard commemorating the crowning of King George VI at Westminster Abbey. The new king's brother had abdicated a few months earlier to marry his American mistress. "Darling June," it says. "Hope you like this card—please write to me. Daddy."

June and Sydney in England, 1936

Sometimes, on breaks from school in London, June would stay near Marble Arch with her great-uncle Michael Adler. A distinguished rabbi, Adler had compiled the 1916 *Prayer Book for Jewish Sailors and Soldiers* at the front during World War I and served as chaplain to Jewish soldiers. It begins with a "prefatory note" signed by him: "This abbreviated form of the Prayer Book has been compiled for the use of Jewish Members of His Majesty's Navy and Army. It is hoped that this book will meet the wants of the very large number of English Jews who are taking part in the present Great European War." On the last page is a personal note from Adler: "The God of Israel keep you all and bring you safely home with victory." The first prayer for the sixteen thousand British Jews on active service includes this line: "Fill our hearts with courage and steadfastness that we may perform our duty to our King and Country for the honor of Israel and the Empire."

The word order suggests Adler's attempt to balance loyalties: first king, then Britain, then Israel, then empire. Jewish loyalty to the Crown had been questioned: thousands of Yiddish-speaking East European Jews in the East End of London were not yet naturalized and so could not serve. In November 1915 *The Jewish Chronicle* reported examples of recruiting officers saying, "Lord Kitchener does not want any more Jews in the Army." But Jews clamored to prove their loyalty.

Writing the previous year, Adler stressed the Jewish commitment to the Crown:

> We have reason to be especially stimulated by the knowledge of the manner in which our Jewish men have proved their readiness to offer their lives upon the altar of duty. Some, like Lieutenant Ronald Henriques, have already sealed their devotion with their blood. Gallantly and eagerly they have stepped forward. From my official statistics I can declare that quite nine-tenths of the eligible youth of the community from all parts of the country have enlisted; they have left parents and homes in order to prepare to show themselves men. We, fathers and mothers who have given our children to this cause, are proud of our boys in the King's service. May God guard them all! If we were proud of being Englishmen two months ago, we are ten times as proud of that title today. The secret of this wondrous enthusiasm that has filled the soul of Anglo-Jewry is apparent to all.

By the end of the war, however, having toured the front several times and seen the carnage, Adler had begun to question his *Dulce et Decorum Est pro Patria Mori*. On July 6, 1918, he wrote: "All this colossal upheaval will have been in vain unless civilized mankind resolves once and for all that every effort should be made . . . that War shall cease henceforth." Quoting the British journalist Philip Gibbs, he continued:

> The conscience of Europe must not be lulled to sleep again by the narcotics of the old phrases about "the ennobling influence of war" and "its purging fires." It must be shocked by the stark reality of this crime of war in which all Humanity is involved, so that from all the peoples of the civilized world there will be a great cry of rage and

My mother's great-uncle Michael Adler, a rabbi to Jewish servicemen in World War I

horror if the spirit of militarism, either in this country or elsewhere, raises its head again and demands new sacrifices of blood and life's beauty.

Adler went on to review the contribution of British Jews to the 1914–18 war effort:

> History will ask, and will have a right to ask, "Did those British citizens of the House of Israel to whom equality of rights and equality of opportunity were granted by the State some sixty years ago, did these men and women do their duty in the ordeal of battle; did that race, which yet remains faithful to the religion of its father and forms but a small community of a quarter of a million souls in the United Kingdom, did its representatives embrace the opportunity presented to them to demonstrate, beyond the shadow of a doubt, their complete sympathy and fellowship with their brother Englishmen, their loyalty to the Empire, both for life and for death, both in the hour of defeat and in the hour of victory?" . . . These are vital

questions and our answer is a clear and unmistakable YES! English Jews have every reason to be satisfied with the degree of their participation both at home and on the battlefronts in the struggle for victory. Let the memory of our sacred dead—who number over 2,300—testify to this.

By the time June met with her great-uncle in 1937, less than two decades later, Adler's words already seemed poignant and forlorn. Militarism had risen in Germany. Hitler was about to plunge Europe into another devastating war. Except in Britain, the loyalty to their nations of newly emancipated Jews, demonstrated by service during World War I, was to count for nothing as Hitler set out to annihilate them. An Iron Cross for valor at the Somme did nothing to keep a German Jew from the gas.

In Adler's emphasis on the loyalty of English Jews, an old disquiet lurks: Do we belong? Are we completely accepted, have all our efforts at integration and assimilation made us citizens on a par with any others? While his brother Sidney had sailed for Africa in 1878, prospected for diamonds at Kimberley, worked in a coal mine, and run a saloon as Johannesburg rose, Michael Adler had stayed on in London and made good. He was an Englishman through and through, or so he wanted passionately to believe. He was a rabbi identified as a "chaplain" and a "reverend" in the armed forces, offering prayers and solace and ways to reconcile their loyalties to Jews serving the Crown at Passchendaele. Later in life my mother would speak proudly of him.

It must have been bewildering for her then, not yet eight, placed in a boarding school, to zigzag between worlds. There was one link she could not have known. On my father's family tree, drawn up in a desperate moment, Michael Adler's three children—Winkle, Ros, and Lilian—all have the black dots of mental instability beside their names.

CHAPTER 4

In the Barrel

M y mother is being wheeled into a stark room in a sprawling, redbrick Victorian Gothic asylum. She is not yet thirty in an England strange to her. She has two infants and is suffering from postpartum depression (or puerperal psychosis, as it was then known) that has afflicted her ever since the birth of my sister, Jenny, in May 1957. Nobody knows now and nobody knew then how exactly electroconvulsive therapy (ECT) works: whether it somehow causes brain cells to be renewed, or changes the levels of chemicals in the brain, or alters the body's system so that stress hormones are kept in balance.

The treatment in the 1950s was often administered without anesthetic or muscle relaxants. The body might jolt so violently as to cause broken bones. I see my slight, fragrant young mother with metal plates being affixed to either side of her head, flattening her dark curls, her heart racing as a doctor straps the plates to her swabbed temples, enclosing her skull in its high-voltage carapace. I can almost taste the material wedged in her oversalivating mouth for her to bite on when the current passes. I can see her imploring eyes and feel her fingers clench.

It is only a year since her emigration to London. The South African safety net has gone. There is no string on the toe of the sleepwalker. She is an emigrant in a cold place with a cool and brilliant man.

Sylvia Plath had the same treatment five years earlier in Boston. She described it in *The Bell Jar,* her semiautobiographical novel: "I shut my eyes. There was a brief silence, like an indrawn breath. Then something bent down and took hold of me and shook me like the end of the world. *Whee-ee-ee-ee-ee,* it shrilled, through an air cracking with blue light, and with each flash a great jolt drubbed me till I thought my bones would break and the sap fly out of me like a split plant. I wondered what terrible thing it was that I had done."

This was the question June asked herself. It was compounded by guilt. She left us with the same question, although she would never have wanted to: *What terrible thing have I done for my mother to disappear and suffer so?*

For a long time she pretended it had not happened. When, in 1983, my first wife and I were about to move from Brussels to Rome with our infant children, we had dinner with my parents in London. My wife expressed some anxiety about the move to a new place with young children. "Oh," June replied testily, "what are you talking about? When I moved to London from Johannesburg with small children, we quickly adjusted and were just fine!"

When I was in Žagarė, I read the letter of a Jewish Holocaust survivor, George Gordimer. In it he said, "I have had and have many health problems. However, the one health problem that has been with me all my life is depression." My mother was spared the Nazi terror Gordimer endured as a small child. She was not, however, spared the strain of upheaval, displacement, and fear. She, too, faced the puzzle of the "genetic" and the "environmental" in her "cyclical" states, alternately manic and inert. She, too, faced the things not talked about.

I tracked down George Gordimer in Cranford, New Jersey. He is a compact, angular man. His large gray-blue eyes are the most prominent feature in a gaunt face. He talks in a gravelly voice, pursuing his point with a methodical insistence. The voice slows and slurs a little when he is particularly down. For a long time now, he has been taking a small dose of Valium, a habit he has tried but failed to break. He still endures episodes of hyperactivity. When things don't go his way, he can also get very depressed, even if the trigger is a trivial thing. He has a tendency to obsess about small things and slights. His mind will race like some infernal machine or freeze as if caught in a paralyzing beam.

Gordimer always looks trim. There is not an ounce of fat on him. His shave is close. He favors gray pants and light blue shirts. Every morning he reads the *New York Times* "A" section from cover to cover. If he needs to go online, he visits the library; he does not have a computer. He reviews his investments in municipal bonds. He and his wife, Dorothy, go out every Saturday night for dinner, but most of the restaurants they liked have closed. If you were looking for someone to fade into a crowd, someone hovering always at the brink of invisibility, Gordimer would be that man.

His life changed, not for the first time, in the fall of 1971. On the way home from his laboratory at Air Products and Chemicals, Inc., in Middlesex, New Jersey, Gordimer had a panic attack. He was on the Garden State Parkway in bumper-to-bumper traffic. A graduate of MIT with a doctorate from the Polytechnic Institute of Brooklyn, he was working on polymeric coatings for a variety of applications, including latex paints and adhesives. Some of the pressure-sensitive adhesives were for Band-Aids. Gordimer's throat dried up as he contemplated the rear lights of the cars backed up on the parkway. His heart thumped; his breathing was irregular. He had no idea what was going on. At the first exit, he found a phone booth from which he called his older brother, Seymour, who came to pick him up. A doctor at the local hospital wanted to give George a shot to calm him down, but Gordimer was not having a shot unless there was something specific wrong with him. He was very insistent about that. Later, after his first heart surgery in 1982, a double bypass, he would get into the habit of saying to doctors, "If it makes any difference, I am actually two years older than my official age." But that was only when he started to open up about the past.

When he arrived home that night, Gordimer was still agitated. His wife, also a chemist by training, had never seen him in such a state. She tried to calm him with a back rub. The next day his panic had eased, but Gordimer felt depressed to the point of being unable to move. When he eventually returned to work, he used local streets rather than the highway to get there, adding twenty minutes to his driving time. If alone, he always avoided the tunnels into Manhattan. They spooked him. Exhaustion and unfamiliar places were not good for Gordimer.

He would get jumpy. Haircuts were also an issue. He would panic in the barber's chair when the apron was fastened around his neck.

Not telling people things was a habit he had slipped into early. When asked where he was born, Gordimer would always respond that he was "raised" in Elizabeth, New Jersey, a subtle evasion that he found passed unnoticed. When asked what kind of name "Gordimer" was, he would answer: "You got me! I have no idea."

He did not want to get into what had happened, and how, anyway, was he to explain? He had two ages, two names, and two places of birth—in short, he was a doppelgänger. These were not facts readily broached with anyone—*Oh, by the way, I'm not who you think I am.* Even with Dorothy it was difficult.

Gordimer's parents had changed his date of birth to October 10, 1940, from the real date of October 10, 1938, in order to qualify him for additional milk rations as a hungry child in a displaced persons' camp in Germany in 1946. The camp was in a converted monastery. Every morning Gordimer would comb the lice out of his hair, until his hair was shaved. That was the hot summer before they sailed away on a transport ship from the port of Bremerhaven, Germany. The vessel was called the *Ernie Pyle,* named after a great U.S. newspaper correspondent killed in combat at the end of World War II. When they reached Elizabeth, New Jersey, on January 16, 1947, the Gordimers submitted the later birth date to U.S. authorities. In the belief that it was easier to get into the United States as Germans than as Lithuanians, they also changed Gordimer's place of birth from Šiauliai to Memel, which was German in 1940, having been annexed by Hitler the previous year. (Memel is now the Lithuanian port of Klaipėda.) Finally, they changed his name from Jona to George.

Thus did Jona Gordimer, born in 1938 in Šiauliai, Lithuania, birthplace of my grandfather and great-grandfather, become George Gordimer, born in 1940 in Memel, Germany, by the time he reached the United States. The family took up residence in the Port section of Elizabeth, a hardscrabble neighborhood inhabited mainly by eastern Europeans, including many Lithuanians and Poles. New Jersey's backdrop of derricks and factory stacks and storage tanks took the place of the Lithuanian woods. His father, Ira (born Icikas), had always been a hustler, one reason for the family's survival. In Lithuania, before the war, he'd travel to Minsk and haul back lumber to sell in his hardware store in Papilė, near Šiauliai. Now, at the age of forty-four, his street smarts were useful in starting over.

Ira Gordimer went to work for an uncle, Morris Lipton, who had left Lithuania in the 1920s and had a successful furniture store. Ira would move furniture, mount furniture, and deliver furniture. Later he went into the dry-cleaning business. People always need clean clothes, he said, just like they need to eat. Then it was property, basic rooming houses. George had to work as a young boy. He and his brother, Seymour (born Šolomas), would sell shopping bags at the local open-air market on Saturdays for five cents each. They used to offload five hundred bags and make twenty-five dollars, good money. Gordimer also worked in the rooming houses, making beds, changing linen, mowing lawns. He picked up English fast. He was an American boy. Nobody knew he came from Europe. Wasn't America one continent-sized exercise in amnesia? The future mattered; the past was dangerous, fraught with shame.

Seymour had a best friend in grade school who was Lithuanian. The neighbors were Poles. Once Gordimer's ball went over the fence, and he jumped after it to be confronted by a dog and an older Polish kid who yelled: "Get the hell out of here, you dirty Jew!" Seymour nearly choked an Italian boy who'd called him a kike. He had him down on the ground with his hands on his throat. George had to pull his frenzied brother off.

Still, Gordimer never talked about being a Jew. He did not want to be stereotyped—"Oh, that's the Holocaust kid" or "That's the Holocaust Jew kid." Jew or gentile, what did it matter? That was what the Nazis had done: peg people. At least that was how he rationalized it. So he was "raised" in Elizabeth, born nowhere, and had a family name he couldn't for the life of him figure out, he said. His bar mitzvah was a complete joke, a recitation of words he could pronounce but whose meaning was a mystery: "I did not want people to stereotype me as this or that. If you say you are a Holocaust survivor, they know everything about you."

He never went out with Jewish girls. His father asked why. George replied: "I go out with the girls I meet. There are more gentile than Jewish girls in the United States."

When he attended the Polytechnic Institute of Brooklyn in the mid-1960s, he roomed with an exchange student from Tashkent who thought Soviet communism was an excellent thing. They argued a lot. Gordimer told the Soviet student what he thought of Stalin's deportations, killing, and tyranny in the Baltic states. But he never mentioned his family's Lithuanian origins or his own suffering at the hands of Nazis and Soviets during World War II.

After the panic attacks began, Gordimer consulted psychiatrists. They told him he was still in hiding because he was afraid to expose himself. He shot back that he did not want to be tagged as Jewish: that was not what defined him as a human being. Besides, he thought the whole religion thing was nonsense. At MIT he took courses in Eastern and Western religion just to find out how full of baloney it all was. In every essay, Gordimer attacked religion with a vehemence that shocked his professor. *George, face it, you are hiding something,* the psychiatrists insisted.

Gordimer, at the age of five, had been hidden in a barrel in the Šiauliai ghetto when, on November 5, 1943, the Nazis conducted a *Kinderaktion,* going house to house to grab 725 Jewish children. They were taken away, stacked in the back of trucks, and then loaded onto freight cars for extermination. After that there were no children in the ghetto. As birds go silent before a storm, children's voices vanished. The Gordimer boys spent three days in a lightless cellar with a trapdoor.

The psychiatrists said he has to get in touch with those emotions. *Pull them out, George, express them. You're still stuck in the barrel.*

In Žagarė, Gordimer is remembered. Zofija Kalendraitė still lives in the house three hundred yards from the village market square where she was at the time of the massacre on October 2, 1941. Aged twelve, she made her way to school that day, but class had been canceled because people were being killed. Zofija tried to find a way back. "I heard a lot of shots being fired and saw Jews running from the square," she tells me. All the streets were bloody.

As we talk, snow lies deep around her home, heated by a single woodstove set against a stone slab in the wall of her living room. Staleness is in the air: cabbage and dampness. In a barn at the back of the house, goats huddle. Their breath is thick in the cold. An overfed cat, Bicas, sleeps on a couch, a ball of ginger fluff. Zofija, her lank gray hair tied back, sits at a table piled with mementos: letters and sepia photographs. She serves fruit tea, the fruit of my grandmother's Žagarė woods. Not a car passes. Her blue eyes are calm and piercing, but her hands are agitated as they sift through papers. Of the Nazi and Soviet forces whose presence punctuated her life, she says: "They came. They burned. They killed. They left."

I have come to Zofija's home with her granddaughter, Dovilė Levinkaitė, who devoted her senior year project in high school to the absence she felt in Žagarė. Her family, because they had saved Jews, talked about Jews. That was unusual. In the introduction to her inquiry, Dovilė writes: "The most interesting thing to me is what the Jews did, how they lived because they were a great influence on the town's architecture and culture, but here at the beginning of the 21st century they are history and I think it's very important to gather and write down this information while there are still people who can recount it." She knows through her research about the iron shop of Zeleman and the slaughterhouse owned by the Skliutauskas family. She can peel away the layers of the Žagarė palimpsest.

Zofija is the link to George Gordimer. Her father, Andrėjus Kalendra, organized the rescue operation that saved the Gordimer family from the Nazis. A farmer, he had come to know them through Ira Gordimer's hardware store in Papilė, which he frequented in the 1930s. A network of his friends, all farmers, hid members of the family after they escaped from the Šiauliai ghetto following the *Kinderaktion* in late 1943. It was too dangerous to hide four people in one place; the Gordimers were dispersed. They stayed at various times on farms owned by the Kalendra, Vaškys, Plekavičius, and Garbačiauskas families. Their survival constitutes a rare example of an entire family of four living through the Nazi slaughter in Lithuania.

Zofija hands me letters she has received from George Gordimer since 2006. After the war, Gordimer's father was in touch with Andrėjus Kalendra to ask if he needed anything. Kalendra responded that he did not save Jews because he expected something in return. Her father,

Zofija says, was the kind of man who was charitable even toward a thief. The Soviets deported him to Siberia in 1951 because he opposed collectivization. He died there the following year at the age of sixty-eight, having fought through small deeds the two totalitarianisms of his age.

Few resist. In a time of terror, the great mass is enthusiastic, compliant, calculating, or cowed. The righteous move to an inner compass. Their anonymous acts, however hopeless, constitute the most powerful rebuke to perpetrator and bystander. Resistance is never pointless, even if short-lived or doomed.

After Kalenda disappeared with his family into the Soviet wilderness, communication between the Gordimers and their rescuers was interrupted for more than four decades. The Cold War cemented a silence built on fear in the East and evasion in the West. Only in 1996 did Zofija's younger sister, Morta Jakutienė, manage to make contact with Gordimer through a physician in California, a hand and finger specialist named Ben Lesin with a particular interest in Lithuanian Jewry. Memory was pried loose from its totalitarian clamp.

A newly independent Lithuania, confronted with the extent of its Nazi collaboration, sought out and celebrated its righteous few. Morta wrote, "Dear George, it is very hard to put down the history which is 50 years long in one letter. I think that we will be in touch for a long time, and our contact will not be broken." Gordimer responded, beginning a late-life return voyage to the childhood he had kept secret. On June 22, 1998, he and Dorothy traveled to Lithuania for the first and only time. They met Morta and Zofija. Gordimer has a relentless character. He began to burrow into everything that had been left behind.

A letter from Gordimer to Zofija lies among her papers. It is dated February 7, 2006, and reads: "The past year has been somewhat of a difficult year for me. Since February 2005, I have been depressed and have also developed a great deal of anxiety. I am now seeing a doctor and have been taking anti-depressants as well as a tranquilizer. Lately my depression has improved and my anxiety level has decreased."

Snow falls with a whoosh from a tree. The cat stirs and then thinks better of it. Zofija is talking about her father: how he called both Hitler and Stalin bandits, how when the Nazis were at the gates of Stalingrad, he said the Red Army would be back; how when they duly came back in 1944, he scoffed at the notion they were Lithuania's "liberators"; how the only happy thing about the Russian return was that the few surviving Jews could emerge from hiding.

In 1989, long after Andrėjus Kalendra died in Siberia, the family had him exhumed, after a protracted struggle with Soviet bureaucracy. His remains were transported the thousands of miles from Soviet Asia to be buried on his Lithuanian farm, beside an oak tree he had planted, beneath a gravestone inscribed with the words "One must do good." Zofija thinks that on the whole, this was a waste of time. After death, she says, the body does not matter anymore.

A second Gordimer letter, of July 28, 2008, reads:

> In the past year I have been treated with 3 anti-depressants and none of them helped me. This depression is cyclical and comes and goes. The psychiatrists and psychologists that have treated me say that my traumatic childhood and/or the genetic inheritance may be responsible for this depression. I basically agree with them. From the age of 3 to 8 years my life was very chaotic. I also recognize that my parents had emotional problems. So from a genetic and environmental perspective I can understand my tendency to have periods of depression.

It falls to his wife, Dorothy, who has a solid disposition, to steady Gordimer. "If I went out with anyone with emotional problems, I'd be gone in a heartbeat," he says. As it is, he has survived a second bypass operation, a quadruple bypass when he was sixty-one, as well as the repair of his mitral valve.

His father died in June 1982, a few weeks after George's first bypass. The last years were difficult. Ira would lash out at people, especially the police. If a cop stopped him and asked if he'd given him the finger, he'd say: "Yeah, I gave you the finger, and what are you going to do about it?"

He would go wild and then get very low: the same bipolar symptoms that affected George, who took a while to realize that. His father had no time for medicine or psychotherapy. A couple of times Ira ended up in jail. George would have to bail him out. For several years he and Dorothy kept five hundred dollars in the refrigerator for this purpose.

After Ira died, Gordimer received checks the German government was sending his father as compensation for his wartime loss and suffering. He established an account in the name of the estate of Ira Gordimer, signed his name to it, and deposited the checks. A year later, having learned of Ira's death, Germany demanded the money back. Gordimer said to himself, *They ain't gonna get this money, no matter what they do.* He sued the German authorities, acting on his own behalf, and wrote down 250 interrogatories for them to answer. What really ticked him off was that the Germans had written "pension payment" on his father's checks. This was no pension. They had the gall to write "pension," as if his father had worked for them voluntarily in some gemütlich office in a suburb of Hanover.

"My father," he wrote, "did not work for you because he wanted to work for you. You take that word 'pension' off the check." Lawyers kept sending letters in an attempt to retrieve the money. Gordimer responded: You answer the 250 interrogatories and remove the word "pension," and we'll talk about it. He knew they would not go through all that work for $5,000. Sure enough, when he went to court, nobody showed up for the German government. The case was dismissed.

Gordimer has a stubborn streak like his father. If Ira had not been as half-crazed and tenacious, he would never have made it through the war. As for George's mother, she was paranoid, always imagining plots against her by strangers or even friends. Once, when she was shopping, a flashbulb went off. She was convinced they were taking pictures of her. "Ma," George said, "who the heck is interested in you? Why would they be after you?"

But of course they *had* been after her and Ira and their two little boys. The odds had been against the Gordimers from the moment the Nazis rolled into the Šiauliai region in June 1941. Ira's mother, Gita, and two sisters were rounded up in Papilė and never seen again. Gordimer believes his grandmother was killed in Žagarė on October 2, 1941, along with other Jews from nearby villages.

At the time of the Nazi invasion, the Gordimers were living in Šiauliai. About six thousand Jews were thrown into the warren of alleys behind barbed-wire fences that formed the Kaukazas and

Ežero-Trakų sections of the Šiauliai ghetto. Ežero-Trakų comprised the area surrounding the smokestack of the Frenkel footwear factory and tannery, established by Chaim Frenkel, a Jewish entrepreneur, in 1879. Because the Wehrmacht needed the output of the Frenkel factory, a category of "useful Jews" was created. Other "useful" Jews worked out at the Zokniai military airfield, which the Nazis were enlarging, or in peat bogs, or on construction sites, or at a sugar factory. A pattern of bribes, sexual exploitation, and vicious humiliation characterized relations between Nazi overlord and Jewish serf.

A smaller tanning and leather workshop was owned by Hirsh Davidov; a few dozen Jews were employed here. One survivor, Leiba Lipshitz, recalled that high-ranking Wehrmacht officials and members of the Security Services and Gestapo were customers. "Germans brought fox and wild boar skins," he wrote. "Large amounts of rat and polecat carcasses were brought by Germans for fur-coats to be made for their wives." *Meine Liebe, mein Schatz, here's a little something from the Lithuanian front . . .*

George, after the first panic attack in 1971, asked his father what happened once they were confined in the ghetto. Ira said little. His attitude seemed to be: "You were there. I was there. Why should I have to tell you?" Only over time did George glean that his father had worked until their escape for the Jewish ghetto police, headed by Ephraim Gens. The small Jewish police force of little more than a dozen men operated under the Jewish Council, or *Judenrat,* which also ran departments for food supplies, housing, work distribution, and health. Jews, Stars of David on their police uniforms, administered Jews in death's shadow. They joined what Primo Levi called "the gray zone," the ambiguous area of a system of terror where a "hybrid class of prisoner-functionary" could succumb to the illusion of having choices.

The dubious bargain gave rise to various forms of self-justification whose essence was that obedience to the Nazis could save lives. Jacob Gens, Ephraim's brother, commanded the Jewish police in the Vilnius ghetto. "When they ask me for a thousand Jews I hand them over," he once said, "for if we Jews will not give them on our own, the Germans will come and take them by force. Then they will not take one thousand but thousands. With the thousand that I hand over I save ten thousand."

George Gordimer, right, as a child. He survived the Nazi onslaught in Lithuania. His parents changed his name, birth date, and place of birth to facilitate his postwar passage to the United States. GEORGE GORDIMER

The Gordimers lived six to a room in the Kaukazas section of the ghetto, which lay between the Jewish neighborhood and fashionable Vilnius Street. George's mother, Sophia (born Sonya), worked at the airfield. On February 5, 1942, the Nazis had decreed that (1) births in the ghetto were no longer acceptable, (2) the harshest measures would be applied against Jewish women who gave birth, and (3) abortions would not be prosecuted. Dr. Aaron Pik, a senior doctor in the ghetto who kept a diary later published in Hebrew as *Notes from the Valley of Death,* wrote, "The day that our representatives were informed of this humiliating decree reducing us to the level of animals will be remembered for generations."

Pik, like another diarist of the ghetto, Dr. Eliezer Yerushalmi, was reminded of the book of Exodus: "And Pharaoh charged all his people, saying, Every son that is born ye shall cast into the river, and every daughter ye shall save alive." Even Pharaoh, in persecuting the Hebrews, had not called for the death of *every* child, and it was Pharaoh's own daughter who took pity on a male infant abandoned in a basket on the river, a child she chose to pluck from his "ark of bul-rushes" and name Moses.

Already, in a Nazi medical decree of November 1941, all Jewish patients had been ordered out of the Šiauliai municipal hospital. They were prohibited from getting medical treatment at any city facilities and from buying medicine in pharmacies. Jews in the ghetto impro-vised. "The only place for the hospital was in the cemetery," Pik records, "in the room used for purifying the dead before burial. This room, with its cement floor, was very cold during our last chilly win-ter." A combination of necessity, initiative, adaptability, and courage conjured a place of healing from a mortuary. Doctors did what they could. The ban on childbirth posed particular ethical problems. All live births after August 15, 1942, were forbidden; any family in which a birth occurred would be "removed" and reprisals taken. The threat was in effect throughout the ghetto. Nazis, perhaps for the first time in history, had brought mass murder of women and children to gynecol-ogy and obstetrics departments.

The *Judenrat* and the doctors urged all pregnant women to have abortions. They were performed almost every day. In the case of a live birth, the baby was to be killed by an injection of poison admin-istered by a nurse. Some doctors said they could not countenance such acts, which amounted to murder. Others argued that according to the *halakah,* or Jewish law, the mother's life takes precedence over that of the child; killing the newborn where its survival would cost the mother's life could be equated with killing a late-pregnancy fetus in the same circumstances.

Sophia told George she got pregnant in the ghetto and was forced to have an abortion.

Pik's diary relates two instances in which he and another doctor had to take the lives of newborn babies. One occurred in January 1944. Pik acted to kill a baby girl just before the visit of a German supervisor:

Injections of potent poisonous drugs powerful enough to kill an adult had not produced quick results with newborns. The previous baby had received two such injections and survived for seven days without food or water! Here the baby had to be killed immediately, without any delay. And so we decided . . . to drown the infant! We took a bucket full of cold water and thrust her head and ears into the water until death tremors appeared and then subsided—a total of six minutes, twice the amount of time needed to kill an adult by suffocation. We pulled out the baby, her mouth open and her nostrils covered with white foam, and covered her with a blanket. By some miracle, the supervisor did not show up that morning, so it was decided to bury the baby, the alleged fetus. How great was their astonishment when, as they went to lower the baby to the grave, they discovered that she was still alive. It was incredible. One-day-old newborns mock the entire theory of medicine, and methods of killing adults are not effective for them.

Remember my uncle, standing before the bedraggled Jews on the floor of a displaced persons' camp in Padua on August 24, 1945, writing in his diary: "Why do they cling so preciously to life? Is it so important to stay alive that one should surrender everything, succumb to any humiliation, in order to preserve the precious spark?" He could not recognize—to his subsequent horror—his Jewish "kith and kin" in such human refuse. The question—why do they cling so preciously to life?—is posed in turn by these acts, at once unconscionable and understandable, of Jewish doctors in the ghetto of my grandfather's hometown. Perhaps the answer lies in the ferocious attachment to the world of that newborn girl: because they had no choice. After all, if the rational mind held sway in human affairs, rather than imperatives of the survival and reproduction of the species, why were so many children, including George Gordimer's aborted sibling, conceived at all in that hell?

On November 5, 1943, the SS waited for Šiauliai ghetto residents to leave for work before going after the children. Conditions had worsened that summer. In July 1943 the ghetto had been transferred to the direct jurisdiction of the SS and designated an "exterior camp" of the Kaunas concentration camp. The Gordimers were moved to the overflowing Ežero-Trakų section. It was from there that Sophia Gordimer left for work that morning and saw reinforcements at the ghetto gates.

Levi Shalit, a survivor, noted that although word had spread of a possible roundup that day, the work brigades seemed eager to be on their way: "Both ghetto gates were besieged. Jews pushed and shoved in their haste to leave the ghetto. . . . Nowhere is the psychologist who will explain to us what psychological complex was at work, or not at work, among the people at that moment. Why did they hurry through the gate, leaving the children and old people alone? Were the mothers and fathers not thinking clearly—was it *the blind impulse to live?*"

It is not clear what Ira Gordimer did that day. He had a back-office police job. The Jewish ghetto police, armed with sticks, were ordered to scour the ghetto and bring children to the gates. Ephraim Gens, the tall and puffed-up Jewish police chief, brought his own infant daughter as an example, *pour encourager les autres*. He saluted the German authorities as he handed over his child for execution, prompting Shalit to note his "dull cowardice and stupidity."

Although Gens had handed over his own daughter, the Nazis did not trust his police, who often tried to mediate in the ghetto. They took on the task of finding all the children themselves.

The previous year, in the Warsaw ghetto, where he was head of the *Judenrat,* Adam Czerniaków had taken his own life rather than obey the German command to deport Jewish children. In his suicide note, he wrote, "The SS wants me to kill children with my own hands. There is no other way out and I must die." Eight months later the Jews of the Warsaw ghetto had risen. Tens of thousands of them had died, either on the spot or gassed at Treblinka. But they had understood—not merely that old habits of malleable compliance were useless against the decision to murder them all; not merely that certain death awaited them whatever their genuflections to might; but also that the salvation of the Jews, and indeed of all humanity, lay in resistance and sacrifice even as the world shrugged at Hitler's annihilation of half of European Jewry.

During the uprising, as the ghetto went up in flames, Shmuel Zygielbojm, the representative of the socialist Bund to the Polish government in exile in London, killed himself in front of the British Parliament in an act of solidarity with Warsaw Jews and in protest at Allied and Soviet inaction. In his suicide note of May 12, 1943, Zygielbojm wrote, "Though the responsibility for the crime of the murder of the entire Jewish nation rests above all upon the perpetrators, indirect blame must be borne by humanity itself." This point about the lessons of the Holocaust for all humanity was taken up later by Hannah Arendt when she wrote: "Under conditions of terror, most people will comply but *some people will not*. . . . Humanly speaking, no more is required, and no more can reasonably be asked, for this planet to remain a place fit for human habitation."

Gens survived the war. He was tried and convicted by the Soviets, who dispatched him to a labor camp in the Arctic. During his trial, he protested his innocence. "The question was to be or not to be," he wrote in letters. "To be meant to survive being continually downtrodden and detested and hope that one day justice would prevail. It was pointless to rebel without guns." Order and work, he insisted, were the only deployable weapons in the fight for survival of the Jewish people. "Today I suffer for saving the majority of the ghetto residents, for their being able to enjoy life."

This is the self-importance of the coward. In fact, all but a few hundred of Šiauliai's Jews had been slaughtered by 1945, as had the Vilnius Jews overseen by Gens's brother.

The Gordimer boys were favored by chance. Their aunt and uncle, Rochelle and David Glickman, lived with them. Rochelle, Ira's sister, was sick the day of the *Kinderaktion* and did not go to work. Hearing of the hunt for children under thirteen, she hid George in a barrel and his brother behind an old mattress in a shed. George was five years old, Seymour six. George recalls climbing out of the barrel and going from the shed into the house. The room his family shared had been ransacked: closets emptied, beds overturned, drawers pulled out, possessions hurled across the floor. He felt panic for the first time, a constriction in the neck, a cold sweat.

The Germans carted children and old people—the innocent and the wise—off to annihilation. Parents came back that evening to find their offspring gone. Ira and Sophia Gordimer were spared the contemplation of that abyss. The boys were alive. They were hidden now in the cellar of another house.

Ira faced a choice: continue to obey, as Gens obeyed, or gamble on escape. Obedience would mean death for his children at least. There were no children's voices left in the ghetto. He thought of Kalendra, a regular customer at his Papilė store, and was able to contact him. On the third night after the *Kinderaktion,* he contrived, perhaps through the privilege of his police position, to smuggle Seymour out of the ghetto in a potato sack. He handed the boy to Kalendra, who took him on a horse-drawn cart to his remote farm. George did not see his older brother again until the end of the war.

On March 30, 2000, in a declaration written for the Commission for the Designation of the Righteous at Yad Vashem in Jerusalem, George set down his recollection of the events that followed:

> The morning after my brother was transported to the Kalendra farm, my mother took me out of the ghetto under her coat while everyone was going to work. With the help of a Lithuanian police-man, my mother took me to a house where Antanas Plekavičius (a good friend of Kalendra) and my father were waiting. Antanas Plekavičius then transported my parents and me by horse and wagon to the farm of Steponas and Marijona Garbačiauskas. Marijona was Kalendra's sister. During the three weeks we were in hiding at the Garbačiauskas farm in or near Žarenai, I developed a severe throat infection. Because it was too dangerous to call a doctor, Marijona held me down while my mother broke up the blisters in my throat with the handle of a wooden spoon.

George kept moving, sometimes with his parents, more often without them. For a time he was at the farm of Augustas and Klara Vaškys, other good friends of Kalendra. In December 1943 he moved alone to the property of their sister, whose boyfriend did not want George around and took to beating him. Six months later he went back, still by himself, to the Plekavičius farm. "I remember the day I found a bullet in the field. I detonated the bullet by striking one end of it with a sharp edged rock. My ears rang for almost a full day. I remained at the Plekavičius farm until March or April 1945, when my parents came by truck to pick me up. I remember that I was afraid to go with them and I hid behind Mrs. Plekavičius."

George Gordimer, at the age of six, ended the war hiding from his father and mother.

The Gordimers' saviors did not fare well. War's end in Lithuania was only the beginning of another struggle, for liberation from Soviet occupiers. On July 29, 1945, Augustas and Klara Vaškys were killed by Red Army forces. Their farmhouse was burned to the ground. Their sister, like Andrėjus Kalendra, was sent to Siberia, joining the approximately 200,000 people deported by Stalin from the Baltic states between 1941 and 1949. Unlike Kalendra, she survived. Selective silence fell on the tumult the Gordimers had lived through. Lithuanian history, and the story of its Jews, was now the Soviet Union's to shape. Memorial obelisks to "victims of fascism" went up under five-pointed red stars rather than Stars of David. The number of Jews killed by the Germans in the Soviet Union remained a state secret.

Today Šiauliai is a dismal sprawl. Unlike Žagarė, it retains scarcely a flicker of the past, apart from the smokestack and warehouses of the Frenkel factory, transformed into a kitschy museum. One Jewish survivor, Boris Stein, oversees a small, drafty Jewish community center where there is not enough money to heat more than a single room at a time. In his shiny blue overcoat and gray woolen cap, he bears the imprint of the Soviet empire that shaped his life. Stein, if he's lucky, can muster 180 Jews from the entire region for High Holidays. Like Isaac Mendelson, the last Jew in Žagarė, he survived in Russia, escaping as a child with his family in 1941 to the Kazan region of Tatarstan.

Stein shows me a file with Nazi lists of the people confined in the Šiauliai ghetto. There's a Reiza Soloveychik, born a few years before my grandmother, in 1886, and a Ginda Soloveychik, born in 1931, and a Simon Soloveychik, born in 1934. The Nazi *Kinderaktion* of 1943 probably took these last two namesakes of my grandmother. There are eight Cohens on the list.

Stein's parents lived to see the end of the war by avoiding the ghetto. His father died in 1954 and was buried in the Šiauliai Jewish cemetery, whose only trace is a handful of overgrown and lurching gravestones. The Soviets closed the cemetery in 1965. They ordered all bodies exhumed. There were scarcely any Jews left for the task. Bone by bone Stein took the remains of his father to the municipal cemetery.

When George Gordimer was an undergraduate at MIT in the spring of 1961, he did nothing for months, immobilized by depression. He would go to sleep around five a.m. and wake up as other students returned for dinner. He was inert, suffocated by a great weight. MIT had a standing offer of five free psychiatric sessions, but he never took the college up on it. He figured he could get by on his own. His father had. Nobody at MIT knew anything about his Lithuanian past; he was not going to start blabbing. Discipline was important. He graduated in September 1961 and was immediately hired as a research chemist by Rohm and Haas Company in Philadelphia.

Three years later Gordimer got a summer job in a small lab belonging to the Kendall Company in Cambridge, Massachusetts. There he met Dorothy Bowdren, who had just graduated with a chemistry degree from Duke. Part of his job was to train her. They started dating. Together they did research on pressure-sensitive adhesives that were to be used in Kendall's Curad bandages.

George told Dorothy nothing about his own untended wounds. She was from a liberal Protestant background. He hid the fact he was Jewish, though he would not have framed his decision that way. He didn't want *anyone* defining him through some extraneous factor, like where he happened to have been born or whether or not he was a Jew. Dorothy laughs about it all now. "George," she says, "face it, you were hiding something."

After dating Dorothy for more than two years, Gordimer proposed to her. He felt the time had come to say something. "Just in case this makes any difference to you," he began, "let me tell you about my background."

It was the same phrase he came to use with doctors, "Just in case this makes any difference to you . . . I am two years older than my papers say." In case it makes any difference, George Gordimer is not who he appears to be. Dorothy, some of whose family came over on the *Mayflower,* had thought he might be Jewish but refrained from asking. When she told her mother about Gordimer's Lithuanian Jewish past, she said: "Oh my God, is he at least a citizen?"

Gordimer had been a U.S. citizen since 1952. He officially turned twelve that year but was in fact fourteen, having lived about half his life in Europe. Between the ages of three and eight, the brain is forming. Connections are made, but if the psyche is under too much stress, the right connections are not established. Gordimer thought some of his own connections—the wiring of his brain—might have gone askew in the barrel or the cellar or the lonely Lithuanian farms where he sheared sheep. It was possible although, as he sometimes insists, not provable.

One of the things Gordimer told Dorothy is that not only did his family have to survive the Nazis, they also had to escape the Soviets. Double occupation, the double man says, requires double evasion. Mendelson's Sixteenth Brigade of the Soviet Red Army had scores to settle: any Jew who had remained in Lithuania and survived was suspect. It was not easy to get out of Lithuania in 1945.

Soviet troops caught up with Ira in Vilnius, where the family had gone by truck from Šiauliai in August 1945. Who are you? Did you cooperate with the Nazis? What did you do? These questions, in some ways, were unanswerable or had many different answers or had answers that made no sense.

His father, born in 1903 when Lithuania was part of imperial Russia, spoke fluent Russian. So did his mother. Ira had a diploma from a Russian school. This helped. Once again, he managed to talk his way out of a tight corner. He was determined now to get to America. George remembers a train journey into Poland and his father hiding money in his shoes and screaming at him: *Just be quiet!*

They traveled westward, past the lines of poplar and birch, the bombed-out villages, the stragglers in their rags. In Stettin, Poland, they found a truck to take them to Berlin. It was midwinter. The truck broke down, and they started to walk, snow crunching beneath their feet, icy wind in their faces. A group of Red Army soldiers picked them up. They threw Gordimer and his father into a dark East Berlin cellar. For six weeks they were allowed out once a day for a brief walk. Food was limited. They feared they would be shipped back to Lithuania. The Soviets did not seem to know what to do with this stray family. Then, without explanation, the Gordimers were allowed passage to the West. An American officer gave Gordimer a red apple.

A half century passed before George was able to go back. The journey to Lithuania in 1998 was a turning point. By then Seymour was dead at the age of fifty-five, and both their parents were long gone. George and Dorothy, who had a mild stroke in 1968, had no children.

"I thought somewhere in the back of my mind that having children might be too much for me," he says. Having corresponded since 1996 with the Kalendra family, he wanted to see for himself. Loose ends needed to be tied up.

His neighbors and friends in Cranford, New Jersey, where they have lived since 1970, were surprised. When they asked why he was going to Lithuania, he told them. The journey was a big production, too much of one for his taste. Everywhere he went—Vilnius, Šiauliai, Žagarė—Lithuanian TV was on hand to record the visit of the returning American Jew and to mark the courageous deeds of Andrėjus Kalendra and his friends. He was happy to meet Kalendra's daughters, Zofija and Morta, and later happy at their recognition in 2009 by the State of Israel as "Righteous Among the Nations." But he has no wish now to return.

Religion, for Gordimer, is still "definitely below zero." He feels no particular identification with his Jewishness. In the end, he still thinks, he's a Jew because that's what somebody else said he is. Still, he feels an affinity with Israel, which he puts this way:

"I do identify to some extent because I think the Jews need some place where they don't have to put up with being in a pogrom once in a while. There are two peoples, Jews and Palestinians, coming from the same place and one said finally, 'We are not going to take it anymore, and we're going back to where we originated, and too bad if people don't like it, because nobody protected us and we went from country to country, and every place we went—be it Spain or eastern Europe, central Europe—wherever we went, including the United States, there was some next-door neighbor who was going to call you a dirty Jew.' That's it: nobody took care of the Jews, and Israel is their ancestral homeland, not Madagascar where Hitler wanted to send them, and that's my feeling on that.

"But I think there's a bunch of crazies in Israel, the extreme religious groups who want to pick on an eight-year-old girl because she's exposing too much flesh—these people are nuts. They are no better than the jihadists. They are like the white extremists in this country. Extreme groups are all the same, they just have different labels: jihadists, extreme Orthodox, whatever. I'm not too fond of people like that, especially when they base their beliefs on absolutes. I don't believe in absolutes. I know only one thing that's absolute, and that's the speed of light."

For the fiftieth reunion of the class of 1961 at MIT, Gordimer was asked to write a brief account of his life since graduation. He hesitated about what to reveal to a class that had known him as a quiet guy "raised" in Elizabeth. At last he wrote:

> In the summer of 1998, Dorothy and I went to Lithuania to visit and thank the families who rescued the Gordimer family during the war years of 1941–45. I am a child survivor of the Holocaust. It required five families to rescue my parents, my brother, and me. On November 5, 1943, after more than two years of incarceration in a ghetto in Šiauliai, Lithuania (my birthplace), a *Kinderaktion* (Children's Action) was carried out by the Germans and their collaborators. Approximately seven hundred children were deported from the ghetto for extermination. My brother and I were hidden in the ghetto for three days after the *Kinderaktion*. Then our family, with the aid of Lithuanian farmers, escaped from the ghetto and was hidden on separate farms by our Lithuanian rescuers.

The hardest words of all for Gordimer were these: "Although we physically escaped, we did not escape psychological damage. In my case I also 'lost' my childhood. From the age of three to eight, my life was totally chaotic and at times traumatic."

The damage was indelible. He was one man in order to conceal the hurt man underneath. I know well enough how that game works. When I gazed at him once in the lobby of a midtown New York hotel, his eyes twinkled: he was in one of his hyper moods. It would be followed by a deep trough, a sagging of voice and skin, depression, and inertia. I have watched such changes all my life in my own family—the chiaroscuro of the bipolar mind. He, too, would crawl into bed.

The Gordimers' simple, two-story house in Cranford is painted pale green with a darker trim called Provincial Olive. Dorothy still finds it a bit "rinky-dinky"—she wanted a more substantial Victorian home—but they have grown used to it over time. The big oak trees in the back cast the yard into shadow. Dorothy's occasional attempts with flowers have failed. Of late neighbors have been putting up fences, first in metal, then another in wood to hide the metal, barrier after barrier where once children roamed free. George hates the fences. The biggest change he and Dorothy have made since they moved in forty-two years ago was to convert the porch into a den.

It is quiet in Cranford except when the flight pattern into Newark Airport disturbs the peace, but George is afflicted with a ringing, or sometimes a buzzing, in his right ear. He thinks it may stem from the day he exploded the bullet he found on the Lithuanian farm. When he is tense, the sound grows louder. Old age, he says, is rough on a perfectionist. Everything has to be just right to overcome the chaos he was in. But his body gathers imperfections. "I'm all screwed up," he says. His prostate is enlarged. He takes statins for his heart. He has to get a finger fixed—an accumulation of collagen has limited its movement, and soon the finger will be bent all the way into his palm.

The decoration in the house is sparse—needlework made by Dorothy before she gave it up, an upright piano she no longer plays, a single sofa, a hi-fi bought in 1958, and an old wooden speaker. There is little light in the small rooms. George prefers to keep the curtains drawn all day. Dorothy misses light. She does not like to live in a permanent penumbra. She is a woman who, in George's phrase, has rolled with the punches.

"Closed curtains keep the house cooler in summer and warmer in winter," he says. "I'm not big on light."

A video records his visit to Lithuania in 1998. It shows him meeting with Morta Jakutienė, the daughter of Andrėjus Kalendra. As he speaks of his late brother to the Lithuanian families gathered to meet them, George breaks down. He tries and fails to repress a sob. Morta, too, starts to cry. It is the first time I have seen Gordimer lose control—a quiet surrender, a crumpling. Gordimer turns from the video to me and says: "I'm still not out of there. I'm still in the barrel."

CHAPTER 5

Château Michel

The mansion, called Amberly, at 44 Fourteenth Avenue, in the jacaranda-shaded Houghton suburb of Johannesburg, was known among the cognoscenti as Château Michel. It was here that my mother's grandfather Isaac Michel, the nineteen-year-old "prospector" who sailed on August 16, 1896, for South Africa, lived the last decade of his life. On his tennis court, in the summer of 1948, my parents first set eyes on each other. She loved him, she said, from that moment.

Immigration is reinvention. Lands of immigrants excise the anguish of the motherland. They invite the incomer to the selective forgetfulness of new identity. Isaac arrived penniless from Lithuania. He died on an urban estate with its arboretum, giant mulberry tree, fishpond, and aviary, surrounded by African houseboys and gold-inlaid bibelots, his turquoise, fishtailed Cadillac parked in the beautiful curving driveway waiting to purr to life in the hands of a tall, slim handsome chauffeur known as Kleinbooi.

Michel had cofounded South Africa's largest retail chain, the OK Bazaars. "I'll meet you at the OK" entered the lexicon. The OK was everywhere, from metropolis to *dorp,* as much part of the landscape as the peppercorn tree or the springbok. Not bad for a former *smous.*

Isaac's children knew wealth rather than the struggle to accumulate it. They were the lulled second generation, easing into the new South African Jewish elite of commerce and finance. The "Peruvians" had been pilloried in some quarters upon their arrival in the 1890s, mocked

Isaac Michel with his wife, Jennie

in the "Hoggenheimer" caricatures of Jewish plutocrats in the years after the Boer War, and branded as Bolsheviks in 1917. As in Europe, they were attacked for being capitalists, and they were attacked for being communists. But with its vast black underclass, South Africa afforded ample space for Jews with acumen to get ahead.

Michel was not one of the towering figures—they included Schlesinger (movie theaters and insurance), Oppenheimer (mining), Ackerman (retail), Lazarus (maize), and Frankel (food processing and milling)—but Isaac was shrewd enough to make his pile and establish a little dynasty. Rapid assimilation is based on a silent bargain—the erasure of the past in the name of a boundless future—that may be less foolproof than it seems.

By the end of his life, it was scarcely possible to explain, even to imagine, where Michel had come from. Yet certain habits from the Lithuanian shtetl and from the years of struggle as a *smous* persisted. Isaac would place a cube of sugar in his mouth and let it dissolve as, in a glass with a metal holder, he drank tea drawn from a samovar. The sweet lozenge beneath his tongue, shrinking bit by bit, was Isaac's *spangoliu,* an open sesame to Lithuanian memory, just as cranberries were to my paternal grandmother, Polly. Other South African immigrants from Lithuania yearned for cherries or, dying, wanted to see the ice skates they had brought with them.

Sometimes Isaac would add a spoon of strawberry jam to the glass. He picked breadcrumbs from the table, pressing his forefinger into them, and when asked why would tell his grandchildren they had no idea what it was to be hungry. After a meal, Havana in hand, black brogues snapping on the polished parquet, he circled the oval mahogany dinner table for his "constitutional." My mother, as a teenager, feared the footsteps would stop behind her if she had not eaten up.

An inventory of Isaac's furniture and household effects drawn up at the time of his death in 1953, and found in the South African Archives in Pretoria, gives some idea of the setting: a Louis XV display cabinet with four hand-painted panels and ormolu decorations; a pair of large ceramic Dresden vases; china and Venetian glass; a four-piece Irish silver tea set; an Empire-style escritoire; a three-piece French clock set and two urns; a large Tabriz carpet (twenty-one feet by thirteen); a Buhl folding card table; a silver-plated card tray; couches and a chair in silk damask; an Empire-style cabinet with china insets; an inlaid Empire table with ormolu decorations.

Years later a Jewish family in Johannesburg who had acquired some of the furniture at auction tried to encourage the marriage of their son to one of Michel's granddaughters. *Play your cards right, and you might get all this back. You see those armoires and that painting—they were Isaac's.*

Fortunes are more easily forgone than forgotten. Once lost, they leave the question not only of how such plenty was squandered but of how far they were imagined. They grow in memory, the chimera of an ephemeral ease.

Photographs of Michel evince a nervous energy. He is coiled, resolute, and brisk. The cut of his clothes is as crisp as the line of his parting. In double-breasted dark suit and Borsalino, umbrella clasped below the handle and carried parallel to the sidewalk, he strides through downtown Johannesburg, his right hand clenched. He could be on Michigan Avenue in 1930s Chicago. In a single-breasted charcoal pinstripe, he

*Isaac Michel, at the height of his business success,
striding down a central Johannesburg street*

appears caught from below against a clear sky at an angle that accentuates the line of his jaw. On the beach at Muizenberg in late middle age, seated in a deck chair, leaning forward, hands cupped in front of him, his expression is as intense as his body is lithe. Big eyes, pale and sensual, dominate his face.

Michel was a ladies' man, but appearances were maintained even if, in later years, he and his wife had little to say to each other. His marriage, just before the turn of the century, to Jennie Rosenberg from Newcastle, England, produced six children, three boys and three girls. The oldest was my grandmother, Florence Blanche (Flossie), born in 1900. There followed Lily, Willie, Bertie ("Googoo"), Basil, and beautiful, moody Alethea, known as "Baby."

After family meals at Château Michel, the men would play whist and the women rummy. A manicured lawn for bowls, a swimming pool, and a rose garden adorned the yard that stretched over two Houghton acres. Old Dad Tomsett, the gardener plucked from England, patrolled with two Irish setters in tow. Michel liked to go hunting with him on weekends. He owned, in the Rivonia area near Johannesburg, a four-hundred-acre farm called Duxbury, the same name he gave to his house in the Cape where I would spend part of my Southern Hemisphere summers. For a while he kept a lion in a cage up there. His favored gun was a Westley Richards twelve-bore with hand-engraved drop lock, cased in oak and leather, a handsome object he bequeathed to his son Googoo, who in turn would teach family members to shoot in his garden, pinning targets to the top of a tomato box among the fruit trees in the orchard. Family legend has it the gun was later sent to Israel to help save the Promised Land. Heaven knows if it ever got there. Like much else, it disappeared.

The gun's dispatch was consistent with Michel's desire to help the nascent Jewish homeland. He would attend shul on alternate Saturdays. He loved Yiddish theater. In his will, prepared in 1950, two years after the foundation of the modern state of Israel, he bequeathed £2,500—equivalent to about $100,000 today—to the Talmudical College, Jerusalem, "with the request that the said College shall cause prayers to be offered up in the said College on the anniversary of our respective deaths." He also left £5,000 to the Hebrew University, Jerusalem, to be invested in such a way as to "devote the annual income to the foundation of a scholarship in such branch of science or learning as they may in their discretion determine, to be known as the Isaac and Jennie Michel Scholarship." (The Hebrew University told me it could find no trace of such an endowment.)

At this distance from the shtetl, Jewish identity still mattered.

The first OK Bazaar opened its doors at the corner of Eloff and President Streets in downtown Johannesburg on Saturday, June 25, 1927, an emporium of goods—from Wedgwood cups to galvanized iron buckets—unlike anything seen before in South Africa. Police patrolled the crowds outside before opening time. An "OK Jazz Trio" played on a balcony transformed into a tearoom. Ladies wore their finest frocks.

Michel's partners in the new business were two younger Jewish immigrant entrepreneurs—Sam Cohen from London and Michael Miller from Lithuania. Such was the shopping frenzy that Cohen cabled Miller, then on a purchasing trip to Europe, with a laconic message: "Buy like hell."

The promise was the fairest and the squarest of fair and square deals. OK would sell goods cheaply but would not sell cheap goods. On opening day everything was priced at threepence, sixpence, or one shilling—a policy soon dropped. New stores followed—in Port Elizabeth, Durban, and Pretoria in 1928; East London in 1929; Bloemfontein and Germiston in 1930; and Springs in 1931. The company went public in 1929, with help from I. W. Schlesinger, who already headed a large business empire. Schlesinger became chairman for several years. Soon people were saying, "You can get it at the OK" or "You can always try the OK." It became the South African Everyman's store, or so it styled itself. For many years blacks lined up at separate counters and could not serve themselves.

A brochure created by the company in 1936, headlined "THEY WERE THREE—An Epic of Modern Commerce" and accompanied by photographs of Cohen, Miller, and Michel, gives a sense of the heady expansion of the OK Bazaars, which by then had eleven branches:

June 25, 1927, will live in a sub-continent's commercial history as a red-letter day in Big Business enterprise. On that date, after perspicacious planning, and patient, persevering preparation, three men, then not over-confident that their undertaking would be crowned with success, opened to the public South Africa's first O.K. Bazaar.

Johannesburg, pulsating metropolis of a sub-continent, and hub of the greatest gold-producing area mankind has ever known, was the birthplace of the business baby, an infant destined speedily to attain to robust, active adolescence, quickly followed by a maturity of surpassing strength.

The three men who rocked the O.K. cradle in a building at the corner of Eloff and President Streets little anticipated, when their infant enterprise was in swaddling clothes, that in the brief space of five years it would develop into the greatest retail stores organization of the Southern Hemisphere.

The "trinity" behind this breakneck expansion was composed of very different men. Miller and Cohen—born in 1893 and 1894, respectively—were almost a generation younger than Michel. Cohen was married to Miller's sister, Dora; the two men had first worked together in Bloemfontein in 1918, setting up a wholesale business called United Commercial Agencies, which moved to Johannesburg and eventually became the New Commercial Trading Company. Cohen was fiery and explosive, a brilliant merchant driven by fierce competitiveness and a boots-on-the-ground feel for retail. Later in life he had his handkerchiefs inscribed with the letters YCDBSOYA: *You can't do business sitting on your arse.*

Miller had a smaller ego, a more even temperament, and a finer sensibility. As the business evolved, he focused on finance, administration, and the design of the stores. Miller's son, Len, who was chairman of OK at the time of its sale to South African Breweries in 1973, described the difference to me this way: "My father was a very quiet man, deliberative, composed. Sam Cohen had a somewhat violent temper, easily riled, made very quick decisions, not always well considered."

My great-grandfather, closer to Miller in temperament, aged fifty when the OK opened its doors (his partners were in their early thirties), was always the outsider of the three, tied neither by marriage nor by long business connection.

In 1937 Michel fell out with his two partners and sold his share of the OK Bazaars. It was left to Miller and Cohen, always the driving forces, to build the business. There followed a concerted attempt, pursued over many years by Cohen and Miller, to write Isaac Michel out of the history of the OK Bazaars. From the time of his departure, official accounts of the OK Bazaars were written as if he had never existed. When acknowledged at all, and that was rare, Michel was a "partner" for some years who "subsequently disposed of his shareholding in the company."

This bizarre insistence led to several corrections in South African newspapers. On March 23, 1980, the *South African Jewish Times* ran a piece headlined "Isaac Michel Was One of the Three Founders of the OK Bazaars." It read: "In a special O.K. Bazaars supplement, which appeared in the SA Jewish Times on March 14, it was stated that the O.K. Bazaars was founded in 1927 by Sam Cohen and the late Michael Miller. In fact there were three founders. They were Mr. Sam Cohen, the late Michael Miller and the late Isaac Michel." Michel's Johannesburg solicitors, the firm of Edward Nathan, Friedland, Mansell & Lewis, wrote a letter to *The Sunday Times* that led to a similar correction under the headline "A Trio of Founders."

Len Miller wrote to me with an attempted explanation. His father and Cohen were the founders of the New Commercial Trading Company. They then met Isaac Michel, whose store was at the corner of Eloff and Market Streets, and agreed to join forces. The OK Bazaars could be viewed as the New Commercial Trading Company under a changed name, so in that sense it might be argued that Cohen and Miller were the founders, even if the three men were the first "directors" of the OK Bazaars.

The problem with this is that the OK Bazaar was a revolutionary retailing concept, a radical innovation: a department store buying directly from manufacturers for cash, so eliminating the middle man and driving down costs and prices. It was *founded* in 1927, not mutated from a wholesaler similar to countless others in South Africa.

As for Michel's contentious departure from the OK Bazaars in 1937, Len Miller shed light, quoting from an unpublished memoir of his father's. The breaking point came over a rival chain store called C.T.C. that Michel tried to acquire without informing his partners. He was asked to leave.

The irascible Cohen never forgave Isaac. He and Miller, and later their U.S.-trained sons, drove the expansion of OK over many years. But Cohen had a flaw: he believed that if he shouted loudest, he would have his way, and that if he insisted long enough, he could change the facts.

His dream of a family retailing empire ended, after Michael Miller's death in 1971, with the sale of the OK Bazaars to South African Breweries. Ultimately, in 1997 South African Breweries offloaded the OK Bazaars for a symbolic one rand to Shoprite Checkers, a retailing chain that then killed the OK name. The brand that had been a national treasure for seven decades was worth a couple of cents at the last.

The demise of the OK became a national legend, a cautionary political and business tale, as well as a family lament. In 2012 the secretary-general of the ruling African National Congress warned that the ANC could meet the fate of the OK Bazaars. "I normally tell people that any brand is as good as its services," Gwede Mantashe said. "If you rubbish the ANC you can destroy it that way. OK Bazaars was a strong brand in the retail sector, so strong that it became complacent and it was sold for One Rand to Shoprite Checkers and that brand disappeared."

Two months after my mother's death on January 2, 1999, my father wrote to me:

> I'm certain you understand that my time with Mum constitutes
> the deepest and most sacred element of my life. It also comprises
> the most sensitive part of my spiritual being and, when injured, the
> pain is deep and enduring. I will never barter or bargain to change
> anyone's assessment of my life with Mum. The complex and often
> tortured web of facts must speak for each individual observer.

Those words were written exactly a half century after he met June. The love that became a "tortured web of facts" began in 1948 in South Africa, on Isaac Michel's two-acre estate. June, who was always immaculate, nursed a dream of perfect family harmony—the comfort and carelessness of 44 Fourteenth Avenue in Houghton, which is where she spent long spells of her adolescence.

They were from different backgrounds. June was a Michel granddaughter, a catch. The Michels were minor South African Jewish nobility. Sydney, eight years her senior, a doctor recently returned from London, was the son of immigrants who toiled to make their way. He was never much interested in status. Laurie and Flossie, June's parents, had in mind a different match from the higher echelons of Jewish retail: David Susman, who went on to run Woolworths in South Africa for many years. Flossie would later say the first time she saw June grief-stricken and inert was when Susman dropped her while they were both students at Wits.

Sydney's father, Morris, from Šiauliai, was good at placing relatives in lucrative businesses. He was less adept at looking after himself. He introduced his brother-in-law Ponk (who had arrived aged eleven in South Africa with his father in 1895) to coal. Ponk thrived as a supplier. For another relative, Morris set up the Ideal clothing company, which

The Michel clan at Château Michel, with June (fifth from right in back row),
grandfather Laurie (standing far left),
Jennie (seated far left in hat), and Isaac (seated left)

prospered. As for Cohen & Sons, his own wholesale grocery, it never generated quite enough income for Morris to stop worrying.

With his beloved wife, Polly, and four children to support—Selma, Ann, Bert, and Sydney—Morris allowed himself only a week of vacation. The rest of the family would go for three weeks to Port Elizabeth and stay at the Pollok Hotel opposite the beach. Sometimes they brought home a wild tortoise to let loose in the yard. A train took them south to the coast. The boys felt terror in the tunnel at Cradock as smoke poured through the window in the dark. At other times they traveled out by car to a small Orange Free State town where Polly's brother-in-law, Jacob Leverton, owned a general store. Leverton's principal source of amusement was scattering change for black clients on a counter to which he had nailed three gold sovereigns. He would smirk as they tried to scoop them up.

The roads were terrible. The family car, an Oakland, would break down, mired in black glutinous mud, and have to be pulled out with a winch.

Morris, who left school at thirteen after his father, Shmuel, had a leg amputated, married self-discipline to hard work. He was honest to a fault. Industrious and cautious, he put all the children through college. He would turn down second helpings with a sweep of the hand and the exclamation "One sixty-five!" His weight never fluctuated from 165 pounds.

Money was made the painstaking way, spent with prudence, and not entrusted to brokers. Morris did not take chances. Debt, he liked to say, never sleeps, and nor do those who have it. The Cohens slept well, but they had no Dresden vases or Tabriz carpets. There was no tail-finned Cadillac parked in the driveway.

Polly's devotion to her husband was unstinting, their marriage one of those rare meetings of souls. She would tend the roses rising on their trellises and take the children to see her father, the humble carpenter from Žagarė, over in the poor district of Troyeville. The boys preferred visits to Morris's depot, always cluttered with boxes and barrels of herring and cucumber.

Six mules and a horse were kept in the yard at the back, tended by a black man called Elias. The horse was used to solicit orders, the mules to deliver them. Morris would venture out in his trap down the rutted roads and tracks of the Rand to retail stores on the fringes of town. As a young boy, my uncle Bert accompanied him through the heat and dust past the spreading mine dumps—some flat-topped, others pyramid-like—of the churning gold city. His job was to tot up sales.

From the trap, Bert sees the blacks on foot, the walkers. Always there is the presence of the other. Whites are in Africa on the rich reef surrounded by blacks. Bert has a Zulu spear called an *assegai,* and he hurls it at the big succulent leaves of the cactus tree. He and my father listen to Zulu songs in the street outside their windows, where the blacks labor. They hear the warning: *Don't talk in front of the blacks.* Their neighbors are called Mandelowitz, Rosen, and Daniel. Some have an anglicized veneer, others the accent of the shtetl. They all get their kosher sausages at Segal's. None, of course, has any notion of the two main Bantu languages, Zulu and Sesuto. Theirs is the English language of the British imperium. In every white, at some level, conscience twitches. Premonitions stir of the inevitable bloodbath.

The boys, particularly Bert, love to play with the English that their parents maul. Everyone has a nickname. Polly is Buddy. Sydney is Larky. Potato latkes are "latchkeys." Matzo is hand-stitched cardboard. When Mrs. Mandelowitz loses her husband, Bert writes a rhyming note to her: "I hear it is said / Your husband is dead / I express my regret / And hope you won't fret." Polly can't stop laughing even as her poor neighbor mourns. When Polly develops a small growth on her ear, Bert writes: "Situated on her ear / You will find a little gear / It's equipped with Syncromesh / So that it will hurt you less."

Sydney would write much later about the family's Honey Street house in Berea, near the top of the Parktown Ridge:

Berea was divided into one-eighth acre plots set in rectangular blocks. Our house, with its red, corrugated iron roof and wooden-pillared front verandah, squeezed into this allotted space. On one side a driveway separated the house from our neighbors, the Lees. At the top of the drive were the green painted wooden doors of the garage. Not long after my arrival in 1921, this gave shelter to a canvas-topped Oakland, T.J. 3350, of erect and dignified contour, which replaced Dad's horse and buggy.

A graveled yard entered from the top of the driveway separated the back of the house from a row of outhouses. The first of these, adjacent to the garage, was the coal store; its periodic replenishment was a notable event preceded by the arrival of a wooden wagon drawn by a team of broad-chested mules. Several black men, rendered blacker by coal and dust and each with a weighty sack molded to bent back, loped in single file up the gravel drive and emptied his load with a resounding clatter and cloud of black dust into the store. Within minutes the swarthy bearers had re-boarded the wagon and the driver on his tall perch flicked the long leather reins, the mules strained their backs and the wagon rolled away down Honey Street.

The coal firm belonged to Mum's brother, our favorite uncle Jack, known as Ponk. On an occasional Sunday Ponk took Bert and me in his Chrysler sedan to the coal depot where we filed along black, smoky paths and faced at close quarters the mules with their blazing eyes and pulsating nostrils.

Dawn would break around five a.m. Sydney was sometimes awake to hear the sound of the cock crowing in the yard, followed by the distant roar of lions, not free ranging in the highveld but echoing from their enclosure in the Johannesburg zoo. The deep vibrating sound silenced the cock. Soon there followed the powerful thrusts of a steam engine puffing out of Park Station, its increasing tempo crowned by an echoing whistle.

Mac entered early. His poker clattered as it delved the innards of the small coal stove that heated the hot water. The powdered ash of yesterday was emptied into dustbins in the yard, wood and coal replenished. There followed a satisfying crackle as the fire spread its warmth upward into the cylindrical zinc tank. Morris, up and about by six o'clock, was assured of hot water for his morning bath and shave. Later in the day Mac cleaned and fueled the big, black kitchen stove, swept and polished the floors, kept yard and drive in order, attended to the small front garden, and waited at breakfast and dining room tables. He wore a short white jacket to serve lunch and in the evening matching white pants.

The room adjoining that of the "boy" Mac belonged to the "maid" Daisy. She dusted, cleaned, and tidied up, made the beds, cooked the meals, and did the washing. Her flat irons, heated on the top of the coal stove, generated a fierce hiss of steam when applied to the damp clothes. Washing involved energetic abrasion on a corrugated zinc washing board, followed by passage through a hand-operated mangle. The mangle's big wheel allowed Sydney's imagination to wander: soon, with its help, he would be navigating a battleship or liner through ferocious seas around the Cape of Good Hope.

Mac and Daisy had one afternoon a week off. Each was paid two pounds a month. Morris maintained that his household of six required an income of one hundred pounds a month. Even for a Jewish immigrant family of modest means, the vast black underclass in South Africa afforded a good standard of living. Because cheap, unskilled black labor abounded, Jews in general avoided manual work and the sweatshop. Jews from Lithuania who headed for the United States rather than South Africa around the same time did not have the same good fortune.

On High Holidays the Cohen family goes to shul. The synagogue is in Yeoville, adjacent to Berea, both predominantly Jewish neighborhoods in the 1930s. The services are boring; the children do not understand what transpires. The men, who sit downstairs, apart from the women, carry the Torah. They read a portion of the law. Then a material element is introduced: congregants announce the size of their donation to the community. Morris gives something, but always less than Mr. Mandelowitz. He feels awkward about not giving more. Sydney perceives the whole exercise as shot through with hypocrisy.

Bert and Sydney are prepared for their bar mitzvahs by a Rabbi Wolf. He is a bad teacher, the object of unceasing ridicule from the four children who study with him. The fruit of their long application to the pantheon of Hebrew literature is knowledge of the word for a broom—*matateh*. (Operation Matateh would be the name given to a Haganah military offensive ten days before the end of the British mandate in 1948; it was aimed at capturing territory between Lake Tiberias and Lake Hula and sweeping it clear of Arabs and Bedouins.) They also learn a single phrase by rote: "Go down from your bed and run to the House of the Book."

They plod to synagogue with dull dread. Years of study have yielded only sounds without meaning. The bar mitzvahs at the Yeoville shul (now the Word of Life Church in a predominantly black neighborhood) are followed by receptions at the Stephanie Hotel, where the recurrent competitiveness over Jewish largesse involves presents. An uncle gives one guinea, another two; all the friends of the family offer fountain pens. Prurient gossip flows over jellied tongue. The boys joke about the symbolism of their rite of passage: *Today I am a grown-up Jew, tomorrow I am a fountain pen . . .*

Bert and Sydney, carrying their pens, go to King Edward VII School, known as KES, founded in 1903, a year after the end of the Boer War, and named after the then British monarch. It does its best to mimic on the faraway Rand the customs of the English public school: the green blazer with school crest of crown and lion; the assemblies in the high-ceilinged, wood-paneled chapel; the classrooms set out around a colonnaded quadrangle of redbrick buildings with a World War I memorial at its center; the "Yes, sirs!" and "No, sirs!"; the rugby and cricket coaches sent from England to impart their message of fair play; the school motto *Strenue*—Strength Going Forward. It would have made a plausible setting for a Harry Potter movie.

The boys know every score and try of the local rugby teams. Every day they listen to the headmaster: *Let us pray. God grant me the courage to accept things I cannot change, to change the things I can, and the wisdom to know the difference.* They cannot change the fact that each morning, along with the other Jewish pupils, they stand outside in the courtyard during Christian prayers. A tower with a clock rises above the quadrangle. The clock, like the one in Bellagio, has two faces, one overlooking the playing fields, the other the school yard.

I look up my father's graduating class of 1938: Kentridge, Kaplan, Meikle, Mendelsohn, Simon. They are huddled there, the excluded Jew Boys. *For our sins we were exiled . . . the fathers ate sour grapes and the teeth of the sons are set on edge.* They never complain: the wisdom, perhaps, of knowing the difference between what can be changed and what cannot.

In the school magazine of 1938, an editorial addresses the state of a world at war's brink:

We are living in troubled times. This editorial is being written under the shadow of vast inchoate happenings in Europe. The stresses set up by the social changes wrought by the advent of technology are straining the structure of civilization beyond the limits of tolerance. The machine does our work for us and meekly comes and goes at our bidding. But it inexorably demands its wages.

The machine has brought men face to face as never before in history. Paris and Berlin are closer today than neighboring villages were in the Middle Ages. In one sense distance has been annihilated. We speed on the wings of the wind and carry in our hands weapons more dreadful than the lightning. Europe has been converted into an elbow-rubbing mass. . . .

Our social sense is only a little less primitive than that of the Middle Ages. But this is the price the machine demands: that we learn to live together in a world where the distance between us and our neighbor is constantly shrinking. The pity is, judging by the events since the turn of the century, that we are learning our lessons badly and with ill grace. . . . Rightly seen, the challenge of the machine is the greatest opportunity mankind has yet enjoyed. Out of the rush and swirl of the confusions of our times may yet arise a majestic order of world peace and prosperity.

Our world of hyperconnectivity, and the strains that accompany it, is not so novel after all. The ghosts of repetition lurk among the preachers of progress. From the "rush and swirl" of 1938 where "distance has been annihilated" and hopes stir of "a majestic order of world peace and prosperity" would follow in short order the slaughter in my grandparents' Lithuanian hometowns, the mass murder of European Jewry, Hiroshima and Nagasaki, and the anguish of all humanity.

The rapid emancipation of European Jewry had offered Hitler rich material for his hateful propaganda. New opportunities opened, and many Jews, through education and industry, seized them. They became conspicuous. Pulled from a self-absorbed shtetl world of Talmudic disputation, they reached the pinnacle of industry and the professions. When frenzied nationalism stirred in a Germany humiliated by the terms of its defeat in World War I, they became targets. The inconceivable proved possible, just when Jews seemed to have broken through the barriers that had long cast them to the margins.

With Jewish self-improvement had come forgetting, in Europe and in Johannesburg. For centuries, in their wanderings, Jews remembered. Rather than disperse anonymously among the nations of the world, they clung with a singular stubbornness to a messianic dream of return and to the rabbinical injunction: *Zakhor!* Remember! Ritual and liturgy, in the frozen shtetl, were, in Yosef Hayim Yerushalmi's words, "orchestrated to transmit a vital past from one generation to the next."

The seder dramatized a living past. For Polly and Morris and Isaac Michel, back in Žagarė and in Šiauliai, and even in Johannesburg, these traditions still lived. As the unleavened bread was raised, the words from the Haggadah were read: "This is the bread of affliction which our forefathers ate in the Land of Egypt." They could still cause a frisson.

To forget was to fall. To remember was the duty of the Jew. As the eighth chapter of Deuteronomy puts it: "Beware lest you *forget* the Lord your God so that you do not keep His commandments and judgments and ordinances . . . lest you lift up your hearts and *forget* the Lord your God who brought you out of the land of Egypt, out of the house of bondage. . . . And it shall come to pass that if indeed you *forget* the Lord your God . . . I bear witness against you this day that you shall utterly perish."

Rites and narrative were set down in the Torah and renewed as traditions with meaning. History was revealed, an eternal present rather than a chronology of events. In the year of my father's graduation from KES, 1938, Freud fled Vienna after the *Anschluss* and addressed this point in a letter to the Fifteenth International Congress of Psychoanalysis in Paris. He wrote: "The political misfortune of the [Jewish] nation taught them to appreciate the only possession they had retained, their Scripture, at its true value. Immediately after the destruction of the Temple by Titus, Rabbi Yochanan ben Zakkai asked for permission to open at Yabneh the first school for the study of the Torah. From now on it was the Holy Book and the intellectual effort applied to it that kept the people together."

Born into the void that comes at the far end of the generational process of forgetting, I can only imagine scripture as riveting, orienting drama. This imagining is also a form of temptation: how consoling it would be to believe in a redemptive God! How comforting to order life around the Torah received by Moses from Sinai and delivered by him to Joshua, and from Joshua to the Elders, and from them to the Prophets, and finally to the Men of the Great Synagogue. So it was for generations—or there would be no Jews.

It is too late. In the upheavals of a century, the transmission broke down. This was progress, or so it was construed. It was emancipation. Yet I see the price of the loss of Jewish ritual as the progressive emptying of the ceremonies that gave cohesion and purpose. It was not enough, in the end, for my immigrant family in Britain to strive to fit in and be like everyone else and push toward the upper echelons of

British society. An emptiness resulted. Already, in the voyage to South Africa from Europe, the world had changed enough for my father and my uncle to come away from years of Judaic study with knowledge of a single thing: the Hebrew for "broom."

An antipathy to Jewish learning in my father, and an ambivalence in my uncle, resulted. In his war diary, under an entry dated March 8, 1945, Bert, then twenty-six and fighting in Italy with the Allies, wrote: "In the truck on the way home Ron Young made a remark about 'fat Jew boys.' I said in as steely a voice as possible, 'I don't like that.' Tangible awkward silence followed."

Six months later, on September 2, 1945, after the Allied victory, Bert visits Berchtesgaden in Austria and goes up to Hitler's mountain retreat, the Eagle's Nest, in a U.S.-led convoy. He writes: "We rested and smoked in Hitler's armchairs. The view from the pinnacle was such that I felt a few months here would make a megalomaniac of anyone. Literally the world lies at one's feet; how easy then to imagine that it does figuratively as well."

Bert etched his name on Hitler's round table: "Cohen, MJ's son." What sweet retribution to have "Cohen" inscribed on the very table where the Führer had presided.

My uncle, back in Europe from Johannesburg, lounged in one of Hitler's private rooms three months after the fall of the Jew-murdering Thousand-Year Reich. He had bridled at the anti-Semitic banter of a fellow officer. He had seen on August 24, 1945, in the displaced persons' camp in Padua, hundreds of desperate Jews sprawled on the floor and felt shame that he could not feel them as *kith and kin of mine*. He does not know the extent of the Holocaust—the almost six million dead—and his parents' now almost Jew-free Lithuania is inaccessible under Soviet occupation, but he knows that as a Jew in Europe, his own vulnerability has been of a particular kind. Yet five days after the visit to the Eagle's Nest, on September 7, 1945, he writes:

"Tonight is the eve of Rosh Hashanah and a service and dinner is being held in Udine. I declined an invitation to attend; this was not easy and may incur the disfavor of some of my fellow Jews but if I am honest I cannot join in such functions."

The intellectual rigor of the nonbeliever prevails over the six million reasons to celebrate Rosh Hashanah with other surviving Jews. I sense some failure of sympathy in my beloved uncle that disappoints me. But I am looking back, and Bert was living forward—and he was acting in accordance with his conscience.

Three months later, just before shipping out from Italy to Egypt, Bert would begin a passionate love affair with a Polish woman named Chalina. On December 2, 1945, he wrote in his diary:

> She is most violently anti-Communist and political argument between us raged . . . for her sympathies in the war lay with the Nazis, although it was the German armies that had first invaded and laid waste her country. Her own adventure during the last six years would make interesting reading. Brief synopsis of why Poles hate Jews is expressed by Chalina: *Polish Jews form a state within a state; they live on Polish bread, accumulate Polish money and wear Polish clothes; but they pay no sacrifice of loyalty to the state of Poland.* She accuses them of welcoming the invaders both from the West and especially from the East when Poland was attacked. She claims they hid away and did nothing to defend Poland.

There is no love like love in the ruins. It springs from, and goes, nowhere. For three weeks in northwestern Italy at the end of 1945, a South African Jew and a Polish gentile of anti-Semitic leanings lived their doomed passion. The world had been cut loose from its anchors. Survival involved desperation. An iron curtain had fallen. It cast half of Europe into shadow. Sometimes I imagine that if my father and uncle had been able to return soon after the war to Žagarė and Šiauliai and see what had happened to the Jews in their parents' former home and throughout the killing fields of central and eastern Europe, where the death camps and the Holocaust were concentrated, they might have felt a stronger Jewish identification. Bert remained childless, and so the transmission of identity became moot. My father had a clear wish: to cast the Yeoville synagogue and Rabbi Wolf into oblivion.

In the Berea district of Johannesburg, near my father's former Honey Street home, stands the Barnato Park School, where my mother was a boarder. A portrait of the eponymous Barney Barnato hangs in the entrance. Cigarette in hand, moustache waxed, gold cuff links and gold watch chain glinting, he wears a pince-nez and a wing collar with bow tie. The Randlord exudes a quiet satisfaction.

Barnato was born Barnett Isaacs in the East End of London, the grandson of a rabbi, the son of a humble shopkeeper. His sister Kate married Joel Joel, the patron of the King of Prussia pub; they had three boys, Isaac, Woolf, and Solly. Barnato, following his brother Harry, left England for South Africa in 1873; formed Barnato Brothers, "dealers in diamonds and brokers in mining property," the next year; and by 1876, at the age of twenty-five, was well on his way to a vast fortune on the Kimberley diamond fields. His three nephews, the Joels, would eventually follow the lucrative trail to South Africa.

A businessman of great cunning, chutzpah, theatricality, and ruthlessness, Barnato amassed wealth in short order. His reputation was dubious. He was unstable, a manic-depressive given to drunken binges, wild bets, and lavish parties. At 25 Park Lane in London, he built a house on a site acquired from the Duke of Westminster; at the same time he embarked on the construction of an estate in Berea, the Johannesburg district where my father was born. Watercolors at the school capture the beautiful park as it looked in the 1890s: fountains splash; a gazebo overlooks a lake; cypress trees give an Italianate air to the rolling grounds within their gates of wrought iron and gold leaf. In hardscrabble infant Johannesburg, this was a thing of wonder.

The paintings are dated 1897, eleven years after Johannesburg was birthed on its blanket of gold. By then Barnato was in a tailspin. His Barnato Bank had failed, despite his assurances that it never would. His mood swings were more violent, his drinking pronounced, his behavior ever harder for his wife, Fanny, to control. In *The Randlords,* Geoffrey Wheatcroft writes of Barnato: "He was delirious, sometimes raving, deluded; at night Fanny found him counting imaginary banknotes or trying to claw diamonds from the walls." At Cape Town, on June 2, 1897, he boarded the *Scot,* sailing for England and Queen Victoria's Diamond Jubilee. On July 23, south of Madeira, in the presence of his nephew Solly Joel, Barnato, aged forty-four, went overboard.

Did he fall, jump, or get pushed? The mystery remains. The verdict was suicide. The Johannesburg stock exchange closed for a day.

My mother, in her uniform of white blouse and dark dress, was a boarder in the mansion of a brilliant, erratic, manic-depressive Jew who killed himself. The place she slept in was known as Joel House, after Barnato's nephew.

The Johannesburg High School for Girls had been founded in 1887 in a little wattle and daub house, moved from there to a corrugated iron church, been dispersed during the Boer War of 1899–1902, before, in the words of its first principal, Fanny Buckland, finding a "fairy godfather" in the person of Solly Joel, who presented his uncle's Berea estate to the school. So was born Barnato Park School (known as "Hags' High" to generations of drooling Johannesburg boys). Its motto was *Vincemus*—We Shall Triumph.

After her return from a year of boarding at Frensham Heights in England, June was sent as a boarder to Barnato Park. She was just nine. Her parents, Laurie and Flossie, had acquired a taste for life without the children around. The school was fashioned, as KES was for boys, in an image of British tradition: empire, church, sports. If the boys were to learn fair play, the girls were to learn to be ladylike. They were to know their way around the classics, embroidery, and lacrosse.

The disintegrating world impinged little on these priorities. My mother was at Barnato Park, my father a medical student at Wits, as the Jews of Lithuania and all Europe were murdered. Classes went on as usual.

Hockey continued, rugby was played, as Treblinka and Auschwitz and Majdanek and Chełmno and Bełżec and Sobibór and the pits of Babi Yar consumed the wretched corpses of Jews from the world my parents' parents and grandparents had left behind. Scarcely a word filtered to the bottom of Africa. The Allies hardly wanted things otherwise. In the joint "Statement on Atrocities" of October 1943, issued by Churchill, Roosevelt, and Stalin, there was no mention of the Jews, although by then more than five million had been gassed or shot.

The deepest lesson was thereby lost. As Timothy Snyder writes in *Bloodlands,* "Jewish resistance in Warsaw was not only about the dignity of the Jews but about the dignity of humanity as such, including those of the Poles, the British, the Americans, the Soviets: of everyone who could have done more and instead did less." My parents were ignorant of the extent of the horror. Others, with the power to make a difference, looked away.

Around the time my mother went to Barnato Park, the school song, "Vincemus," was composed:

> We've a bath for swimming and a hall for gym
> For we must be supple and fleet of limb
> In a land where such sports are conducted in style
> By the springbok, ostrich, and crocodile
> And at seasons proper we stake our fate
> On a contest grim, but devoid of hate,
> And we cheer the victors with this refrain:
> "Vincemus! Vincemus! We'll win yet again."
> Oh years of freedom, how fast ye flee!
> We shall yearn for you in the years to be
> For the joy of striving with all our might
> To play as a team, with the goal in sight;
> For the love of a friend who will see us through
> Whatever the hazardous things we do;
> Yet we'll greet the future with this refain:
> "Vincemus! Vincemus! We'll win yet again."

June would indeed yearn for the years of freedom. Joe Teeger, who would go on to a distinguished career as a Johannesburg physician, met her on the beach at Durban in 1942. Her father was a commander in the South African Medical Corps and about to go to Cairo, where he would spend the rest of World War II. Teeger was at KES, knew several of his Barnato Park contemporaries, and was taken with thirteen-year-old June, who was always adjusting her lovely thick hair. "She stood out from the other girls," he says. "She was intense, clever, direct, ebullient, forceful, and impressive." They began a correspondence that would endure over several years. Her letters were beautiful, he recalls, and he found it an "intellectual challenge" writing back.

David Lopatie, a family friend of the Michels, also exchanged let-

*The Barnato Park prefects, with June in middle row at right,
slightly removed from the rest, 1947*

ters with my mother. He had met June at family gatherings on Sunday evenings. Lopatie was equally struck by June's burning vitality: "She was vivacious, alert and most intelligent, and a bright, successful, happy future seemed to be ahead for her. There is absolutely no possibility that I would have guessed that she was going to suffer from mental illness."

School records from Barnato Park, including June's transcripts, were lost or destroyed during the last years of apartheid. Berea had become an overwhelmingly black neighborhood by 1990. There were not enough white girls in the area to justify the school's existence. So it was closed down by the government, and the history of more than a century lost. Barnato Park later reopened as a school for boys and girls of all races.

One school magazine from 1989 that attempts to trace the then-102-

year history of the school survived. Its cover reads: "In my end is my beginning." I have a photograph my mother kept of the twenty-three Barnato Park prefects of 1947. June in her last year stands slightly apart from the others at the right side of the picture. There are many smiles around her. She holds back from one with a detached, knowing air. Her gaze is inward-looking. At the age of eighteen, she is about to step out into the postwar world, a child of privilege. She would always fear abandonment and had hardly known, as a boarding school girl first in England and then in South Africa, the physical reassurance of parental love.

Isaac Michel died on July 9, 1953. More than three years later his solicitors, Edward Nathan, Friedland, Mansell & Lewis, wrote to the master of the South African Supreme Court to explain delays in the settlement of the estate: "The accounts in the Estate I.D. Michel cannot be drawn until such time as the valuation of the deceased's shareholding in Isaac Michel Holdings (Pty.). In this connection we refer you to our letters of the 29th October in the Estate Late I.D. Michel, when we advised you that the Auditors are at present busy upon this valuation—*which is a most complicated calculation.*"

There were large bequests—to a host of Jewish institutions and to various charities and hospitals (£4,000 for Johannesburg General and £1,000 for the "non-European" hospital). Michel had owned farms sprawling over hundreds of acres and seaside properties in Durban and Cape Town. His wife, Jennie, had valuable jewelry; his "Château Michel" Houghton home had "four brick servants' rooms." He had a large interest in a shoe manufacturer, Edworks. He was a partner in the brokerage firm of L. Bowman & Michel, where his son Googoo would work. He had stakes in several South African blue-chip mining companies.

Yet he had contrived to make his liabilities outweigh his assets, an apparent ploy to avoid death duties. He was indebted at the time of his death to the tune of £78,549 to his own holding company, Isaac Michel Holdings, corresponding to "monies expended by the company" for him. His company funded his lifestyle. In all, his official liabilities came to £118,832, exceeding his assets by £1,140, a sum his heirs agreed to pay.

The Michel will mentions various trusts, apparently established well before his death. These were the apparent source of the dolce vita of his offspring, most of whom lived in luxury in Houghton, traveled the world when they wished, and generally chose the path of least resistance to apartheid. But the family scourge that would afflict my mother did not spare them.

Willie, who co-owned an upscale men's store called Manhattan's on the corner of Eloff and Jeppe, was a gentle soul, a keen bird-watcher, who suffered from manic depression and periodic breakdowns. Basil was a playboy who liked to buzz the beach at Muizenberg in his private plane to announce his arrival to the babes. He was always fooling around with the shopgirls at the OK Bazaars. Brave and reckless, he was happy to get cut to ribbons in the surf as he searched for lead sinkers off the rocks at Duxbury that he could take into Fish Hoek and sell.

On July 17, 1961, the Johannesburg daily *Star* carried a story on its front page headlined "Girl Aged 19 and Brother Die as Car Hits Tree." The dead were Basil's children, Linda and Brian, my mother's first cousins. They had gone for a spin with two eighteen-year-old friends, David Aronsohn and Duncan Macdonald, both of whom survived. Their car swerved out of control on Witkoppen Road in Rivonia, the area where Isaac Michel owned property. Basil then took to drink. His marriage broke up, and his mood swings became violent.

Googoo labored on as a stockbroker at L. Bowman & Michel but, like his brothers, lacked the drive and ambition of his father. He found consolation in cricket and bowls, his daughters, and his beautiful home and garden.

As for the three girls, Lily had trouble with her children: her son, Clive, was murdered in the Hillbrow district of Johannesburg, his penis severed, the victim of a crime of passion; her daughter, Yvonne, was mentally unstable and married a half-dozen times; Clive's youngest son shot himself.

"Baby" Alethea, the youngest of Isaac's children and the most gifted, pursued her gorgeous, solitary path from Johannesburg to Paris and

June in South Africa (a happy moment) with her parents, Laurie and Flossie

finally London. Her first husband was killed in Libya in World War II, leaving her with an infant son, Erroll. Her divorce in the late 1940s from her second husband, John Sive, the heir to a pharmaceuticals fortune and father of her daughter, Jane, precipitated a family crisis. Isaac Michel cut her out of his will, then at the last tried to reinstate her, only for his five other children to vote against dividing the patriarch's estate six ways rather than five. The feud over this vote never abated. Alethea, disinherited and ostracized, once told Erroll how "Googoo walked in front of my car and I could have run him down—but in the end I didn't."

Like my mother, Alethea could keep up appearances in public but was two people, sparkling at times, dark and destructive at others. She went places and ran up bills. If appearances demanded a party she could not afford, she went ahead anyway. Money would take care of itself, except of course that money, like beauty, does not last forever. She was among the top six bridge players in South Africa, a gifted decorator, a charmer; and then her destructive side would come out and she would leave friends dangling and run away to Paris hotels she could not afford. She died of brain cancer in London at the age of sixty-one.

My grandmother Flossie was the most stable of the six. She was also a shrewd investor. A document dated March 9, 1954, shows her marking her independence from the intractable Michel estate. It states that although certain shares had been registered in Isaac's name only "for the sake of convenience," they had in fact always been recognized as her property: holdings in West Rand Consolidated, Spring Mines Ltd., Harmony Gold Mining, Grootvlei Proprietary Mines, Edworks, and Blinkpoort Gold Syndicate. She would later acquire a lucrative stake in De Beers. The oldest of Isaac's children, she outlived them all and died at 104. She also outlived her daughter, my mother, June, whose mental instability curtailed her will to live and left her aching for the sunlit land that had made Isaac Michel, the *smous* from the shtetl, rich enough to create her African house of dreams.

CHAPTER 6

Picnic in a Cemetery

She is tall with an easy stride. I have passed her on this street before, at about this time, with the trees casting the same etched shadows. There is no sidewalk—only blacks walk in apartheid South Africa. They do not need sidewalks. Yesterday she smiled, I slowed the car, we talked for a moment, and the air between us quickened. From a fenced yard came the barking of a dog.

Today she is there again with that same languor to her gait, in her hips and her arms. Now she looks around—toward the house where she is employed, perhaps. Making up her mind, she signals for me to stop. She slides low on the backseat to conceal herself. Her long slender legs push up against the front seat. I see the outsize inoculation mark in her left arm, the dimple in her cheek. We are caught in the swoon and lull of the middle of the African day and in breach of the color lines set down by racist law.

Her story: She is going to meet her sister in town. They will take a bus together out to one of the townships; their mother is sick, but the bus service has been erratic, and she has to be back at work early tomorrow morning. Hers is the catalog of practical difficulties that is black life in South Africa, the endless back-and-forth imposed by legislation with anodyne names like the Group Areas Act (aka Blacks Out of White Areas Act).

We climb into an expanse of vacant lots, skittering garbage, and unpaved roads. The light is blinding. We pass a white homeowner, red-faced as an oyster shucker outside a Paris brasserie, berating his black gardener. She tells me the way. Her voice is quiet but clear. We turn onto a track and pull up behind dusty shrubs.

I had been at a *braai* a couple of days earlier, where a Jewish industrialist friend of my mother's, stoked by a couple of gin and tonics, had begun to expound on the impossibility of desire when it came to the natives, who, after all, were "only just down from the trees." The phrase was spoken as if it were a self-evident historical fact. In feature and smell, he went on, as he tried to dislodge a piece of beef from between his yellowing teeth, they were closer to animals than humans. "I mean," he said, withdrawing the toothpick at last with its dangling prize and peering at it through his bifocals, "can you imagine ever touching one of them, let alone—?"

There was more than a touch of thou-doth-protest-too-much in his boozy exposition. He'd probably been daydreaming for years of bedding the maid as he drove out to Houghton golf club. I said that I could very well imagine desiring a black woman—indeed, I did not have to *imagine* it. He spluttered, smirked, and suggested I could not be serious, at least not about the kaffirs here in South Africa.

Now in the car there is nowhere for us to go, a young white man and a young black woman—no café, cinema, house, or even bench. The businessman's attitude is enshrined in the Immorality Act of 1957: any white male person who "has or attempts to have unlawful carnal intercourse with a colored female person" or any colored female person who "has or attempts to have unlawful carnal intercourse with a while male person" is guilty of a crime.

The offense is punishable by imprisonment with compulsory labor for a period not exceeding seven years. It is, however, "sufficient defense to any charge under this section if it is proved to the satisfaction of the court that the person charged at the time of the commission of the offense had reasonable cause to believe that the person with whom he or she committed the offense was a white person if the person charged is a white person, or a colored person if the person charged is a colored person."

There is not much latitude there. The chiaroscuro of our intertwined limbs on the car seat offers scant basis for a plea.

In 1955 and 1956, years that my father was dean of the residence for black students at Witwatersrand University and I was in South Africa as an infant, a rabbi named André Ungar caused a stir. Born in Hungary, a Holocaust survivor, he had arrived from London to head the Reform congregation in Port Elizabeth, the coastal town where my father used to vacation with his family. Blacks were then being cleared from white areas under the Group Areas Act. Ungar was appalled.

"There was a sense of déjà-vu in many ways," Ungar, who lost dozens of family members in the Holocaust, tells me. "I remember being ordered into a ghetto in Budapest in 1944, and the attitudes of racial superiority in South Africa seemed to me to be cut from the same cloth. Even if there was no systematic extermination, black life was cheap. I arrived in January. A few months later Passover came, and I made some comparisons about our slavery in Egypt, liberation and the condition of oppression of black Africans. The parallels seemed inescapable."

Black life was cheap: that was the way it struck my father, returning from England and having to extricate his students from the clutches of Afrikaner cops, and how it always seemed to me. My other relatives, however, viewing the system from within, did not react in the same way. They were attached to their traditional way of life—the so-called TWOL—and the rest of the world was anti-TWOL, even if the lifestyle existed in a permanent state of suspension, and the consignment of the black majority to the status of *Untermenschen* was the cornerstone of their circumscribed South African world. I never heard from them a remark of the "just come down from the trees" order, but prejudice was so ingrained, it was part of their unconscious.

For Ungar, himself an outsider, a young man who had survived in hiding in Budapest before escaping communist Hungary for England in 1948, South Africa's racist laws cut to the quick. The Reservation of Separate Amenities Act was striking in its echo of the rules that had kept Jews out of certain Hungarian stores, off certain benches, outside certain parks, and away from certain sidewalks: "Any person who willfully enters or uses any public premises or public vehicle or any portion thereof or any counter, bench, seat or other amenity or contrivance which has . . . been set apart or reserved for the exclusive use of persons belonging to a certain race or class, being a race or class to which he does not belong, shall be guilty of an offense."

In Hungary it had been the yellow star. Here it was the passbook that tagged the persecuted. From the pulpit of the temple, Ungar railed against the injustices of apartheid. He called the National Party government a bunch of "arrogantly puffed-up little men." He said it was the moral obligation of Jews, based on their scripture and millennia of exclusion, to stand against the social engineering of a racist system. "I knew I had a clear mandate to say what I was saying from the Jewish experience itself," Ungar, who went on to work as a rabbi in Woodcliff Lake, New Jersey, recalled.

His forceful condemnation of white supremacy made the majority of the South African Jewish community, then numbering about 110,000, or about 4 percent of the white population, uneasy. My family was representative enough in its general, but not universal, desire to keep their heads below the parapet. The Afrikaners might turn on them.

The National Party had been shot through with pro-Nazi anti-Semitism in the 1930s. The Immigration Quota Bill of 1930 took direct aim at Jews by strictly limiting new arrivals from Latvia, Lithuania, Poland, Russia, and Palestine. D. F. Malan, the National Party leader, attacked the Jews in a speech in 1937 that was explicit about their menace: "I have been reproached that I am now discriminating against the Jews as Jews. Now let me say frankly that it is so. . . . There are too many Jews here, too many for South Africa's good and too many for the good of the Jews themselves." Jews were attacked for their success in business and the professions, for "buying" the press, and for refusing to assimilate. The Transvaal section of the National Party banned Jews. Prewar *völkisch* Afrikaner nationalism advanced by placing Jews in its sights.

But after Hitler's defeat and their own electoral victory in 1948, the Nats changed tack. Now it was the preservation of power rather than its acquisition that concerned them. They toned down the anti-Semitic rhetoric, decided to co-opt the Jews as fellow whites in the confrontation with the black majority (the Afrikaners sensed they needed the

Anglo and Jewish communities to bolster their position), and were forthright in support for the new state of Israel. Prime Minister Malan would be the first head of government to visit the Jewish state. The Afrikaner in a sea of blacks looked with sympathy on the Jew in a sea of Arabs. This bond—composed of Old Testament sympathies, shared isolation, Cold War alignments against communism, and plain survival instinct—was not without its strains, even as it provided the backdrop to significant military and nuclear cooperation between Johannesburg and Jerusalem.

Still, the Jews could be targeted again. Relegation was always possible: perhaps to the status of Indians, an underclass of apartheid but, like the mulatto coloreds, a little less *under* than the blacks.

Blessed with the color of the ruling caste, and now accepted as paid-up whites in an apartheid system, South African Jews nonetheless lived in an unease they seldom avowed. Jews told Ungar he was putting himself, the congregation, and the whole community at risk. There were threats, anonymous letters, phone calls, and visits. The president of the South African Union of Progressive Judaism defended the government as "men with outstanding careers behind them."

The South African Jewish Board of Deputies, the umbrella organization serving as the mouthpiece of the community, declined to intervene. Since the coming of apartheid, it had adopted a policy of nonintervention, urging individual Jews to act according to their consciences but rejecting political opposition to apartheid. This position was in effect one of acquiescence. It would endure for decades: the silence was pretty deafening.

Arthur Suzman, a vice chairman of the board and a liberal who agonized like many Jews over their passivity before evil, summed up the approach in an address to the National Congress in 1974: "The nonintervention of the Board in political issues does not imply that we are indifferent to the inequities of our existing political, social and economic structure. We are not, however, a political body and we cannot take up the cudgels for or against the policy of any particular political party."

Such statements, of course, sought to finesse the fundamental issue: that apartheid was not simply a "political" question. It was a moral and ethical question involving basic human rights and dignity. The Jewish Board of Deputies strove hard to ignore this fact.

Ungar, unsympathetic to the semantic contortions of South African Jewish caution, continued to wield his cudgel. He was struck by the sense of terror in his congregation. Fear had the upper hand. In late 1956 the rabbi, then twenty-seven, received an order from the Interior Ministry to leave South Africa. He had become persona non grata by urging Jews to resist apartheid and treat blacks as equal human beings.

The Jewish community did not lift a finger over Ungar's expulsion order. "There is no occasion for the Board to intervene to make a statement," said the Jewish Board of Deputies, arguing that Ungar had taken his message to the "political platform" and must take personal responsibility for his utterances. Relief was general, with one or two exceptions.

South Africa's brave chief rabbi, Louis Rabinowitz, sent Ungar a telegram congratulating him on his stand. Rabinowitz used his sermons at the Great Synagogue on Wolmarans Street in Johannesburg to argue that man's inhumanity to man was a political as much as a religious affair (so disturbing the members of my family who felt the pulpit and politics did not mix). In a Yom Kippur sermon, Rabinowitz would say:

> There are some Jews in the community who attempt to do something . . . and when as a result they fall foul of the powers that be, the defense put up by the Jewish community is to prove that these are Jews only by name, that they do not belong to any synagogue. . . . Have Jewish ethics ever descended to a more shameful nadir? I have practically abandoned all hope of effecting any change in this matter. The power of fear and the possibility of security being affected are too strong.

Rabinowitz once called apartheid "an abomination that desecrates the sanctity of life." His telegram comforted Ungar but did nothing to change his fate. In December 1956, the rabbi left South Africa.

At the time, my father, overseeing black students at Wits, also found himself appalled by the tightening noose of the apartheid laws. His students would be forced out of the university in 1959; the drift in that direction was already clear. Prime Minister Hendrik Verwoerd explained to parliament some years later, "There is no space for the native in the European community above certain forms of labor. . . . Until now he has been subjected to a school system which drew him away from his community and misled him by showing him the greener pastures of European society where he is not allowed to graze."

Jews often ask how the Holocaust was possible, how an entire civilized nation could turn on them, how so many people could look away as their neighbors were herded toward train stations and boxcars that would usher their doomed loads to the gas, how indifference could overcome outrage and ordinary folk become murderers. South Africa is instructive in this regard. Of course, Hitler's rise to power occurred in specific historical circumstances. German humiliation and disarray fed the search for a scapegoat, just as the postwar rise of the National Party in South Africa exploited Afrikaner insecurity and grievance. But the human traits that buttress violent systems of racist oppression—fear, envy, tribalism, resentment, conformism, opportunism, acquisitiveness—are universal and enduring. Inject the virus of hatred, with violence if need be, and it will find tissue on which to propagate.

The attempt to annihilate European Jewry had been vanquished only a few years earlier when, in South Africa, a system built around the systematic relegation of the blacks to wretchedness in the township ghetto or "Bantu Homeland" was put in place and extended piece by piece—through the passbook, job reservation, exclusion from higher education, and repression. Most Jews looked on and kept quiet. As in any such situation, where to resist is to put your freedom and perhaps even your life at risk, the majority opted to join the impassive onlookers who tried not to see too much as evil was done.

Some Jews were active backers of the order from which they drew great benefit. (Abraham and Solomon Krok, through their company Twins, made a fortune from skin-whitening creams sought by blacks who saw a whiter look as the path to advancement.) But a significant number did resist, no matter the risk or likelihood of exile, because their consciences could not be quieted in a land where pigment determined the value of a life.

Perpetrator, bystander, and resister: the pattern repeats itself. The cowardly will always outnumber the courageous. I have seen this in every conflict I have covered and been left in no doubt that what is most precious in Jewish ethics and teaching was distilled by Rabbi Hillel into three sentences: *What is hateful to yourself, do not do to your fellow man. That is the whole Torah; the rest is just commentary. Go and study it.* Or there is the phrase repeated thirty-six times in the Mosaic book: *You were exiled in order to know what it feels like to be an exile.* Jews are to treat the stranger well, for *you were a stranger in a strange land.*

The year after Ungar was expelled, in 1957, a young South African Jewish newspaperman, Ronald Segal, took up these themes in an article for *Commentary.* "No form of oppression," he wrote, "is as intimately an experience of the Jew as the ghetto. Yet no Jewish organization, let alone the bugle of the community, the South African Jewish Board of Deputies, has attacked or even delicately protested against the savage Group Areas Act, which will segregate the races of the country into separate residential pockets at immeasurable sacrifice always to the non-whites."

His view was contested by Dan Jacobson, a young South African Jewish novelist living in London:

> As a result of their upbringing in a passionately color-conscious society, South African Jews in general actually *share* all the color prejudice of their fellow whites. When I think in the simplest possible way of my innumerable relatives, friends and acquaintances in South Africa going about their business and pursuing what they believe to be their interests, in all conscience I can only wonder what people Mr. Segal thinks he is talking about when he issues his appeals for disinterested sacrifices and martyrdoms, and then grows angry because there is no reply. Is he talking about people at all?

In my own family I saw this failure of imagination—this inability, busy with one's own interests, to conceive of the suffering at the foundation of South African society. As Nadine Gordimer (no relation to George, although her paternal family hailed from Žagarė) observes in *The Lying Days,* whites were busy having "a picnic in a beautiful cemetery where people were buried alive." Sit on the fence, and people get killed behind it. Indifference is midwife to iniquity.

But I also saw anger and resistance. Prejudice and obliviousness were far from universal. On arrival in South Africa, Ungar felt the compulsion from millennial Jewish experience and from his own recent persecution to identify with, and speak out about, the stranger. Expulsion then became inevitable. Only in 1985, almost forty years after the National Party came to power and apartheid was imposed, did the Jewish Board of Deputies, seeing which way the wind was blowing, state its rejection of apartheid and express its "commitment to justice, equal opportunity and removal of all provisions in the laws of South Africa which discriminate on grounds of color and race."

The silence of the majority of South African Jews over Ungar's fate and their long acquiescence to a racist system suggest how careful Jews should be in invoking the lessons of history. Jews learn selectively from the past, just like everyone else.

One of the congregants listening and shaking his head in the Wolmarans Street shul as Rabbi Rabinowitz criticized apartheid was my grandmother Flossie's brother Willie Michel. He was a conservative man who liked his bridge and bowls, and he took the view that Rabinowitz had no business talking politics from the pulpit. "Why must he busy himself with things that don't concern him?" Willie would mutter. "Shame, it will only bring trouble for us all."

Willie had more than enough politics at home, a reason for his prickliness. His wife, Joyce, née Levy, was a member of the Black Sash antiapartheid movement, founded in 1955 by a group of white women, and an outspoken intellectual. She went only once to synagogue, for the bar mitzvah of a nephew. The occasion was doubly memorable because she smoked in the lobby.

Joyce had been to college, Willie had not. But a Michel was a catch. Willie's men's store, Manhattan's, was the second best in Johannesburg. Willie sold Pringle's cashmere sweaters, fine Italian suits, and fedoras. He worked upstairs where the suits were hung. His busi-

Isaac Michel with his three sons: Basil, Willie, Googoo

ness partner, whom he couldn't stand, sold socks, ties, and underwear on the first floor. When the security services raided Manhattan's on account of Joyce's political activities, Willie was not happy. That was the kind of trouble you got into by rocking the boat.

There was worse. On Yom Kippur Willie emerged from shul to find his wife having a picnic lunch by the pool with two prominent anti-apartheid figures, Julius and Tamara Baker. It was one thing to pooh-pooh religion, but this defiance, Willie felt, was in his face. He was fasting, wasn't he? Still, he was not confrontational; he kept quiet. He soaked it up. They played bridge together. That was the family way: stoic silence.

Their daughters, Sue and Peta, born in 1942 and 1944, were not given any religious education, at Joyce's insistence, to Willie's dismay. He was happy when Sue, at the age of eleven, influenced by some girls who were having bat mitzvahs, suggested they keep a kosher home. Joyce replied, "You can be kosher if you want to, darling, but I don't believe in all that, and our home will not be." Shame, Willie thought, but so be it.

Julius Baker, who picnicked on Yom Kippur, was a lawyer and

adviser to the African National Congress, revered by both the ANC and the South African Communist Party; Tamara was a Black Sash activist. They would both be hounded out of South Africa in the 1960s. Joyce helped them make good their escape to London.

Joyce's intelligence and engagement earned her a special place in my parents' hearts. She was the sane one among South African relatives. We would often stay at her lovely house at 22 Second Avenue in Houghton, ten blocks from the old Isaac Michel mansion. Joyce smoked and talked; Willie listened. She moved in a milieu of resistance that included several prominent Jewish figures, most of whom were atheist leftists like her and the Bakers, people who looked to Marx, not Moses. Joyce, a great beauty in her youth, busied herself with street collections for the protracted Treason Trial, which began in 1956 and was conducted partly in Pretoria's Old Synagogue, vacated a few years earlier by a suburbia-bound Jewish community. Of the 156 defendants accused of treason, 23 were white, and of these 14 were Jewish, a disproportionate number indicative of the determined minority that broke from the compliant attitudes of the Board of Deputies.

Nelson Mandela was successfully defended at the trial by Israel ("Issy") Maisels, assisted by another Jewish attorney, Sydney Kentridge, a member of my father's 1938 graduating class at King Edward's School. Joyce's circle also included Joe Slovo, a Lithuanian Jew who became a leading figure in both the ANC and the South African Communist Party, before, after long exile, becoming a minister in Mandela's first postapartheid government. Helen Suzman, another descendant of Lithuanian Jews, who represented Houghton for decades in Parliament and was a fearless opponent of apartheid, was a friend. Joyce and her daughters would go to reelection meetings in the Houghton school hall. They were involved in all Suzman's political campaigns. Suzman, accused of posing questions in Parliament that embarrassed South Africa, famously responded that it was not the questions that were embarrassing, but the answers.

There was a lot of unease at home. Sue and Peta carried books about Lenin to their grandmother, Dora Levy, to be hidden when there were raids by the security services. Dora disapproved. At times the whole house seemed like a workstation in the cause, full of pamphlets and activity. When blacks refused to board buses because of rising fares,

Joyce would pack the young girls into the car as she drove black work-ers back and forth to the townships. Her action and Willie's inaction, her conviction and Dora's disapproval, demonstrate how South Afri-can politics inhabited every family.

Tensions rose after the 1960 Sharpeville massacre. Slovo moved into the armed struggle. Three years later security forces raided Lil-liesleaf Farm, a property on the outskirts of Johannesburg in Rivonia acquired as a safe house by a communist named Arthur Goldreich. The five whites arrested were all Jews, a fact that led to renewed rumblings in the National Party. The Rivonia trial sent Mandela to prison and Joyce into a state of great agitation, but she managed, unlike some of her friends, to walk a fine line that kept her in South Africa, out of the ANC, and out of incarceration.

Willie tried to rein her in, but he was the weaker character. He vol-unteered at the Jewish orphanage and old age home. Increasingly he retreated into his silences, his depression. Sue and Peta grew up with one thing clear in their minds: this was not a normal country. Both would emigrate, Sue to Israel, Peta to the United States.

Tens of thousands of Jews, about a third of the South African com-munity, have upped and left since my childhood, because they could not see a future. They could not see Mandela walking out of jail with a message of reconciliation.

My parents made their decision to go in early 1957, as the Treason Trial got under way and the poison of apartheid infiltrated deeper. It was a hard choice. They had gone back to South Africa with me in 1955 because that was where they felt they belonged. My father later said of this return, in a newspaper interview, that he went "as a son and not as a scientist, I love Africa, it is in my bone and marrow and it is there for good." This love was a victim to hatred. It could not withstand the ambient racist venom of the Group Areas Act. My parents departed a couple of months after Rabbi Ungar. They never again lived in South Africa.

Asphyxiated by a country where now only white brains counted, my father felt he had no choice, despite what he felt in his bone and his marrow. My mother was pregnant with my sister, Jenny. Over the previous two years, she had given birth to me in England, returned to

South Africa, and now, at the age of twenty-seven, headed for London again. So it is that political gusts buffet personal lives, leading in my mother's case to the shock of displacement and breakdown.

We were in South Africa, and we seemed happy there, with all the family around us, yet back we went to England, where life was lonelier. And even in South Africa there was something not quite right: that fear and disorientation I had first felt in the arms of the black nanny who placed me on the parapet in Cape Town and intimated I could fall. When the disorientation faded and I discovered words, I understood the uneasy state in which South Africa lived, its double character, with the underclass always out there at the horizon on the brink of eruption. For a while I refused to go. When I went, I strayed across the lines, I touched the troubling flesh of the stranger. I wanted to know the other side.

It would all end badly because it had to, with the hot embers from the *braais* rammed down white throats, the country clubs on fire, the gold-birthed European annex on the Witwatersrand reef upended, and blood spilling red across the swimming pools of Houghton. The barefoot black mob would trudge out of the dust to take back what was theirs. This was what we believed. Calamity was inevitable.

So return was out of the question. My mother lived in her own painful state of suspension in Britain. Keeping the surface intact after her breakdown demanded a lot of energy. Below her was a maelstrom, as terrifying as any black storm gathering at the horizon. She dreamed of going back to South Africa, ever more so as she grew older. But we had decided to become English. Sometimes in life it is just too late. To forge new British identities, it seemed better, or at least easier, to forget. In the family we were not good at talking about the toll of "the situation" in South Africa and the consequent flinging of Isaac Michel's grandchildren and Polly Cohen's children back across various oceans. We were not good at tracing matters back to their roots.

The apartheid South African state was watching even its exiles. Sue and Peta Michel traveled to Europe in the mid-1960s. They saw my parents and the Bakers, now in London. In Paris, Sue fell in love with a Frenchman and decided to stay on for a while. She called at the South African Embassy and asked if they knew of any jobs. Yes, as it

Ruth Michel (Googoo's wife), June, me, Joyce Michel (Willie's wife), and Flossie in London

happened, the embassy needed a receptionist. Every day Sue would answer the phone: "Ambassade d'Afrique du Sud."

She made a few calls of her own. The embassy listened in. She contacted the Bakers, who were like surrogate parents. "We note, Miss Michel, that you have been in touch with people who are enemies of the South African government, and we must ask you to leave at once." Fortunately, her love affair was ending anyway.

The situation at home in South Africa had become very difficult. When Sue and Peta were in their late teens, Joyce called them into her bedroom to tell them something important.

"Your father is going to have electroshock treatment tomorrow to treat his depression."

"Electroshock treatment! Why? What's wrong?"

"The psychiatrist, Dr. Perk, says it's the only way to get him out of depression. Shame, he's been very bad."

Willie had seemed low and forlorn to Sue, but she had not guessed the extent of his anguish. Depression was a nonsubject. Joyce took Willie to the hospital. When he came back, he looked dazed. His personality had changed. He seemed jolted, far away. After a few days he rallied, but the depression returned in its cyclical way, and back he went for more electroshock treatment. When their father came home, the girls always pretended that the ECT had not taken place. For the rest of his life, they never talked about it. Sue knew Willie to be a warm and loving person, so his withdrawal was particularly painful. Silence became a family reflex, a survival mechanism, whatever its cost.

Shame, depression brought trouble for us all. Willie's ECT in Johannesburg in 1959 followed that of his niece, my mother, the previous year in London.

CHAPTER 7

Patient Number 9413

June Cohen was a woman hollowed out like a tree struck by lightning. She had been blighted. I wanted to know why.

On a blustery February morning I boarded the 8:50 from Waterloo to Woking in Surrey. The train was empty, commuters headed in the opposite direction. Ever since my mother's first suicide attempt in 1978, I had been trying to fill in gaps. She was gone in my infancy, and when she returned, nobody spoke about the absence. She had suffered an acute depression after my sister's birth in 1957. I learned much later that she was in hospitals and sanatoriums and asylums being shot full of insulin and electricity. The resulting spasms, seizures, convulsions, and comas were supposed to jar her from her "puerperal psychosis."

In 1957 my mother was treated at a psychiatric hospital in Wimbledon. For several weeks during the early summer of 1958, she was injected with insulin at London's St. Mary's Hospital. After each session she would be revived with a nasal feed of liquid glucose. When she failed to respond, she was discharged on July 8. Soon afterward she was admitted to the Holloway Sanatorium, the sprawling Victorian Gothic fantasy of a nineteenth-century tycoon, Thomas Holloway, who amassed a fortune through the sale of dubious medicinal concoctions.

None of Holloway's remedies was any more than a placebo. Joy Whitfield, a nurse at the sanatorium during the time my mother was confined there, told me his ointments were composed of olive oil

(44 percent), lanolin (30 percent), resin (15 percent), and a mixture of white and yellow beeswax. The pills consisted of aloes (37 percent), rhubarb root (18.75 percent), ginger (18.75 percent), potassium sulfate (9.5 percent), and small amounts of cardamom, cinnamon, salt, and saffron. But Holloway understood marketing. London trams were covered with his ads. They promised miracle cures. Sales of his bogus stuff soared. Holloway went global. He had an office in Manhattan. Only in France was he not represented, because the French insisted the composition of medicines be disclosed.

Childless, Holloway and his wife, Jane, pursued grandiose philanthropy with their fortune. They built a ladies' college inspired by French châteaux and a sanatorium in the likeness of the Cloth Hall at Ypres in Belgium. The Prince of Wales, in the company of a few friends who had been attending the nearby Ascot Races, opened the sanatorium at Virginia Water, west of London, in a ceremony on June 15, 1885. The great heap of gabled redbrick buildings were filled with paintings, a nod to a nineteenth-century French theory that the mad respond to visual stimulation. In some rooms small devils lurked in the exuberant design, as if to remind patients of what they were there to excise.

A square redbrick tower rose 145 feet into the damp air of Surrey. The lugubrious dining hall boasted stained-glass windows and a magnificent cantilevered timber ceiling. Hand-painted medieval bestiaries adorned the overblown Gothic entrance hall, with its oak wainscot and blue and red medallions in the ceiling inscribed with "TH" and "JH," the initials of the founders. In the Great Hall, where tea dances were held once a week, a picture of Holloway was flanked by portraits of Queen Victoria, Oliver Cromwell, Lord Nelson, William Shakespeare, Queen Elizabeth, Francis Bacon, Benjamin Disraeli, and other English notables—the company the founder felt he should keep. Every inch of space was decorated. Images of philosophers weighing the world's cares on their scales abutted elaborate floral patterns. On the recommendation of the Commissioners in Lunacy [*sic*], a chapel was added in French Gothic style. Matins and the Eucharist were celebrated every Sunday. The sanatorium had its own chaplain. A rabbi would come only if specifically requested or in case of a Jewish death.

It was into this establishment that my mother was admitted

seventy-three years after its opening. Run initially as a private institution, the Holloway Sanatorium became a mental hospital within Britain's National Health Service after World War II. It was not closed until 1981, after lightning struck a gable and caused a fire. Many of its records and casebooks were burned by Spanish orderlies. The chapel organ pipes were broken up and used as javelins. The gutted sanatorium became the setting for horror movies. Directors could not believe their luck. Holloway's Gothic caprice found its natural calling a century on.

The premises adjacent to Virginia Water railway station were, however, too valuable to be passed over by Cool Britannia's real estate moguls of the 1990s. The property was acquired, renamed Virginia Park, and transformed into a gated community of high-security luxury homes, complete with underground garage and a state-of-the-art health complex. A swimming pool was built where the mentally ill once thronged the dining hall. The vestry was turned into a shower room. The chapel became a sports hall. Lines of a basketball court were painted on its wooden floor. Behind a Ping-Pong table and a basketball hoop, a reredos survives, like a guest who has outstayed his welcome. It recalls another time, as do the wooden plaques with gilt lettering commemorating the Holloway Sanatorium's dead in World Wars I and II.

So ends nineteenth-century philanthropy—in a twenty-first-century suburban fortress for the rich. It is situated opposite the Sunrise Senior Living Center (known locally as the Sunrise Home for the Bewildered). Children in bright bicycle helmets and pregnant American moms unwind in Virginia Park where lunatics once performed the gardening detail. The statue of Thomas and Jane Holloway has been removed.

Joy Whitfield notes that the two cast-iron weather vanes on the former chapel point in different directions. In the more than half century she has known them, they have never pointed the same way. In the Great Hall, she remarks that some of the lights are turned on by flicking switches up, others by pressing switches down: "We are in a mental hospital, after all."

Not all the Holloway records disappeared. Some were preserved at the Surrey History Center. In the faint hope that a trace remained of my mother, I wrote to inquire. A letter came back a few weeks later.

References to June Bernice Cohen had been located in the admission register and in ward reports from July 1958. These showed that "she was patient number 9413, was admitted on 25th July 1958 and was discharged on 12th September 1958." The ward reports for August and September had vanished. I applied under Britain's Freedom of Information Act to see the records.

It is a fifteen-minute walk from Woking Station to the history center. The streets follow like Eliot's "tedious argument." England in February weaves its misery into a gray curtain. Cafés in the Home Counties now do toasted panini and espressos. The mimicked "continent" is no longer the faraway place of my youth, where various forms of unpleasantness (rabies, garlic, and intellectuals prominent among them) lurked ready to invade England.

My reencounter with my mother was the object of a painstaking negotiation with an archivist. It left me struggling to maintain an appropriate library whisper. At last I was presented with the weighty admission register for female patients. Entries are written with fountain pen in cursive script. In columns across the page my mother is identified. *Name:* June Bernice COHEN. *Ref Number:* 9413. *Age:* 29. *Marital Status:* Married. *Religion:* JEW.

The admissions register for female patients at the Holloway mental hospital recorded details of my mother when she entered it on July 25, 1958.

I stared at her age—so young—and at the capitalized entry under religion: "JEW." The noun form has a weight the adjective, *Jewish,* lacks. It seems loaded with a monosyllabic distaste redoubled by the strange use of the uppercase. June was not religious. She is the youngest on the page. She is also the only non-Christian.

The first ward notes on my mother read: "History of depression in varying degrees since birth of second child, now fourteen months old. Husband is engaged in medical research. Patient has some private psychotherapy and also modified insulin treatment at St. Mary's last month, being discharged July 8th. On admission she was depressed, tearful and withdrawn." The doctor examining June was struck by how "her tension increased remarkably on mention of latest child."

Guilt, especially over my sister, Jenny, would pursue my mother, a shadow that could not speak its name. I ran my fingers over the page and paused at "JEW." I wanted to take a soothing poultice to her face.

On July 28, 1958, June was visited by a Dr. Storey. He "confirms diagnosis of post-puerperal depression and advises Electro-Convulsive Therapy (ECT), which patient and husband are *now* willing to accept."

What painful reflection and discussion must have preceded the electricity that left June in a permanent state of brittleness. She first underwent ECT on July 30, 1958. The treatment was repeated a second time on August 1, 1958, one day before my third birthday. At least now I know where she was.

At the time of the disaster, my parents had been in England for a couple of years, but my father had known the country longer. They had unequal experience of their adoptive land. Perhaps this discrepancy goes a little way to explain why he shed South Africa and embraced Britain, its climate and habits, in a way that proved difficult for my mother.

Fun-loving and bubbly, June struggled with the British understatement she had first known for a year as an eight-year-old boarder at Frensham Heights. She belonged in South Africa, the privileged child of a close-knit Jewish community in Houghton, where the trees in the yard dropped their fruit, apricots blushing into ripeness. She would gaze at the muddy winter fields of England with gulls hovering over them, the color of goalposts, and wonder.

There was no equivalent community for her to join in London. For Sydney, the obscurantism of the Jewish religious instruction he had received in Johannesburg was part of what he wanted to leave behind. He was uninterested in, if not hostile to, Jewish identity. As in many things, June followed him. She quelled whatever doubts she nursed. Sometimes she talked with pride to her friends about her distinguished great-uncle, Rabbi Michael Adler, but that was in private and sotto voce.

Sydney had arrived in England on May 18, 1945, ten days after the end of the war in Europe. Like many others in the West, he knew less of the Holocaust than seems imaginable today. The Nazi death factories— Auschwitz, Treblinka, Majdanek, Sobibór, Bełżec, Chełmno—were all liberated by the Red Army, not by the Allies, who saw the horror of Bergen-Belsen much not the much ampler horror farther east. A month-long sea voyage brought my father from South Africa to Britain. A circuitous route, charted to avoid lingering German U-boats, took him in a great westward loop almost to the coast of Brazil. Sydney, recently qualified as a doctor, with some experience in remote stretches of Zulu-land, spent much of the journey aboard the SS *Nestor*—"a huge funnel surrounded by a little boat," as he described it—gazing at the Atlantic. It was a journey from balmy breezes to biting winds. When a depth charge went off during a meal and caused a panicked rush for the exits, he opted to go on eating. Merchant sailors slept on deck as a precaution. They had already been torpedoed. They called Sydney crazy for preferring the comfort of his bed down in the ship's bowels.

Early experience as a doctor had made him fatalistic. Working in the Transkei before he sailed for England, my father had been called into the bush to help an African girl who had been in labor for two days. He drove as far as he could and was met by men with horses. They rode for about an hour. When he entered the hut, he found the girl, encircled by elderly women of the tribe, with a baby's arm dangling from her vagina. The baby was crossways. He reached in, managed to turn the baby around, and it was born, dead. He examined the mother and found her uterus hemorrhaged. The elders put him back on a horse and made a litter to carry the girl, taking turns to run with her. The journey lasted for more than two hours. Every ten minutes the team carrying the litter changed.

The little hospital, when they reached it, was run by nuns. They laid the mother out and did what they could, but she died soon after. With the baby and her mother dead, Sydney felt he had achieved nothing. He was astonished when the men of the tribe insisted on giving him a small, beautifully engraved wooden box.

"But the baby's dead and the girl is dead and I wasn't able to help you," he said.

No, they explained, he had helped them achieve the essential, which was that the girl should not die with the baby inside her. If she had, an evil omen would have hung over them for many years.

Britain, its treasury mortgaged to the hilt by Churchill in the fight to defeat Hitler, was overrun with war injured. Doctors from the Dominions came to mitigate its burden. The backwash of empire bore talent as well as travails to British shores. Sydney was accompanied by three young South African doctors who would be lifelong friends: Allan Kark, Paul Marchand, and Pat Denehy. They had written to Jan Smuts, the South African prime minister, to appeal to be allowed to work for the Emergency Medical Service in England.

Victory in war camouflaged looming British decline and the passing of the torch across the Atlantic. For my father, raised in Berea on the Johannesburg reef, his first sight in 1945 of London's monuments and the crowds thronging its great iron-and-glass railway stations still provoked the frisson of presence at the nexus of global power.

By a strange quirk, his older brother, Bert, arrived in England for the first time a day later, on a plane from war-ravaged Italy. On May 19, 1945, he wrote in his diary:

All of a sudden land was below us. This was England, very green and orderly. The sky was dull as we flew over the Sussex Downs. The Englishmen in the plane lost their *aloof restraint* and peered avidly through the windows. We landed in Croydon, passing over a green cricket field and white-flannelled players. A truck took us to London. Familiar names were everywhere. I saw the Houses of Parliament, Big Ben and got off at Trafalgar Square where Nelson stood atop his pinnacle unbowed. I deposited my luggage at Charing Cross Station and set off to find Larky.

Sydney had owned a violet jersey of the same color as larkspurs in the yard at Honey Street. Bert coined the name. It stuck: Larky Cohen of Johannesburg, brother of Bertie Cohen. Bert was "burning with eagerness" to see Sydney, whom he had left in South Africa eighteen months before. Through a friend he located him at the Tuscan Hotel in Shaftesbury Avenue. Sydney was out. Bert settled into the room, read a paper, smoked a pipe, and drank tea. Coupons were needed for sugar, flour, and Mars bars—but not for the sacred British "cuppa." The reunion was emotional. "I was very happy to see the Boy," Bert wrote, although the news Sydney bore—of their father's sharply declining health—was worrying. "It's time I got home to the old folks."

Uneasiness between the brothers set in the next day: "There is something strange; I looked forward with such passionate eagerness to meeting Larky but, perhaps as an anticlimax, I do not feel thoroughly happy with him. There is something disquieting. I cannot put my finger on it. Is it that he is not '*simpatico*'? Perhaps this is imaginary." My uncle's musings on my father continue in the diary that week: "It occurs to me that he hardly knows me and that I must be patient and earn his respect and affection instead of expecting it as a familial due."

A few weeks later, after Sydney has found his first job at the Royal Berkshire Hospital in Reading, Bert went to visit him. Sydney had encountered an astounding sight at the hospital: a *white* woman on her hands and knees cleaning the floor.

My father had also discovered the need for rapid improvisation as he treated a range of war injuries. Up and down a spiral staircase from the ward he scurried to consult a weighty medical manual. His supervisor was a stiff English doctor whose brother had been a renowned big-game photographer. Sydney had treasured a book of wildlife photographs as a child. The photos, it transpired, were by the doctor's brother. He was invited to the doctor's house. In the hallway were photographs of a rhino and a charging elephant. "That's the elephant that killed my brother," the doctor remarked. *You mean, killed the rhino?* "No, the photograph was found in my brother's camera after his death."

Bert, arriving at one a.m., found "my hardworking little brother still awake." He writes: "We chatted for a while and then I lay down on a mattress on the floor and went to sleep. Lark has a fine room all to himself and seems to be most happily situated."

Bert's reflections presaged the highs and lows of an intense, often difficult relationship between two brilliant men who would go on to illustrious careers in British science—both reaching the pinnacle of their respective fields, both appointed Commanders of the British Empire by the queen for their pioneering research, both pursuing vaccines that were never found, Bert for dental caries, Sydney for malaria. They never put to rest the combination of sibling rivalry and character difference that troubled their bond. My uncle, emotional and demanding, a born raconteur, a spellbinding weaver of thought and feeling, often found my father detached, cool, or remote. Sydney, with his intense inner world, silvery wit, loner's self-sufficiency, wry deadpan humor, and distaste for displays of feeling, was the more introverted personality, wary of an older brother he sometimes found overbearing or controlling, a sibling who in his diary called him "the Boy."

In early August 1945, on the eve of departure back to Italy from England, Bert writes, "I asked Lark if I should cable him from Rome but my strange brother said that a letter would suffice." Then an afterthought: "An atomic bomb has dropped on the city of Hiroshima in Japan today." My uncle is peeved with my father as the first atomic bomb falls. Perhaps he experienced a fraternal affront with more intensity than the mushroom cloud over Japan.

These two successful men stood at two poles of my life. I felt their competing natures vie within me, warmth and coolness. Bert never had children. His wife Hazel's several pregnancies all ended in premature births, probably as a result of a backstreet Johannesburg abortion she had before they were married. One fetus, a boy, lived for a couple of days. He would have survived if born a couple of decades later. I filled that absence in some measure.

Perhaps I also filled another. On July 8, 1945, my uncle made this entry in his diary: "Of late I am obsessed with a desire to write—but I lack inspiration. If it were forthcoming, if I could unleash my pen, I might perhaps if blessed by Fortune be able to redirect my life away from the prosaic channels along which dentistry leads." Later

My uncle Bert, who dreamed of becoming a writer before pursuing an illustrious career in dentistry

that month he returned to the theme: "I am becoming obsessed with a burning desire to write well. Perhaps literary achievement is the unknown goal for which I have been feeling, groping in the dark recesses of my muddled mind." At the end of the year, back in Italy awaiting a boat to Egypt, he declared 1945 to be the year of an important realization: "I will not be able to practice dentistry happily unless I have been successful in writing."

It was not to be. The young man who wrote in Italy that "falling snowflakes remind me of a Botticelli virgin—pure, leisurely, fragile, very delicate and almost casual in their indecision"—became the first Nuffield research professor of dental science at the Royal College of Surgeons of England. In his diary he wrote: "The Barrier of Fact—the bigger you grow, the bigger the barrier. Beyond the barrier lies the land of colorful imagination. When you are young you can go there yourself, when you are older someone must describe it for you."

My mother returned to Gillespie Ward after her first electroconvulsive therapy. The ward notes for July 30, 1958, say, "Normal recovery, a little improvement noted. Visited by husband. More talkative. Said she felt rather better after ECT. Slightly restless during the night." She is prepared for a second ECT on August 1. A nurse writes, "She seems much improved. Well occupied and interested in other people."

Then silence: the record of my mother at the Holloway Sanatorium stops, the ward notes lost in upheaval just like her transcripts from Barnato Park School. Her mood swings during the following six weeks of that English summer can only be guessed at. She always referred to the place as hell. I do not know how many ECT sessions she had after that second one. My father blotted out, as best he could, the memory of this nightmare.

Perhaps June visited the hairdressing salon once a week, or attended a concert in the recreation hall, or did regular needlework, her delicate hand poising in the air as she tightened the thread. Or perhaps she was too heavily sedated for any of that. Perhaps she was led around like a child or waif. Perhaps she sobbed in guilt and pain before her daily meetings with Dr. Storey, recalled by Joy Whitfield as "your typical mad psychiatrist, odd, short, very difficult to make eye contact with." Nor do I know how my third birthday was celebrated without her on August 2. Sydney went to visit her most days. I was often with my uncle Bert and aunt Hazel.

Patients in Gillespie Ward did not eat in the main dining hall. A heated trolley came around from the kitchen. A nurse would serve the meals. The ward was close to the ECT room. There electrodes were placed on either side of the brain and attached to a transformer. Staff would hold the shoulders and hips of patients to avoid dislocation when the current passed. By 1958 a general anesthesia was often administered so that, in Whitfield's words, "patients did not jump around so much."

The surviving ward notes have my mother in Holloway for seven weeks. My father's notes at the time of her first attempted suicide say four months. She may have returned to the sanatorium later that year. In any event, June came home from Virginia Water to our house at the end of a cul-de-sac in Mill Hill on September 12, 1958, six days before my father's thirty-seventh birthday.

Eight years had passed since their sunny meeting on the tennis court at Château Michel in Johannesburg.

Our house was in the north of London, close to the National Institute for Medical Research, where my father worked. My first memory is of standing at the far end of the Mill Hill garden looking through a picket fence at the allotments and field beyond. There were horses in the field. The shadows of trees played on the whispering grass. I can still feel the sensation of smallness as my hands gripped the fence. Once in that house I was very ill with flu. High fever caused me to hallucinate. This was during the absence of my mother. My father cared for me. He told me he was sick with worry. I laughed in my delirium at the sight of creatures garlanded in tinsel and mistletoe frolicking across the door of my closet.

Life resumed. My mother found some tenuous equilibrium. Her mother came from South Africa to help—to what degree, I cannot say. June's collapse became a nonsubject, the mute stranger in the house. A friend, Mary Warshaw, told me June hated life in Mill Hill because she felt cut off. She found relief going into town for lunches with friends. They would meet at Debenhams, a department store. June would go straight for the hats and fascinators and try them all on and hoot with laughter. She was *bright*—and when she was not, she hid away. She never forgot a birthday. She was full of kitchen tips. Always keep the butter paper—you can cover the vegetables with it and keep them warm. Leave the skin on the onions when you make a stock, it will give the soup a nice golden color. She darned and gave dinner parties. She tried to repair the broken bond with her husband and children.

My father completed his Ph.D. thesis in 1959. Bound in blue leather, it sits on his bookshelf to this day, with its startling photographs of the backsides of baboons—he always pronounced them "BAY-boons"—swollen to a great size at ovulation. (This he relates to the level of protein in the blood.) Sydney was the first to bring baboons to Britain in the 1950s for medical research. He would go to Heathrow to meet them and bring food. Once he got an odd look from the grocer when, having asked for bananas and been told they were out, he said he wanted carrots instead. Later the baboons were given to the London zoo. A year or so after the donation, he went to visit, and the females started chattering in high excitement, pressing against the bar of the cage. They had always liked him, but not his assistant, whom they once pushed to the ground.

In 1961 we moved to the house on the hill in Hampstead that my mother came to love. That was also the year my father began work at

St. Mary's Hospital with his friend Rodney Porter, who would win the Nobel Prize for Medicine in 1972 for determining the chemical structure of an antibody. Sydney was a gifted immunologist. Porter, later killed in an auto accident, recognized his talent and opened doors for him. His career leaped forward as June tried to find some ballast. He later told me that after a shipwreck you cling to the wreckage, you do not strike out for shore. But my parents, young Jewish immigrants recently arrived in Britain, did not have much to cling to when June broke down. Their families were in South Africa. They had embarked on an arduous adaptation only for my mother to buckle.

A photograph from July 1958 shows June in a small boat on the Norfolk Broads. It was taken during the seventeen days between her discharge from St. Mary's Hospital and her admission to the Holloway Sanatorium. She is seated. Her smile is expressionless, an outward show overwhelmed by inner torment. I would come to know similar expressions well, a straining to reach the surface. Aged nearly three, I am behind her in a white shirt, my anxious look directed straight at the camera. Behind me a Danish au pair, Jette, holds my fourteen-month-old sister, who looks down in apparent distress.

June has two infant children but is holding neither of them. Depression has buried her gaze. My father must have taken the photograph. His life henceforth would never altogether escape this tension.

My mother liked to quote Othello: "What wound did ever heal but by degrees?" And William Walsh: "I can endure my own despair / But not another's hope."

I was born in 1955, midway between the atomic bomb and the release of the Beatles' *Rubber Soul,* at the start of a postwar boom that would endure decades, on the free side of the iron curtain, in a Europe embarking on the "ever closer union" that stopped the self-destruction of the first half of the twentieth century, safe from the Nazi death factories, too late for the trenches, not too late for flower power, in time for the hippie trail to the subcontinent, and in line for the sexual sweet spot between the arrival of the Pill and the onset of AIDS. This was a good time to be born. One grew up without device distraction and got

*June between sessions at psychiatric hospitals with me, my little sister, Jenny,
and our au pair, Jette, 1958*

into the habit of reading. As Philip Larkin noted, "Sexual intercourse
began \ In nineteen sixty-three." For me it began five years later in a
Chelsea town house, a couple of hours after watching the Pink Floyd
free concert in Hyde Park and feeling, to my surprise, Sarah's toes touch
mine in the grass. I can never listen to "Set the Controls for the Heart
of the Sun" without recalling the moment I realized her toes were not
mingling with mine *by mistake*. She knew a lot more than I did.

Such luck could not but build forms of amnesia. Weren't things
always this good and love always this free? The distance between the
generation that had known the war and my own insouciant band of
baby boomers was not easy to bridge. Especially because my father, in
a word my mother often used, was a loner. Or at least he became one.

June once wrote to me of him:

He may not be able to show and express what he feels because such is
his nature. But I *know* that he has a vast depth of feeling, understanding and true love for me and you. Life has taught me that very often
highly intelligent and gifted people are loners—their work and the

genius they are able to apply cuts them off from us lesser mortals. Theirs is an esoteric and somewhat unique life force. Try therefore to allow for his occasional appearance of detachment. I *know* that he feels with passion. He *cherishes* us and if we need him—as I have often done—he spares no effort to support, to love and to care.

I knew the love beneath my father's severity. But after boyhood it was a prize to be earned rather than a sure harbor. My father could not fill the empty space left by the electricity jolted through my mother. Each of us has his limits. I could not count on love. So I sought it where I could. Always, within me, there was a dreamed-of reconciliation, in effect, as I came to understand much later, the restoration of my mother to life.

Children are ingenious even in their complete dependence. They build worlds that allow them to cope with fears they cannot understand. My father, in his notes on my mother's depression, kept a photocopy of a chapter from Anthony Storr's book *Human Aggression,* with certain passages underlined. One reads:

Young children are, of course, totally dependent upon their mothers. If they are uncertain of their mother's affection they soon learn to behave in such a way that they could not possibly offend or irritate her; but on the contrary, they are compelled to placate her in order to get what they need. Such children become very sensitive to their mother's moods and feelings; and it is this early and skillful adaption to her which makes them able to adapt and identify with others later in life. More robustly confident persons with a greater conviction of their own value are often less sensitive to the feelings of others. On the other hand, when they do become aware of them, they have more to give.

My father, the apple of Polly's eye and object of her unstinting love, had an immense amount of love to give—when he chose to. I had a gift—one I would later put to professional use—for entering others' psyches.

I was a resourceful child with a strong will to survive. Jette, the Danish girl in the back of the boat on the Norfolk Broads, was the first

My father in his midforties

of a succession of Danish au pairs—Inge, Manja, Marianne. In their late teens or early twenties, they lived at my end of the Hampstead house. They bathed and cared for me, gave me the goodnight kiss I craved, and took on the brunt of what my mother could not or would not do.

I discovered as a boy that I had power over them. I could, it seemed, bend them to my child's will. *A storyteller is what I am. I may have driven my mother away. At least that is how I understand the mystery. I may dwell in a cold house. But I can escape. By dividing myself, I can have two women, my dead mother whose touch I long for and my vital close-by girl. Division is a small price to pay for the elixir of escape.*

Manja Fristoft came to work in our house in early 1965. I tracked her down in Minnesota, and she recalled her time with us almost a half century earlier. She found my mother to be "a lady all the way through, very thoughtful and sweet," but also a little lost, as if "she had a wall built around her or is a person living in a big grayness." June often rose late. Sometimes the cleaning lady informed Manja that "Mrs. Cohen is not feeling so well." Then the door to the bedroom remained closed.

When June ran out of the Rothmans King Size cigarettes whose lipstick-tinted filters were always in the ashtrays, she came down the corridor to get one from Manja. She was scrupulous about returning these "borrowed" cigarettes. June seemed to Manja to live in some fear of my father (known to the au pair as "the doctor"), as well as at a distance from her children that she could not altogether understand.

In June 1965, a couple of months before my tenth birthday, Manja went to a Danish midsummer evening celebration party outside London and met Jörn Loberg, who had just arrived from Denmark. They fell in love. When Manja told me she and Jörn were engaged, my fury knew no bounds. Manja tells me I "climbed the walls" in a frenzy at her decision. I would never speak to Jörn.

Manja was soon pregnant by Jörn, and their engagement was announced in haste. My mother, concerned about Manja's dignity, insisted that she should get a ring at once. Appearances mattered. Convention existed for a purpose. She directed her to a small antiques store at the bottom of the hill. "That's better," my mother said. "You could not possibly go back pregnant without a ring." In November 1965 Manja returned to Denmark.

Bereft, I stumbled from one infatuation to another but assembled my outward world with a fierce concentration. In the classroom, on stage, on the sports fields, I excelled. What else defines the success of an English boy? I conjugated my Latin verbs, declined my Greek nouns, converted the half-chances in the squelching, waterlogged goal mouths, cleared balls off the muddy line, captained the cricket team, read voraciously, and cultivated an aura. I wrote a poem about the patterns the clouds make. Beneath the shifting sky, I invented ball games that held me captivated.

Of course, I could not altogether escape the physical punishment then de rigueur in an English public school (my headmaster beating me with a cricket bat at age eight, for telling a lie, as I recall) or the abuse of twisted educators (my French teacher telling me, as I bailed out of his school trip to France, that he hoped my plane crashed because he was certain I would then go to hell). This was just part of growing up in pre-touchy-feely Britain, that long-lost country where nobody had special dietary needs, or knew what gluten-free meant, or was afraid to use the accent they were born with.

London unfurled for me along its misty canals, in the sulfurous tunnels of the Northern Line, on the single-decker Green Line bus (quicker but more infrequent than its double-decker Red cousins). From Hampstead tube stop, I walked down to my house past the church of St. John-at-Hampstead and its cemetery. From the Green Line bus stop, I walked up past St. Andrew's church. It was often damp and gusty. I kicked the wet leaves. I varied the route home from school, not wanting to settle on one. It never took less than forty-five minutes, more often closer to an hour. I began making this journey when I was eight or nine; I was alone a lot.

My mother was often in bed. I came home one late afternoon to find her sobbing, inconsolable. Our dog, a cocker spaniel called Smokey, had died. Smokey had adored her but held back from my father, a mirror image of the baboons' affection. June's grief troubled me even in my own house because there was something *disproportionate* about it.

She was a shadow of the woman who had had me, yet she was there for me in extremis. Leading the cricket team as captain to a game in Highgate at age thirteen, I protected our equipment against skinheads who assailed us on an underground platform. As we turned to board the train, one of them smashed me from behind on the right side of my face. I *crawled* into the tube, the bones around my eye broken and my cheekbone crumpled.

At Camden Town I left the rest of the team to take the other branch of the Northern Line to Hampstead. I waved down a car. June was in her bedroom, alone. It was the middle of the day. She dressed the wound and comforted me. We went first to a local hospital, then, as the gravity of the injury became clear, to Guy's, where my father became professor of chemical pathology in 1965. There were concerns about my eye. The surgery was long and delicate.

My father was away in Scotland. He returned the next day. Much later, in a scribbled annotation of harbored resentments, I found a reference from my mother to Sydney's absence. Such feelings got locked in a storehouse. It took me a long time to measure the weight of the silence or pinpoint its roots in Virginia Water.

Much later, in a letter to my first wife, Katherine, in 1981, I wrote about the childhood feeling I could never quite articulate: "The fear of death was with me once. Objects resisted all harmony, clamped to their corner of space. Faces fled into their private tunnels. A dull hum pressed on my temples in mornings that were too long. I wanted out from the cold. Only the cold awaited me. Alone on this street I can still feel what the fear was like but the fear has gone. The stars are beautiful, each one in its place, and as the world turns, we find in the end where we will rest. There was a scent of sweet peas on our bodies in the sun. You said, I could die right now and be happy."

CHAPTER 8

Jews in a Whisper

The compromise in Britain seemed to be: you kept quiet about it, and you could rise just about as far as anyone else. The "it" was being Jewish. Of course there was anti-Semitism—was it not everywhere? But this was not *annihilationist* anti-Semitism, after all, the continental kind that had pushed many Jews toward British shores in flight from Russian pogroms and Hitler's Reich.

No, the British were genteel, even affable, in their prejudice: a comment here about pushiness; an aside there about money; a drunken, embarrassed confession from some ruddy squire about a half-Jewish grandparent; a grumble about flashiness ("All that gold jewelry!"); a casual reference to a woman looking Jewish with her "great conk of a nose"; an allusion to "Jewish behavior," whatever that might be; a murmur about stinginess ("Don't be so Jewish!"); a harrumph about how "these people are very clever"; a suggestion that a Jew could be "British" but certainly not "English"; variations on the old self-contradicting themes of Jews as arch-capitalists and arch-communists and, whichever they were, a little uncouth.

All this could be irritating, but it was not threatening, flotsam on the tide of an ingrained bigotry that was harmless enough. Compared to the real thing, this was mere condescension, a trifle when set beside Britain's unusual tolerance. The posture was not actively hostile, and it was quite likely tinged with envy. Britain's quarter of a million Jews did all right. Many did very well. There were few, if any, societies in

Europe where you were better off as a Jew. You turned your back on full-throated Judaism, changed your name perhaps (not de rigueur), and opted never to make a fuss. You swept all that nasty silliness under the carpet. Almost all the time there was nothing to make a fuss about. Britain was ample, open to all comers. The motto was: Keep quiet and carry on. You could even become prime minister.

Yet the prejudice was there in the background, enough—if you were being honest—to feel not quite comfortable, to feel excluded from the heart of whatever it was that was going on. Philip Roth, in his novel *Deception,* has his American protagonist say to his British lover: "In England, whenever I'm in a public place, a restaurant, a party, the theater, and someone happens to mention the word 'Jew,' I notice that the voice always drops just a little." She challenges him on this observation, prompting the American to say, yes, that's how "you all say 'Jew.' Jews included."

My parents were quiet to the point of silence about the Jewishness I stumbled on at school through the taunts I faced. Many factors contributed to this effacement of identity: the immigrant's push for assimilation, the subliminal shame of the diaspora Jewish survivor, a scientist's rational rejection of Jewish religiosity, and the habits of fellow Jews in England who opted to keep their heads down. I recall my father shaking with rage at the murder of Israeli athletes during the 1972 Munich Olympics and announcing he would watch no more of it. But we never talked about what it meant to be Jews. Tradition and custom and ceremony were absent. No days were different from any other days. There was none of what the Israeli novelist Amos Oz and his daughter Fania Oz-Salzberger have called "the intergenerational quizzing that ensures the passing of the torch." Our apostasy was complete. There was no wrestling with God. We were chopped liver. We did not have a Christmas tree. Nor did we have anything else. Our deity was academic and professional achievement. My father's rise in a country he had reached only in his midtwenties was meteoric.

My mother's core role, in line with her times, was to support him and raise us. She had collapsed but tried to rally. Her closest friends in London were almost all Jewish—Noreen Webber, Mary Warshaw, Eve Pollecoff. They were smart, witty women, born a generation too early to realize their potential. June felt comfortable with them.

But English life was complicated, infinitely more so than among the Jews of Houghton in South Africa. If she thought differently about how we should be brought up—if she felt, for example, that we should know about her grandfather's brother, the rabbi who served as chaplain to Britain's Jewish soldiers during World War I—she did not speak up. Sydney knew best. "Syd and I think": so began many sentences, to the occasional annoyance of her friends, who felt the marital tension suppressed by my mother in the name of loyalty and love. She kept her own views (at least those not in a state of conjugal fusion) to herself.

In Howard Jacobson's novel *The Finkler Question,* an aging London Jew and widower makes an awkward confession: "I have discovered in myself a profound necessity to think ill of my fellow Jews." He is sick to death of "the Jew business," which has only become more complex with Israel's growing power and bellicosity, a subject of increasingly unpleasant London dinner-party conversation. He says that he would not be "so quick to see the Jew in the Jew if the Jew in the Jew were not so quick to show himself. Must he talk about his wealth? Must he smoke his cigar? Must he be photographed stepping into his Rolls?"

His companion, a Jewish woman and old flame, is incensed: "We are not the only people to smoke cigars." No, he concedes, "but we are the very people who should not." To which she retorts, "You have the Yellow Star mentality, Libor."

The response is sharp: "I have lived in England a long time."

My mother's difficulties as an immigrant trying to adapt were of many different kinds. She had been deracinated. In mildewed England there were no more Shabbat gatherings, no more beef on rye, none of that sunny ease where friends from the neighborhood popped in. One of her problems, although she never framed it that way, lay in how to be that whispered word—a JEW, as she had been registered in the ledger of that British mental hospital—in the land of Lewis Namier's "trembling Israelites," a nation whose message to Jews often seemed to be: Lose yourself to join us entirely, and even then fall just a little short.

Westminster School, founded in the sixteenth century, stands on the premises of the Abbey in central London, a stone's throw from Parliament and a short walk from Piccadilly. Geography is history. Certainly it goes some way to explain Westminster's unusual combination among British public schools of tradition and worldliness. An establishment so close to Soho could scarcely aspire to the hearty discipline of a remote country boarding school, least of all in the permissive late 1960s and early 1970s, when I was there.

What Westminster offered was academic excellence. It was scholarly and civilized and tolerant. In the days before inspectors and academic league tables and all the deadening modern mechanisms of control and accountability—accompanied by parental hysteria over children's performances in the global educational marketplace—it was also a place of extraordinary liberalism. Teachers whose eccentricities were indulged allowed boys (and by the time I left, a few girls) great leeway to pursue whatever inspired their passion. Exam curricula were no more than a contemptible passing consideration, it being assumed they could be covered in short order before delving deeper into Ovid or Kerouac. I recall my English teacher, John Field, writing three words in chalk on the blackboard: "Property is theft." He then uttered one: "Discuss." When we had dealt with that little matter, it was on to Joseph Conrad's *Nostromo,* a novel dense as a tropical forest. Westminster taught how, not what, to think.

Freedom nurtures individuality while indulgence may undermine it: the balance is never easy. I arrived at Westminster in January 1969. A year later a young headmaster of great energy and strong convictions, John Rae, took up the reins and, as he relates in his memoir *Delusions of Grandeur,* grappled at once with how to prevent the descent of invigorating tolerance into destructive permissiveness. Rae had an unusual combination of qualities. He valued Westminster's sophistication and excellence while bridling at the elitist snobbery he had first encountered in the army—state schoolboys never became officers— and feeling unease at what he called England's "clearly delineated social strata." He prized merit and hated prejudice. He wanted as far as possible to treat students as adults—all the evidence of adolescence notwithstanding—and so preserve Westminster's distinctive urbanity. At the same time, he abhorred the toll drugs in the school were taking on a quality that defines an adult: the capacity for sustained exercise of the will. Even his strong stand against marijuana was not enough to prevent some members of the school's board of governors from regarding him as an incorrigible radical: Rae the Red. One of his last acts before departing in 1986 was to name a black girl as captain of school.

I first set eyes on Rae, a handsome man of upright bearing and chiseled features, in his long red cassock striding into the Abbey for the daily service. He had his own stall in the Abbey, inscribed with his Latin title: "Archidedasculus." The cassock, as Rae explains in his memoir, was "the outward sign of his membership of the collegiate body of the Abbey and the school." Henry VIII had expelled the monks at the time of the dissolution of the monasteries in England in 1540 and established the Abbey and school as a joint foundation: the dean was chairman of the school governors, the headmaster a member of the Abbey collegiate body. These were Westminster's interlocking institutions.

The past was palpable in the flickering flame of gaslights, in the uneven paving stones of the cloisters (today they would merit a danger warning to visitors), in the nocturnal silence of Dean's Yard (broken only by the chiming of Big Ben), and in the magnificent Abbey itself, where the fifteen-minute morning services were brief enough to be bearable but just long enough to establish some dim connection between learning about William the Conqueror and imagining his coronation there in 1066.

A child of repetitive Jewish displacement, I had somehow arrived, in the space of two generations, at a Christian epicenter of continuity. This irony was lost on me. I was unaware that my paternal grandparents and much of my mother's family came from the shtetls of northern Lithuania; or that my upbringing, while bestowing the gifts of a superb liberal education, had also been devoted to the expunging of this past, as well as to the suppression of the not-unrelated history of my mother's mental breakdown shortly after she reached England. On arrival in the school, I had just turned thirteen without having the bar mitzvah that was the rite of passage of generations of my forebears in the Cohen line. Sydney's convictions and June's brittle perfectionism informed my makeover.

Pot was everywhere, and stronger stuff not hard to find. We mocked the notion that one might lead to the other before discovering its truth. Rae writes of the late 1960s, "The use of cannabis was so widespread at Westminster that the drug was sold openly in Little Dean's Yard and across the tables in College Hall." There was cannabis growing in window boxes. It was everywhere. What, after all, was the point of listening to Dylan or the Grateful Dead or Jefferson Airplane or Van Morrison without a joint?

An anonymous boy interviewed in *The Sunday Telegraph* said he had "worked out that half of the senior boys in the upper school take or have tried cannabis. There is nothing wrong with smoking pot, but if you think there is, then a situation exists at Westminster which you would consider serious." Rae spoke out; there was even a police raid. A few boys were expelled. Orders went out for hair to be cut so that it was off the shoulder, a stipulation that meant we held our heads up high when confronted by a teacher while adopting a hunch at other times to be cool. The notion that Westminster would somehow roll back the tide of swinging London was far-fetched. We laughed—and went off to the 1970 Isle of Wight rock festival to watch Jimi Hendrix, the Who, the Doors, Chicago, and Joan Baez. It rained a lot, and we were in heaven. For a fifteen-year-old, there was no arguing with the liberation in that music.

Of course, turning on and tuning in did take a toll. We noted that our all-conquering under-fourteen football team had somehow, by the time we reached senior level, become incapable of winning a single match. We had oozed languid class. Now we were simply languid. Our plummeting form drove our coach, Stew Murray, a dour and diminutive son of Yorkshire, to paroxysms of red-faced exasperation.

His was a losing battle against sex, drugs, and rock 'n' roll. In our last team picture, I, as captain, should have sat in the middle of the five players on the bench in the foreground, but this seems to have been too much for our distracted minds to calculate because I was off by one. We were rebels. We still had the footballing talent, but we no longer had the will. We had acquired the amused detachment that was a Westminster trait. Our pink team shirts summed up our effete turn.

I came to love the school. In English and history I was inspired by brilliant teachers—John Field and Jim Cogan. I formed lifelong friendships. Westminster was still a school attended by the children of London's cultured professional middle classes; it was not yet coveted by the hedge-fund honchos and assorted masters of the universe who make up the global elite now bivouacked in the houses of central London with their multistory basements.

Still, adaptation took some time. I had to assert myself and emerge from a cloud. In my first term, the suppressed Jewish past came back. I kept hearing the old "Yid" insult from the boys in my dormitory. If there was a disagreement, I was a "fucking Yid." There was more. I had earned a scholarship but not the one I would have had if Jews had not been barred from College, the house where Westminster's forty Queen's Scholars resided. As Rae wrote of the school he found on arrival there in 1970: "Another deterrent to prospective parents was Westminster's reputation for anti-Semitism, a reputation that was not undeserved."

The examination for election to a scholarship at Westminster is called The Challenge. I took the exam, which is appropriately named, at the age of twelve, between May 28 and May 30, 1968. Among the questions was: *Are the Ten Commandments out of date? If so, why?* I also had to translate into Latin elegiacs these lines of Dryden:

> Soon after, Homer the old heroes praised,
> And noble minds by great examples raised;
> Then Herod did his Grecian swains incline
> To till the fields and prune the bounteous vine.

That I was able to coax those swains to incline in Latin elegiac form, as well as wrestle various mathematical problems to the ground (*Can you say anything about the number of lines of symmetry for a regular n-sided polygon?*), seems astonishing today, to the point I feel the need to get reacquainted with this talented boy. Who was he, and what did he know about polygons?

I did well enough to place sixth in The Challenge, an exam in which the top ten or so performers earned a Queen's Scholarship and entered College. But I sat the exam in ignorance of the fact that its rules stipulated that "candidates for Queen's Scholarships must profess the Christian faith." My parents had signed an entrance form acknowledging this requirement. My failure to satisfy it was evident. So I was awarded an Honorary Scholarship, a kind of sop to conscience that entitled me to wear the scholars' ankle-length gown but not enter College or afford my parents its financial advantages.

I thought nothing of this at the time. Such matters belonged to the vast realm of silence. When I inquired of Westminster's archivist, Elizabeth Wells, how this requirement had arisen, she wrote back saying that in 1958 two new sentences had been added to The Challenge's regulations. The first was: "No boy who is not a British subject shall be eligible to compete for Election as a Queen's Scholar." The second was the Jew-barring condition: "Candidates for Queen's Scholarships must profess the Christian faith." Nothing in the school's statutes justified this change. The school's records do not clarify who instigated it. The governing body never discussed the matter.

By 1958 many of the children of the Jewish immigrants from Europe who came to England to escape persecution before World War II were of an age to apply to Westminster. My English teacher, John Field, framed the issue this way: "The demography of London began to change markedly in the 1930s with refugees from mainland Europe, and when the school returned to London after five years' evacuation, the number of Jewish applicants slowly began to increase. The bursar and registrar was an ex–Indian Army colonel with the kind of views you would expect such a background to provide. I recall archiving his notes on Nigel Lawson"—later Britain's chancellor of the exchequer—when his parents brought him for an interview. "On the lines of 'Undoubtedly a bright and clever child; very Jewish of course.'"

The colonel in question, who controlled Westminster's entry over many years, was Humphrey Carruthers of the Tenth Gurkha Rifles. Concerned about Westminster's reputation for anti-Semitism, John Rae looked into the colonel's notes of interviews with Jewish parents of prospective pupils. Among them, as he relates in *Delusions of Grandeur,* he found:

I thought her an unattractive parent, ugly voice and really Jewish in appearance.

The mother came to make the registration (jaguar and chauffeur) nice clothes but the bangles! Very common speech and talked through her nose.

Both parents came to make the registration. They brought the little boy with them. They were vulgar and unattractive.

Personally I thought the father was conceited and obnoxious. In fact I took a violent dislike to him. I am sure he is very wealthy.

With Carruthers gone—he left in the mid-1960s (too soon to pass judgment on my mother's South African accent and "Jewish appearance")—Rae set to work to rescind the conditions introduced in 1958. They offended him personally; they also limited Westminster's ability to attract the broadest talent. He wrote in his diary—posthumously published as *The Old Boys' Network*—that the effect of the rules was to "exclude candidates, including Jewish boys, who are honest enough to say they are not Christians." He raised the matter in 1971 with the school's governing body. The statutes committee began an investigation. It submitted its conclusions on July 14, 1972, six months before I left Westminster for Oxford: "A boy is not precluded from admission as a Queen's Scholar on the ground either that he is not a British subject or that he does not profess the Christian faith."

Rae still had to make the case before the governing body at a meeting the following November. He encountered stiff opposition. One knight of the realm, Sir Henry Chisholm, declared that he would resign rather than accept the change. Rae countered with the argument that, as he puts it in *Delusions of Grandeur,* "we needed all the bright boys we could get." Chisholm had second thoughts. If pragmatism demanded the change, he might not resign after all. "With no further discussion," Rae writes, "the requirement that a Queen's Scholar must 'profess the Christian faith' was swept away." Jews could now go openly to College. So could pupils of every faith. They no longer had to convert to Christianity or lie low.

The change was enacted for The Challenge of 1974. By then I had already made my way to Balliol College, Oxford, after a diversion of several months on the hippie trail to Afghanistan. The Afghan king was deposed in a coup during our stay in the summer of 1973, not that we noticed much or could possibly have imagined the world-changing turmoil that would follow over the ensuing decades.

In those days you could drive around Afghanistan for months in a VW Kombi, named "Pigpen" after the keyboardist of the Grateful Dead, and nobody bothered you. We sat on the heads of the Buddhas of Bamiyan, since destroyed by Taliban fanatics, and got high. We drove through the Salang Pass at almost thirteen thousand feet, returning from Mazar-i-Sharif to Kabul, only for the engine to blow as we emerged from the tunnel. We rolled down the other side in neutral for fifty miles. Every time I read about the battles of the 1980s for the Salang Pass between the Soviets and mujahideen fighters, I imagined us heedless hippies in our downward glide. The pass was not yet "strategic" in our time. It was just too much for our engine.

My friend Martin Orbach—the goalkeeper on that soccer team of slow-fading glory—was also on the hippie trail at that time. He had attended College and was also headed for Oxford. His great-grandparents, Hungarian Jews who had converted to Catholicism, were killed by the Nazis in the camps. Conversion made no difference, of course, to Hitler's murderers. Not remaining a Jew was impossible. His grandmother committed suicide in flight from the Nazis. His father's family was also mostly Jewish. Martin, however, had been raised a Catholic and so passed muster to enter the scholars' house at Westminster.

The whole sixteen-year interlude, from 1958 to 1974, during which Westminster allowed a form of British prejudice against Jews to infect its regulations, was a betrayal of the values the school embodied and Rae defended: the civilized openness that forged questing and questioning minds. Still, among the manifold gifts it gave me, I have Westminster to thank for opening my eyes, however inadvertently, to the fact of my Jewishness and the slight discomfort, like a recurring twinge, that accompanied being Jewish in England—a country, then at least, of quiet Jews, many converted or wholly assimilated. They would never make a commotion about some slight that was, they tried to persuade themselves, not quite anti-Semitic, even if it did carry the faint but unmistakable reek of the sewer.

In 1938, on the eve of the outbreak of World War II, my uncle Bert wrote a short monograph called *On Being a Jew*. He was twenty years old and had lived all his life in Johannesburg. It begins:

> The problem of being a Jew is one that has teased my mind. I have been vexed. I have been puzzled. I have been proud. To the depths of despair I have been plunged by petty humiliation, and alternately I have been strangely raised to crests of silent exhilaration, I have felt a surge of strength at the thought of an imposition I bear— a magnificent stigma, the magnificent stigma of being a Jew.
>
> My first recollection of being a Jew was that it caused me fear; this was when I was a child, for Jew boys were singled out to be especially bullied. This was my first taste of a status of inferiority bestowed upon me by my very birth, an unpleasant phase it was, but which served to foster a spirit of sturdy independence. Successively fear was followed by resentment, despair, steadfastness, and indeed a tumultuous gamut of similarly conflicting emotions. Until eventually I reached a state of mental equilibrium, a balance, inward harmony. I am now no longer actively and persistently conscious of the fact that I am a Jew. Aware of it, yes, but no longer am I ashamed of it, or afraid of it, nor indeed proud of it.

There is something agonizing about my uncle's struggle to cast off the humiliation of repetitive school-yard insults—the daily ritual of huddling outside class with other pariah Jews while morning prayers were held—and declare himself at peace with his Jewishness. He ponders how to navigate a middle course between the loud and "objectionable Jew" and the "cringing and cowardly Jew." Neither "unnatural assertion" nor "servile subjection" is the answer. The Jew must "go to even greater heights to overcome the handicap imposed on him" and achieve greatness, while avoiding the "vaulting ambition" that would be another form of excess. His fundamental dilemma is that "society as a whole has not risen above judging by a primitive or fundamental dogma—a single Jew is regarded not as an individual to be separately appraised but as an example of a type." Or, as he puts it in another passage: "A Jew may be brilliant, he may be an intellectual genius, he may be one of mankind's most perfect productions; he will be recognized as such by a precious few, but eventually it will be said of him that he is a Jew, one of the same category as any other Jew, be that Jew the most wretched individual."

My uncle was then about to begin his studies at Witwatersrand University. There an anti-Semitic professor would fail him twice in pathology, holding him back a year, before eventually allowing him through and commenting to a fellow student who did not make the cut: "I'm sorry I had to fail you and pass the Jew."

Three decades and a world war and several thousand miles separate Bert's South African experience and mine of England, and yet there is something recognizable in his sense of not quite belonging. In America, where Jewish shallow-rootedness existed beside the shallow-rootedness of just about everyone, the situation was different. As Karl Shapiro observed, "The European Jew was always a visitor and knew it. But in America everyone is a visitor. In this land of permanent visitors, the Jew is in a rare position to 'live the life' of a full Jewish consciousness." Yet a struggle still existed. Irving Howe said of the Jewish writers published by *Partisan Review*: "We wanted to shake off the fears and constraints of the world in which we had been born. When up against the impenetrable walls of the gentile politeness we would aggressively proclaim our difference as if to raise Jewishness to a higher cosmopolitan power."

The Jewish experience over millennia demonstrates that no amount of scholarly questing, of religious devotion, of determined emancipation, or of proud patriotism and service could provide security. People and entire nations might turn on you. Scrolls without swords did not work. Zionism was born of that reluctant conclusion. It was prescient, given the fate of European Jews in the Nazi camps. Israel, by giving Jews at last a small piece of earth, was supposed to create what David Ben-Gurion called "a self-sufficient people, master of its own fate," rather than one "hung up in midair."

Bert, in 1938, was hung up in midair all right. Considering my family story—the pits in the Lithuanian forests, the repetitive school taunting, the displaced persons' camps where my uncle Bert saw the bedraggled Jews in 1945, the frustrated attempts to fit in whether in South Africa or England, the Jewish precariousness, the annihilation angst, the inner exile—I can only concur with the necessity of Zionism. Israel, for all its failings, helped assuage at least some of my uncle's fear. The state's message has been clear: Know your history, be proud of your history, and end Jewish meekness and shame, the acquiescence that took your forebears to the ditches and the gas. Never again would Jews be so diminished as to inspire the revulsion my uncle felt on seeing his desperate Jewish "kith and kin" in Italy in 1945, just seven years after he penned *On Being a Jew*. By this time his words had redoubled resonance: "The Jews crave equal treatment. Let them take their place then amongst the peoples of the world and seek no preferential consideration from their fellows."

Fifteen years after I left Westminster, in 1987, Jonathan Katz was appointed master of the Queen's Scholars. Katz, a lapsed Anglican, had a Jewish father from Leipzig who fled the Nazis, a Christian mother, and a Hindu wife. In order to marry Kalyani, he had officially become a Hindu, a persuasion that, like being a Jew, mixes belief and ethnicity: even if you stop believing you do not stop being one. Katz had stopped believing. He had no religion. He was deeply conversant with several.

This rumpled and eclectic man—a brilliant classicist who had taught at Westminster early in his career before becoming the Indian Institute librarian at Oxford's Bodleian Library—represented a departure for College. The scholars' house was intimately associated with the Abbey. It had begun admitting Jews who were open about their identity only a dozen years earlier. So there were bound to be hesitations. Katz received a polite letter before his appointment from John Rae's successor as headmaster, David Summerscale, inquiring about his religion. Somebody on the Abbey end of the governing body had raised concerns with the dean, Michael Mayne, about appointing this fellow called Katz.

Katz wrote back to Summerscale asking that his letter be passed on to Mayne. He said he was equally interested in several religions but could not profess any; that he would encourage scholars to follow their own conscience in such matters; that he would be happy to lead students into Abbey for the by-now-twice-weekly services or run a compulsory compline; and that if any of this was a problem, he would remain in his job at the Bodleian.

Mayne invited Katz down to London for a chat. He had been reassured by the letter and asked Katz not to take the inquiry amiss. His concern was that Katz be a good teacher and look after the scholars well and have cordial relations with the Abbey. All was now in order.

"Michael," Katz responded, "put me right if I'm wrong. What you seem to be saying is that what is saving the situation is that I have no religion. But what if I *did,* and it was the wrong one?"

Well, Mayne suggested, the less said about that, the better.

In 1921, at the age of ten, Bernard Katz, the father of the future master of the Queen's Scholars at Westminster, takes an exam similar to The Challenge for entrance to the Schiller-Realgymnasium in Leipzig. His own father, a fur trader, is one of fifteen children from an Orthodox Jewish family in Russia that has fled persecution a few years earlier and settled in Germany, where the environment seems more liberal. They live above a bakery on König-Johann-Strasse in an area of Leipzig with a large Jewish population; the future Israeli novelist S. Y. Agnon lives on the same street.

Bernard Katz is a brilliant student, who will go on to win the Nobel Prize for Medicine in 1970, one of countless Nobels of which Hitler deprived Germany. However, when the list of successful candidates for the Schiller school is posted in Leipzig, Katz's name is not there. His family is informed that his failure has nothing to do with his grades; they are excellent. But priority for places has to go to "full-blooded ethnic Germans." Katz is admitted to another school, the König-Albert-Gymnasium.

Here this gifted boy excels. The following year he goes home for Yom Kippur. When he returns, a friend tells him that some pupils have been talking about what should be done to the Jews. One has boasted about his father's idea: all the Jews should be gathered, taken down into an underground shopping area in central Leipzig, and asphyxiated with poison gas. Katz later tells his son Jonathan that it was at this moment that he knew he would eventually have to get out of Germany. Heinrich Heine, the German Romantic poet, had noted, "Wherever they burn books they will also, in the end, burn people."

A student of medicine at Leipzig University, Katz is forced from the student union by Nazi pressure in 1933. He considers going to Palestine. A chance meeting in Karlsbad in 1934 with Chaim Weizmann, the future president of Israel, changes his plans. Weizmann has contacts in the scientific community in Britain. With his help, Katz secures a position with Professor A. V. Hill of the biophysics department at University College, London, and escapes Germany in 1935. Hill is a Nobel laureate in medicine. He has made it his business to welcome refugee scientists from Germany and takes the young Katz, who soon becomes known as "BK," into his home in Highgate in north London.

After completing his doctorate at UCL in 1938, BK is offered a job in Australia. He has managed at last to get his parents out of Germany. Shopkeepers, they resisted leaving until Kristallnacht dispelled the last doubts about the Nazis' intentions. Together the Katz family sails for Sydney in 1939. Here BK spends the war in the Royal Australian Air Force. He meets his wife, Marguerite Penly. Together they return to England in 1946, eventually settling in the Kenton area of northwest London, where Jonathan Katz is born in 1950.

To BK, who had arrived stateless and penniless, England is a haven of tolerance. He would later say that coming to Britain in 1935 felt like David Copperfield's experience of coming "home" to Aunt Betsey Trotwood and being given a good, warm bath.

Jonathan Katz is sent to a London junior school with what he calls "a clear Christian profile" but no restrictions on children from other religious or ethnic backgrounds. Here he encounters "a moderate British style of racist attitudes"—including taunts about rich Jews, at which he bridles: "My dad is a Jew."

He has been prepared. His Leipzig-born father has told him to expect to hear comments about Jews but brings him up to distinguish between conventional British anti-Semitism and people who want to kill you. The British version, to his father, is not much more than a form of insensitivity. It is only the other, lethal kind that matters. Katz takes his father's teaching to heart.

The question, of course, is whether the mild does not contain within it the seeds of menace. Britain's discreet anti-Semitism seemed a good bargain to Jews in the postwar years. But the real distinction is between bigotry, even mild, and tolerance.

BK takes from the Holocaust not the need to assert Jewish identity but the paramount need for understanding between people of different beliefs. A scientist-immigrant nurtured by British liberalism and academic freedoms, like my father, he lives his Jewishness in a minor key. He sends Katz to University College School, a liberal day school in Hampstead, and tells the headmaster that the capacity of distinct traditions to respect each other is critical.

His parents, perceiving the Church of England as a benign and tolerant institution, decide to have Katz confirmed as an Anglican. On the night before his confirmation by the Bishop of Willesden, Katz has identity crisis. He says to his father: "I think I might have got it wrong and I'm really a Jew and I'm not sure I believe in what I am about to take on."

In response his father, in the German accent he never overcame, tells the story of a Jewish boy who says to his rabbi just before his bar mitzvah that he is afraid he does not believe in God. The rabbi smiles and says, "Do you think He cares?"

Katz goes to church regularly until he starts at Oxford. There he finds that "the metaphysics of it no longer convinced me at all." What he is left with is a residual affection for Anglican worship, music, aesthetics, and theology.

Just before Katz took up his job in College, he was visited in Oxford by the parents of a Jewish boy, James Fulton. Their son had had his bar mitzvah; they were worried about his Abbey duties. Katz responded that he did not have the experience to allay their concerns but imagined that the services and prayers in the splendid Abbey setting could be viewed as a beautiful metaphor for something worth deep consideration by anyone. You did not need to believe in hell, he noted, to read Dante with appreciation. Fulton went on to become captain of College. He presented Katz with a book on Israel as a leaving present.

By 1987 there was already a large Jewish presence in College— perhaps as many as 30 percent of the students in Katz's recollection. Rae's fight had been won. Katz recalls teaching Yiddish songs to Jewish boys and girls, telling jokes, insisting they sometimes go home Friday night, and attending Passover seders with them. He once made the mistake of scheduling a charity event on Yom Kippur, got berated by a Jewish parent ("You of all people!"), and had to rearrange it. Asked if the school should add Jewish High Holidays to the almanac along with Easter, Ascension, and so on, he responded that, yes, that would probably be a useful reminder for most of Westminster's Jewish parents. He put up a mezuzah on the front of the college master's house in Dean's Yard. It is still there. Katz thinks the works department views it as some sort of intercom.

Katz remained as master of College for more than two decades, departing in 2010 to return to Oxford as a lecturer in classics at St. Anne's College. Of late he has been studying Hebrew. "You get more Jewish as you grow older," he says. The idea of conversion is quite attractive to him, but he is not sure yet. People say they feel him to be a Jew, whatever that means. "But I still feel a bit of an outsider or a fraud when I go to synagogue," he says.

In 2013 Katz gave a Latin sermon at the University Church of St. Mary the Virgin in Oxford. He quoted a verse from Hebrews: "Do not neglect to show hospitality to strangers, for by doing that some have entertained angels without knowing it." He said, "Paul knows that sometimes angels do come in the guise of humans to test the hospitality of those they visit; they do so in both the pagan and the Jewish tradition." And he noted, "There is a common thread of an idea that strangers come from God, are indeed perhaps a gift from God, and yet we know that entertaining them may bring risks as well as rewards. And here again, moral behavior, to be worth the name, presumably has to involve at least some risk of inconvenience."

The Katz family, like mine, came as strangers to Britain. They have been treated well, low-level anti-Semitism notwithstanding. "One takes this shit," Katz says, "because there is so much shittier shit around. And it's what has produced, in reaction, a lot of Jewish culture. It's the manure."

My sister, Jenny, grows up believing she has been adopted. She does not need to ask; she *knows*. She stands at the bottom of the beautiful yard in Hampstead and says to herself: *Imagine if this really was my house and these really were my parents.* My mother had given birth to her only to disappear into mental hospitals. A stranger is now in the house.

She recoils from my mother's touch. She lies in bed and thinks: *If Dad dies, I will die.* June cannot explain what has happened. She cannot tell her daughter how she suffered on being forced to abandon her, how her pulse rate shot up when the doctor at the Holloway Sanatorium asked about her baby in 1958. If she had talked of her postpartum depression, things might have been different.

Sydney is my sister's lifeline. She adores him. My father has the capacity to elicit fear as well as love. His warmth is irresistible. His severity is frightening. She knocks on his study door with trepidation. If her school report is bad, he swivels in his desk chair and asks if she really wants to grow up to mind the cash register at Woolworths. Then he swivels back to his lab notes and Mahler.

Sadness hangs like a pall. When I go off to board at Westminster, Jenny finds she cannot bear to be at home alone with my parents. At thirteen she goes to St. Catherine's, a boarding school in Surrey about a dozen miles from the Holloway Sanatorium where my mother had been confined. Jenny is in chapel every evening for services, twice a day on Sunday. All her friends are being confirmed into the Anglican Church as they turn thirteen. She is the only Jew in the school. Listening to the hymns, loving the services, aware of the void inside her, she feels faith stirring. The school reverend is a cadaverous man, bald, hollow-cheeked, small and slight, with hooded eyes. His name is Irving. He listens intently to Jenny in a back room of the chapel as she explains her desire to convert and be accepted into the church. Gently, he encourages her.

Irving drafts a letter to my parents: *Your daughter has discovered Christianity. She has found faith. She wants to know the consolation of God.* My mother is upset. She feels it is wrong; she is worried what our grand-parents would think, particularly my Žagarė-born paternal grand-mother, who is now living in London. My father says to Jenny: "Wait a year. If after that you still want to do this, we will not stand in your way." The advice proves sound. Within a year the urge has subsided, nudged aside by the discovery of the Grateful Dead's *American Beauty* album.

"It was about belonging, simple as that," Jenny says. "I felt this des-perate need to belong."

Without belonging there is loss, a seed of depression. Once, when down in London on a break, Jenny goes to dinner at a friend's house. The father is a high court judge and an alcoholic. Halfway through the meal, well oiled on whiskey and wine, he asks where Jenny lives. Her reply—Hampstead—sets him off: "Oh, I see, along with all the other rich, flashy Jews. Think you're the chosen people, don't you? Chosen people who can do what they damn well please. Fingers in every pie, making a killing, that's the Jews. Tell me, Jenny, do you think you are a chosen person? Do tell us. . . ."

Nobody at the table stirs, not his wife, nor any of the children. Jenny, blotchy with embarrassment, runs upstairs.

Back at St. Catherine's, Jenny sometimes calls home in tears. It is hard to adapt to the school. My mother can only respond with tears of her own. Yet she wants to help. When Jenny has to study George Eliot's *The Mill on the Floss,* June reads it, too. Then Jenny thinks: *She cares about me enough to read the book.*

June has lost the ability to sustain the giving of love. She veers from the shrill to the shrinking. My mother could be impossible; when she was not impossible, she was heartbreaking.

The truth does not emerge until Jenny is sixteen. She is back home by now. I am in the midst of my year off between Westminster and Oxford—not yet called a gap year—and after working as a driver for a carpet salesman have departed for Italy and then Afghanistan. June has been very down, often bed-bound. My sister returns from school with a friend. It is a hot summer's day. She picks up a bottle of Coca-Cola and is trying to unscrew the cap when the bottle slips and smashes on a marble shelf. Shards of glass mixed in sticky Coke spray everywhere. June screams in an uncontrollable way—the telltale disproportionate reaction again. Her father, Laurie, visiting from South Africa, storms in: "I warn you, Jenny. If you carry on treating your mother like this, she will end up back in hospital."

Back in hospital? What does Laurie mean? When has June been in hospital before?

My father comes home from work that evening and, confronted by Jenny's questions, reveals what has gone unsaid in my family for sixteen years: *When you were very young, your mother was in hospital for a long time suffering from depression. She is fragile. There have been signs of the affliction returning.*

Only then, as the curtain lifts at last on our story, does everything start to fall into place.

CHAPTER 9

Madness in the Brain

I will begin with my mother's suicide note to my father of July 25, 1978, found in the Hampstead house on the hill she loved; the house she had, in an access of manic activity, agreed to sell the previous March to buy a Georgian terraced jewel on Lord North Street in central London, only to cancel the sale when she plunged back into a depression in June.

> *Darling Dearest and Most Precious, Never ever think you weren't very good and kind and wonderful. It's as though I've turned to stone. I can't relate, I can't communicate and I can no longer bear the pain and gloom I cause to those I love most. . . .*

In January of that year, before the manic March phase, she had been depressed and delusional during a visit to South Africa. She revealed to the British consul in Johannesburg that my father, Sydney, had been appointed Commander of the British Empire and that the honor would be conferred by the queen at Buckingham Palace on March 7, 1978. At the time, this information was not public. June began to fear arrest for her indiscretion, an anxiety compounded by the fact she had told a South African friend of her mental turmoil and convinced herself this information would reach the lord chancellor. He, in turn, would dismiss her from the position of justice of the peace for the South Westminster Division, to which she had been appointed on May 24,

*The author in Paris, working as a freelance journalist,
at the time of his mother's visit in 1978*

1976—a year in which she had suffered from a combination of symptoms: weight loss, dizzy spells, hot flushes, blurred vision, paroxysmal tachycardia, and polydipsia, combined with alternating hyperactivity and inertia, or manic depression.

All this she had kept to herself. She had to pursue her work as a magistrate and maintain the outward appearance of familial stability. What if she were found to be bipolar? What if the dark secret of her mood swings was uncovered? She had returned to London from South Africa on January 23, 1978. The sound of the doorbell at the Hampstead house terrified her. It could only be the police coming to scoop her up for divulging official secrets in South Africa. She would end up incommunicado in some lightless cell. She had a dream of birds of prey circling, like bloated flies, over a small child.

Six days after her return, the American gentleman who lived in the apartment upstairs was killed in a freak accident. A car swerved out of control onto the sidewalk as he posted a letter at the bottom of the hill. This was ominous. She had been fond of him. He had collected antique music boxes. And that aquarium of his: the stern-eyed fish, the silvery fish in schools, the ridiculous armored rectangular fish with spikes and no tail. A few days later, in early February, a doctor suggested electroconvulsive therapy for my mother. No! Two decades on from her Holloway Sanatorium confinement, she would not return to that hell.

Laurie, far right, "up north" in Egypt during World War II

By early March her condition had improved. (There was often a fleeting moment between the depressive and manic phases where she seemed, as my father sometimes put it, "just right.") At the palace for Sydney's CBE, she beamed in her dusky salmon-pink knitted outfit and pretty mink hat. She looked a picture of pert pride beside my top-hatted father. A week later, on March 14, papers for the purchase of the house on Lord North Street were signed. On March 29, the sale of our house, her English anchor, was agreed. In May, buoyant, June traveled to Paris with her parents to see me. I had been living in the French capital since graduation from Oxford the previous year, teaching English and writing for a start-up magazine called *Paris Métro,* an ersatz *Village Voice* then enjoying a *succès de mode* among Parisian Anglophones. The year abroad was an escape. Being an outsider, I found, suited me. I was most comfortable in the role of observer.

On the Boulevard St. Michel, June was bubbly, her sharp girlish eyes almost popping out from behind her glasses, bright as a rabbit's at night. My grandfather Laurie wanted tripe. She laughed and averted her eyes as he wolfed it down, mopping the juices off his moustache with gusto. *Tripes à la mode de Caen.* She had a soft spot for his mischief— any mischief in fact. During the war, when he was "up north" in Egypt, Laurie had become legendary for his turtle-meat kreplach. He loved them, but they were generally considered the ne plus ultra of emetics.

I offered June a ride on my motor scooter. She declined. She always hated the wind in her hair, a cause of arguments over open windows during family car rides.

Within weeks, back in London, familiar signs of a mood shift appeared: eyes turning inward and puffy, smooth skin beginning to sag. My father noted in a journal, "Acute onset depression. Houses cancelled." Voiding the real estate deals was neither easy nor cheap, and for June it came with guilt at the time and money wasted. One thing about mania, with its rashness and rages, is that it provides plenty of legitimate reasons for remorse during the ensuing depressive phase. She started on a new drug, Tofranil, an antidepressant, on July 5, 1978. It did not help.

Her anxiety had been growing since 1975. That year my father injured his finger mowing the grass in the beautiful Hampstead garden he had created. The cut from the rotor blades caused a severe infection. After recurrent rigors, he was admitted to Guy's and then St. Mary's Hospitals. He remained intermittently ill for eighteen months. June, then aged forty-six, started on low-dose estrogen in 1975, which she took for about six months. Depressed, she was admitted to University College Hospital in late 1976, weighing one hundred pounds. She was prescribed amitriptyline. In September 1977 she entered Archway Hospital with an attack of tachycardia. It reverted after sixteen hours. The next month she was in a severe depression.

All this turbulence coincided with the approach of menopause. Jenny and I had left home, Jenny also moving to Paris, falling in love, and staying on. The family maintained its code of silence. Rigors and racing hearts were not recounted. My home had become forbidding. Paris was a release. My first sojourn there, teaching English in a lycée, culminated with the boiling summer of 1976. City fountains dried up. People sat dazed on park benches staring into the haze. Not a bottle of water could be found. The only subject of conversation was *la canicule,* or heat wave. It went on and on. All barriers evaporated. Strangers opened to each other. The city was as romantic as a war zone. Pensioners died in little airless maids' rooms under the zinc roofs. Nobody knew. Brittle leaves on plane trees dangled motionless. Old people huddled in the patches of shade on the Place des Vosges watching listless children in the little deserts of their sandboxes. I sat at my window and took notes.

I pray dearest Roger and dearest Jenny will bring you comfort and joy—they are both very special. I feel I'll never completely throw off this mood and hope-lessness and depression. I know I have everything *to thank God for and be thankful for, which only makes my ordeal worse and worse. . . .*

In June's purse were her Rothmans filter-tipped cigarettes that would be stained with her lipstick; her lighter; scraps of paper picked up here and there with notes scrawled on them; Ysatis perfume by Givenchy; ads for trips she thought of taking or trinkets she thought of acquiring; car keys and house keys; her makeup compact; a special offer for a hotel in Acapulco (she loved Mexico); articles about the law and the role of magistrates; a diary filled with her flowing handwriting; and lines of Coleridge from *Christabel* ("And life is thorny; and youth is vain; / And to be wroth with one we love, / Doth work like madness in the brain").

Madness in the brain, everything raveled and no way to untangle the web. Better a horse that rears than a horse that bucks. The madness was a bucking horse. It made a mockery of control. You were always under the harrow. I wanted so much to clear away the clutter in my mother's mind. I dreamed of calm and ease between us and her return to life.

The suicide note was beside her bed, folded in an envelope:

You are made to do <u>great</u> things, make immensely useful discoveries to aid all mankind and I'm leaving you to continue unimpeded by my burden. I so much hoped to help you and to help you and to love and adore you . . .

My father had come from work and found the bedroom doors closed. He thought nothing of it. June was often in bed. He fixed himself a whiskey, sat down with the papers. It was a mild summer's evening, sunlight glinting through the trees, bees circling the roses, clouds of gnats against the fence. June's cycles were running at three-month intervals. With luck, come September she would be active again. But, truth be told, was there any luck in this matter? If she veered manic, she would be full of ideas—another house, a small Old Master drawing, or a long weekend in Venice—and by the time the ideas came to fruition, they would both be ruing them. He saw himself in a beautiful room at the Gritti Palace in Venice overlooking the Grand Canal. June would have a single thought in her mind: drowning herself.

Sydney tossed the papers aside. You never knew in life. That, on balance, was a blessing. He tried the bedroom door, leading onto the L-shaped hallway of my childhood fears. It was locked. He raced around to the other door, from the bathroom. It was locked. He ran outside. The net curtains were drawn. The windows looked sealed. On closer inspection, one was very slightly ajar.

My mother lay sprawled on the bed, a bottle of gin beside her. She had taken large doses of Doxepin and Valium, washed down with the alcohol. (Its emetic effect probably saved her.) Her arms were thrown back behind her head. Her pupils were scarcely responsive, her breathing shallow.

At present I am filled only with self-hate. I do love my family and dear friends but I can't go on and on and on like this. God bless you sweetest dearest angel.

Jenny happened to be back from Paris for a few days. She was out with a friend, whose father gave her a message to call home immediately. She had dreamed the night before that June had tried to take her life: white sheets flapped in the wind on a washing line in an empty yard. My mother, when she last saw her, had been in her room with the curtains drawn, smoking a lot, filled with hopelessness. Now Jenny ran down a broad staircase onto Albemarle Street in Mayfair. The thought in her head was: Let the agony end, let her be dead.

Can my body—any part of it—be used for research? I wish I did not have to cause you pain but it will pass—you're a survivor my brave good love. Wish and pray I could have been better. Thank you. Bless Floss and Laurie for so much kindness and love.

Jenny found my father in a disembodied state, draping stained sheets over chairs. All the lights were on. "Mom's in hospital. She took a large overdose. They've pumped her stomach. She seems to be stable now." I remember his ghostly voice when he called me in Paris that night. It was two months since my mother, in high spirits, had visited.

My mother's first words to Jenny when she walked into the Whittington Hospital the next day were: "What a lovely cardigan! Have I seen that before?" She was no longer depressed.

By the time I reached London that day, she was already home. We gathered in the lounge, the room reserved during my childhood for special occasions. I suppose this was one. We hugged and cried. June wanted to move on. As soon as the deathly darkness lifted, she was brisk and businesslike. She wrote to me soon after: "I realize full well that you have my interest at heart. Remember, darling, I love you all deeply and dearly and devotedly. I realize the pain I've caused but it is DONE—we *must* now look forward PLEASE."

In early September, she wrote to my uncle Bert and his wife, Hazel:

I want you to know how grateful and sorry I am that you were involved (for a second time, alas) in such a traumatic drama. Both Sydney and Jen have told me of your kindness, help and understanding. I alone have to bear the pain of knowing how I involved those I love and I have to come to terms with the knowledge over the years as best I can—I can assure and promise you that now, knowing the pain and hurt I caused, NEVER again will I resort to such a drastic step.

I *know* that when one's in a trough of black despair one is either on the brink of insanity or suicide. This time I felt sure I'd never recover, be committed to a mental home and there was no fight in me. There *has* to be some *quality* to life to make it worthwhile. I had become a mental and physical shell and a burden to those I love.

Virginia Woolf wrote to Leonard: "Everything has gone from me but the certainty of your goodness. I can't go on spoiling your life any longer."

This precisely reflects what I felt had happened except in my case the children, too, were involved. I was certain that Sydney's health and work would suffer forever and the beloved children would be obliged to carry an intolerable emotional burden. This was too much for me to bear.

With love and endless gratitude,
June

On September 18, 1978, my father's fifty-seventh birthday, she wrote a letter to him promising a new beginning:

My Darling,

Think of your birthday as a new year—a fresh start. Please, please let the trauma fade into your unconscious. Put your mind at peace—it's never going to happen again. You have nothing to blame yourself for. You have been my best and truest friend, a loving, caring husband and you did more than could have been expected over a long test of endurance that would have broken most noble spirits. We are together with so many things to look forward to—that's what matters—and our darling children are united in our mutual love.

Something is always gained from anguish and pain if one has the strength to survive. We have a deep understanding and the children shared our troubles—how I'd have wished to spare it all—but it's made them stronger and given them an insight into what life can throw up unexpectedly.

On November 5, 1978, three months after her suicide attempt, my mother contemplated the fireworks in the night sky over London. She wrote: "Guy Fawkes night—bonfires, sparks and a catastrophic fire once planned, yet many, many years after here we are and Parliament stands yet."

She watched the trails of light falling down the sky. At the last they were like tears. As sure as death is sure, she told herself, her love for Sydney was everlasting. She had been reading Dylan Thomas. His marriage to Caitlin was fraught. "They fought physical fights," she noted, "threw verbal spears to pain and hurt, and yet their love was very deep and their need for each other great." She told my father: "I worshipped you and our children at the brink of death and I'll love you always, always and always."

I circle back to my mother as I imagine her, the curl and bounce of her hair in her fleeting passages of happiness. There is no trace of her now but in memory. I could not abide the blankness of her burden. Of course she would again "resort to such a drastic step." That was in the nature of things. In her condition, death was always the cajoling voice in her ear.

I have tried to give form to the facts of my mother's life and death. Part of the unraveling that followed her first barely thwarted attempt to take her life became clear at once. The undercurrents took longer to emerge and were more devastating. Mental illness is a charnel house from which nobody escapes unscathed.

Orhan Pamuk has written: "What is important for a painter is not a thing's reality but its shape, and what is important for a novelist is not the course of events but their ordering, and what is important for a memoirist is not the factual accuracy of the account but its symmetry."

At the far end of the garden, next to the greenhouse where my father's African cuttings bloomed, I see him piling objects on a fire. A frenetic determination marks his movements as he stoops and straightens, sometimes half hidden by smoke, and the fire grows. Smoke billows upward into the plane trees. Onto the flames go old toys, battered suitcases, furniture long stored in the cellar of the house, files of papers, and the weathered, much-loved "Don Bradman" cricket bat I had used as a child and he had used before me. His frenzy allows no interruption. The fire consuming my childhood, in the very place it was most intensely lived, would burn for a couple of days.

The blaze was intended to prepare a move away from a place now blighted with Valium and gin. June, within weeks of her suicide attempt, had found an apartment in central London, a few blocks from Lord North Street. It would be "easier to maintain," closer to Sydney's work, and smaller, of a size more appropriate for the two of them. This time the move went through.

It was a disaster. In an apartment, my father, starved of the wide skies of his garden, suffocated. On a gloomy balcony, overlooking other redbrick apartment buildings, he managed to coax a number of lush plants into life, creating a tiny midtown jungle. In the midst of this greenery, he looked like a morose lion peering out from a Douanier Rousseau painting. One day, when the light in his study remained unchanged as a dull day gave way to sunshine, he decided he could stand his confinement no longer. Very soon, in November 1979, my parents moved back to Hampstead, to a house they both liked less than the one they had left.

In the space of twenty months, they had bought a house, only to change their minds; an apartment near that house, only to find they loathed it; and a third place a stone's throw from our original home (the only house they really loved). This commotion amounted to the physical expression of my mother's mental turmoil. Of course, given the self-aggression involved in depression, she ended up in a house that "punished" her through its proximity to the true object of her affection and attachment.

As they moved into the second Hampstead house, with its wisteria and much smaller and shaded garden, June wrote to my father:

> I realize the great pressure—emotional and physical—that has been placed upon you these last few years. Only someone of your strength and courage could have put up with the strain so nobly— your love and devotion never swerved and, God knows, it was sorely put to the test.
> I can only hope the ghastly illness is really receding, if not disappearing altogether. At present I do feel an inner calm and a great joy in life and all it has to offer.
> The new house has a welcoming and charming atmosphere. We will be *together* with room for our loved ones if they want to stay. So I view the future very optimistically. My innermost love for you is everlasting—let us pray that the black clouds have disappeared and be happy in creating a peaceful, harmonious new life in a beautiful new setting. I adore you.

Sydney's sense of confinement did not abate in their new home. June had become multiple, one "me" morphing into another "me" overnight. He never quite knew where he stood. None of us did. As a husband and a physician, he tried to care for my mother. That he loved her, I have no doubt. Only a deep love could leave a man so stricken at his wife's loss. But each of us has limits. Caring could easily give way to impatience or become an exercise in control. Stern, in an upright chair, my father was punishing and intimidating by turns. He felt he could not leave. After July 1978 the danger was evident. He had to stay. Like everyone, he also had to live.

The June he had known had been progressively hollowed out. His response was to adopt a double life, a substantial part of it hidden. This dual existence had, as I learned much later, begun in 1967, midway between my mother's postpartum breakdown and her first suicide attempt. The solution was damaging, its fabric deception and silence. The idea was not to share troubles but to evade them. June, despite everything, was always fiercely loyal, at least in public.

He was gone and unreachable much of the time, the absent figure at family gatherings, the gap in the photograph, the invisible puppet master. His controlled resentment was often palpable. I tried and failed, more than once, to breach his armor. My father preferred me at a distance. He could not tell me everything and so preferred to say nothing. There was no middle ground. I suppose I wanted him to offset a pain it was no longer in his power to assuage.

The warm father he had been in my early childhood and the chilly figure he had become seemed unrelated. He was inaccessible. He managed June's split life in function not only of her well-being, as far as it could ever be assured, but of his need for relief. Were there better possible outcomes than this mutually reinforcing suffering? No easy resolution offered itself. It rarely does as life closes in. My father, in his human frailty, did what he could, confronted by the "ghastly illness" afflicting his wife.

June was far too intelligent and sensitive not to know what her loyalty forbade her to say. More honesty, whatever its initial cost, would surely have helped. I know that what goes unsaid festers and wounds. That had been part of the problem ever since June first collapsed on arrival in Britain in 1957. The pattern was never broken. We knew little of love as a gift freely given. A recriminatory silence settled on our home as my mother's illness took its long toll.

On January 1, 1979, June began treatment with Silvio Benaim, a psychiatrist whose Jewish family had fled Fascist Italy for England in 1938. Benaim, three years older than my mother, was a fellow immigrant. They had both come to rainy shores from sunlit lands. A trial he conducted early in his career on insulin coma therapy helped sound the death knell of a treatment from which my mother, at the age of twenty-eight, had suffered. He was interested in the phenomenon of hysterical epidemics. One appeared to occur in 1958 among the nursing staff at his own Royal Free Hospital.

Benaim, whose relationship with my mother would become close (he was at her funeral), was an early advocate of lithium carbonate in the treatment of bipolar illness. My mother started on lithium at once. Benaim, in a letter of May 10, 1979, described June's depressions as times "when every day is a challenge and tends to be worse in the morning." There followed emergence "into a state of hypo-manic activity during which she is excited, elated and over-active." He wrote: "It is my impression that during the last few months, both her depressions and her hypo-manic phases have been milder, shorter and less disabling."

Lithium often causes deep ambivalence in patients. It saves countless lives. It is also a muffler and a deadener, robbing manic-depressives—at least as they often see it—of the elixir of their mania, those times when sleep is unnecessary, the mind leaps in giddying bounds, ideas proliferate, desire swells, confidence bubbles, assertiveness abounds, sensitivity is acute, and anything seems possible. Virginia Woolf noted, "As an experience, madness is terrific I can assure you, and not to be sniffed at; and in its lava I still find most of the things I write about. It shoots out of one everything shaped, final, not in mere driblets, as sanity does."

My mother, in general, took her lithium. She broke off for a while after she developed a transient cerebellar lesion (which resolved completely) but never found any more effective treatment. It attenuated the highs. It did less for the lows. Of course she disliked the regimen, feeling muted and often despairing.

She would lie in the bath and let the water run out. She lay there, blank. She was numb in the empty bathtub. When she could cry, it was a relief because crying constituted feeling. At the same time, she recognized that the alternative to lithium would almost certainly be worse.

Even when taking it, her manic phases could involve paranoid delusion that brought mayhem in its wake. She was given to rages in which all her accumulated frustration at being "monitored" by my father burst out. *Don't, please, WATCH and TIME me.* She bought a ticket for a Concorde flight to New York, only desisting at the last. She was honest and brash to the point of tactlessness. She bought all sorts of small gifts, sometimes giving the same one more than once to the same person. There was at least one incident of shoplifting in South Africa that required a delicate intervention from her brother. She screamed at him for getting involved in her business. A relative against whom she had conceived a grudge received enough harassing late-night phone calls in London to contact the police and have the calls traced. June screamed in outraged denial when the police came to the door. She would be up all night calling family and friends in the United States. Once, during a period of regular IRA bombings, she left a bag unattended in the middle of the food hall at Fortnum & Mason. She was questioned and—such was her hysterical outburst—detained for a spell in a locked room. She screamed at the startled security staff. *I am a magistrate, how dare you do this to me!* The next day the store sent a beautiful bouquet by way of apology. Despite my father's pleas, she would have none of it. The flowers were returned with a furious note.

As her moods careened, June had little in the way of regular psychotherapy. My father viewed her condition as biological or endogenous. She had the far-flung, recurrent family gene whose antecedents he had plotted on a chart. In Benaim she had a wise and sympathetic physician who was treating her with the most effective medicine available. Pharmacology was the answer. But as Sydney noted in a letter to a colleague in 1983, "conventional medical therapy has, in my view and despite the unfailing support of Silvio Benaim, been almost totally ineffective."

Was there some complement to a "conventional" approach that might have helped? As Anthony Storr has noted, "The adjective endogenous is merely a confession of ignorance, since all that it implies is that the condition of depression takes origin from within the patient, and that the psychiatrist cannot detect any obvious cause for it." I thought my mother—in her loneliness and guilt and anger and inertia—needed regular psychotherapy to serve as an outlet for the expression of the turbulent feelings that went with the various disasters and fractures of her condition. In June 1981 she had been obliged to quit as justice of the peace, an awful blow to her self-esteem. She could not even explain the reasons for her resignation. Being a magistrate had meant a lot to her. The more I thought about her, the more I saw her as a figure in isolated exile. Therapy would not cure her, but it might ease her pain.

In her personal account of the manic-depressive condition, *An Unquiet Mind: A Memoir of Moods and Madness,* Kay Redfield Jamison writes:

At this point in my existence, I cannot imagine leading a normal life without both taking lithium and having had the benefits of psychotherapy. Lithium prevents my seductive but disastrous highs, diminishes my depressions, clears out the wool and webbing from my disordered thinking, slows me down, gentles me out, keeps me from ruining my career and relationships, keeps me out of a hospital, alive, and makes psychotherapy possible. But, ineffably, psychotherapy heals. It makes some sense of the confusion, reins in the terrifying thoughts and feelings, returns some control and hope and possibility of learning from it all. Pills cannot, do not, ease one back into reality; they only bring one back headlong, careening, and faster than can be endured at the time. Psychotherapy is a sanctuary; it is a battleground; it is a place I have been psychotic, neurotic, elated, confused, and despairing beyond belief. But, always, it is where I have believed—or have learned to believe—that I might someday be able to contend with all this.

My mother had no safe place where she could learn to contend. She had no sanctuary. She was a transplant that did not take. Fresh soil invigorated my father. It overwhelmed my mother in the end. Too much of her was left behind in South Africa.

June tried to kill herself again on April 15, 1982, almost four years after the first attempt. Again she took an overdose. There was another note to my father.

I see no end to our pain. You talked of five years of purgatory—it could be endless. You are too fine and noble a person to be deeply worried about me so much. You've done all (and more) to help. I'm just too tired now to fight anymore.

That morning June had called her old friend Noreen Webber, who lived down the road. Noreen, whose husband, Harry, was a psychiatrist, had followed my mother's mental struggle over a quarter century. Words June had spoken to her in a psychiatric hospital in 1957—*I've got a perfect baby and I don't know why I'm crying but I can't stop*—never left her. When they first met, in 1954, Noreen had wondered if they could be friends. June was "Mrs. Perfect." Her husband was perfect, her life was perfect, her clothes were perfect, everything had to be *just so.* Then she discovered June's rapier intelligence, her honesty, her humor—and finally her pain.

There had been occasions in recent years when June, in her dressing gown and nightdress, would come running down to Noreen's house at night, saying she could not stand to stay at home anymore. One of the problems in the marriage, as Noreen saw it, was that June developed. She discovered assertiveness. Now all June said was: "I just want to tell you how much I love you."

As she thought about the conversation, Noreen had the uneasy feeling June was saying goodbye. She grabbed a key my mother had given her and rushed up to the house. My mother was on her bed with a bottle of pills beside her and a plastic bag over her head. Noreen pulled her upright and called for an ambulance. She reached my father at Guy's. June was rushed to the Royal Free Hospital, where she remained for several days.

You, I hope, will find a worthy companion to enjoy the beauty of the farm— the rugged walks, the bracing air, the solitude and gorgeous garden.

My father, in 1973, had bought a 240-acre farm in central Wales, a beautiful property set in rolling hills. Here he could be alone with the sheep, the kestrels, the streams, the silence, and the pitch-black nights. He worked his magic in the form of a garden that flourished even in the rare sunlight. He planted pines. He built himself a carpentry workshop in a barn from which beguiling benches and tables emerged. For my mother, with her longing for the South African sun of her youth, the house was hard to love. It was not what she would have chosen. The soft air of the Mediterranean was more her habitat. She did her best. But cold sapped her. The wind always seemed to be up.

I wanted so much to help you always, but it is now no longer possible. I am sure our children will be a great comfort—they have grown into fine people. But our Jen needs a lot of love and understanding.

Just six months earlier Sydney had written to Benaim to say how delighted he was with June's progress since her discharge from a mental health facility: "She is lively and energetic, but sleeping very well with minimum sedation and altogether a delight to be with. I am at last optimistic that the nightmare might be over. If it is, then her recovery is due in my estimation almost entirely to your unfailing support and skill through all the dark years."

Such spasms of hope—that the turbulent horror might forever recede, that June might be liberated from her demons—occurred for some time before the repetitive pattern became too set to allow serious contemplation of uninterrupted relief. Most long marriages, at some stage, need at least the mirage of a new start. There could be none. The infernal illness had to be endured. It allowed only moments of lightness and laughter. She loved children, who adored her in turn. I see her seated on the carpet, legs folded back behind her, playing cards for hours with my daughter Jessica, born in 1981, and son Daniel born the next year. Treasures, she called them.

My mother spent more time in South Africa. When in London, long silences were punctuated by occasional explosions as June emerged from depression into a manic phase and expressed all her bottled-up rage. Then plates would be smashed. Sometimes she would call friends to come "rescue" her. Her fury was the obverse of her devotion to my father.

You are ashamed of me for reasons best known to yourself! I do not know who your friends are! You blame me for something I cannot

*My mother in South Africa six years before her death,
September 1993*

control! You REALLY want to pursue your own life unhindered by
my presence! I am not a laboratory specimen!

My mother's second suicide note ended with these words:

*My precious, forgive me, forgive me. I never meant to hurt you or anyone for
all the world. I will always be near you in spirit—always my love—my dearest, dearest love, my beloved.*

"At the moment June is somewhat euphoric," wrote my father in
1983, "and on past experience this state is likely to persist for perhaps
a few months, after which her spirits and level of activity will gradually decline and then quite swiftly severe depression will take relentless
grip of her mind."

I have tried to measure the agony he went through and concluded that I do not have an adequate frame of reference.

⁓

I walk with my mother on the beach at Muizenberg. It is a calm, clear morning. We can see Simon's Town and, stretching beyond it, the Cape of Good Hope pointing its green tongue toward Antarctica. The sand is ridged and firm at water's edge. The bracing sea washes now and then over our feet, planted here at the bottom of Africa. The laughter and voices of children mingle with the sound of the surf. June is wearing sunglasses and a floppy white hat and a pink swimsuit. The jingle of an ice-cream van drawing up next to the mini-golf course reaches us in the warm breeze. A plane leaves its softening vapor trail across the immense blue sky. My mother slips her cool hand into mine and speaks.

"What is it, darling?"

"Well, it's a long story."

"You can tell me." A little squeeze of the hand . . .

"Shall I begin at the beginning?"

"Or in the middle, it doesn't really matter now. Les jeux sont faits! Oh, how Laurie loved the roulette tables in Monte Carlo."

"Those were good times."

"You know I tried my best, wanted everything to be right, even perfect. And I failed, but perhaps it was not my fault."

"You never wanted to leave, did you, Mama?"

"Leave?"

"South Africa. It was your home."

"Yes. I suppose it is. I had my bearings here. And I lost them. I got uprooted. Absence is terrible. You know, darling, what Mole says in The Wind in the Willows: *'Home! That was what they meant, those caressing appeals, those soft touches wafted through the air, those invisible little hands pulling and tugging, all one way!' "*

My mother stops, smiles, breathes the salt air in, contemplates the faraway horizon, as if asking how anyone could exhale all this and inhale the forbidding north.

"Ever since I lost you," I say, "it has proved hard to love. The loss was a catastrophe, you see, it took away all meaning. The temple collapsed. My love was frozen. And now I find myself alone."

"*Lost me? But darling . . .*"

"*Yes, they took you away. I know now what happened. Because I was not old enough to have an explanation, I could only blame myself. It was a brutal change. I could never restore you to life, nor let go of you. I could not trust enough to love. In the end I always had to punish those who tried to love me, avenge myself somehow for the bereavement you caused. I had to find vitality at any price. Every relationship was a mausoleum in the making.*"

"*I was alive and with you. I came back to you,*" she says.

"*You returned like a faint echo.*"

"*No more than that?*"

"*Like the light from a dead star.*"

"*Still, I was there,*" says my mother.

"*My mourning continued. There was a gaping hole. You had been buried alive. And Dad was too preoccupied to fill the gap.*"

"*But there were happy times, darling. We recovered. You were a golden boy. You did so well!*"

"*The doing was also a cover-up, Mama. It is time to say that now. The hectic achievement was a distraction from an empty core. Ambition and imagination were the best sanctuaries I could find; and passion, physical pleasure, the surest distraction.*"

"*I tried to resume our conversation. I know how much words matter to you.*"

"*You did give me the gift of loving closeness. I knew what it was before I lost it. To have lost it is better than never to have had it. I have understood how you gave love and how it was taken away. I have also learned through you how stubborn and fixed love can be. Perhaps that gift has saved me in the darkest times.*"

"*Darling . . .*"

I looked up. My mother was gone.

A decade after her second suicide attempt, during a visit to South Africa, my mother was diagnosed with cancer of the liver and lung. She told my sister, who burst into tears on the phone. "Darling, you must not cry for me," June said. "As far as I'm concerned, this gives me a legitimate way out."

She was brave. Cancer to my mother was a derisory thing, even a solace. The cajoling voice in her ear had become an insistent intruder.

Yet the illness moved slowly. She lived far longer than expected, testimony to the force of her spirit. As for her will, I am sure that it often tugged in the opposite direction.

Her chatty letters would arrive from time to time at my homes in Paris and Berlin.

We leave on Sunday for Madeira—the sight of *blue* skies and feeling *warm* is a joy to relish. It's been quite arctic here with the usual chaos and disruption.

Or this:

The cancer is moving *VERY* slowly. As you know I accept it and refuse to let it interfere with what I want to do. Pain can be controlled with drugs so I have little to fear.

And in the same letter:

I'm sorry—I forgot to bring you the mats for glasses which go with your set. I'm rather forgetful now!

As the illness ate away at her, and she became thinner and frailer, she gave parties at which there was no room for sadness. In Johannesburg and London she gathered friends for tea and cakes in the Killarney Mall or at the Ritz, and she would say, with a disconcerting joie de vivre, that she wished to thank everyone for their kindness and patience. Her zest was hard to reconcile with the message delivered: she was dying. Cancer was doing what it does, feeding on her flesh. But nobody should worry too much about that. She was in good hands.

Her private torment continued. When she was down, she hid away. She kept her dignity. She was now almost a half century into the marriage that had begun on her family's fairyland Houghton estate back in 1950. Close to half of it had been under the manic-depressive cloud. Once, over lunch in the West End, she confided in a close friend, Eve Pollecoff: *There's somebody else. It's somebody at the hospital.* Eve, another Jewish woman who had grown up in Africa (and who had been told on arrival at Cheltenham College that she was one over the quota of

*My parents' wedding in Johannesburg on June 29, 1950. My uncle Bert is standing
left. Next to him, my grandmother Polly. In the center are my parents,
June and Sydney. My maternal grandparents, Laurie and Flossie, are standing at
right, my grandmother looking pained. The bridesmaids, left to right, are my mother's
cousins Peta and Sue Michel, my father's nieces Linda Gillman and Barbara Fink,
and my mother's cousin Jane Sive.*

1 percent for Jews), insisted that she was wrong. That could not be.
June waved her away. She *knew*.

She wrote letters to Sydney she never sent, made resolutions she did
not keep.

> You need to admit to yourself that you see me as an enormous
> burden, as someone with whom you are unable to emote or to
> share your thoughts. However, after so many years together I can
> read your thoughts very well. Your manner and expression tell
> me all.
>
> I want you to know and to believe that I consider you to
> have many great and *wonderful* virtues for which I respect and
> love you. You have stood by me when I'm ill and you've always
> been extremely generous. You are reliable, dependable, capable,
> honest and highly talented, both in your chosen field and in your

pastimes. I have never been able to measure up to your standards however hard I have tried. I have felt myself to be very much in your shadow and under your constant scrutiny and judgment.

I *WANT* you to feel free and to pursue your own interests when and how you please. As long as I am fit I now intend to be away from you as much as possible. Should you ever need me (for *whatever* reason) you will find me by your side. I will never stop loving you—as you once said, "Love is not love that alters when it alteration finds."

We need to see whether our lives will be happier when we are apart. I suggest we put this to the test in the following six months and then review our situation. I certainly do not intend to stay trapped in an unhappy relationship where you look at me with utmost displeasure and you keep your life very apart from mine. I take this decision with a very heavy heart but I am quite firm in my resolve. You obviously need and want your own lifestyle and you find me and my lifestyle a serious obstruction to your peace of mind. I only wish you well. May you find peace and be happy. I am yours when and *if* you want me.

They stayed together. My father cared for my mother day after day. She lay in bed propped on pillows. She showed no self-pity and, when she could still muster it, a good deal of gaiety. June was good at dying. It was her grand finale, her last and irreproachable act.

A few months before she died, on August 4, 1998, Sydney wrote a poem about her:

> I have lost my way
> And can only stare at the stars
> I drift in neuronal void
> And lament forgotten days.
> I crave the faces I knew
> And the clatter of tongues
> Yet those about me
> Seem voiceless and grey.

Thoughts revolve in a shrunken shell
And silence is the throb of despair
Oblivion tugs at my hand—
For I have lost my way.

He called the poem "JBC"—her initials. He might have called it "SC." It was as much about his pain in that moment as about hers.

She was quiet but resolute. In that small frame, reduced almost to nothing now, she summoned some indomitable force that would not be quieted even with her passing. When she opened her eyes and saw me, three days before the end, she took a moment to focus—and then happiness filled her eyes like morning sunlight filtering through a curtain. Her breathing was thin. We are all Lazarus for a moment. Death does not come unannounced. Liminal states precede it. Cancer had tamed at last the crippling gyration of her moods. For June there could be no greater peace. She held my hand and would not let go. My sister fed her a last meal—half of a canned pear and chocolate ice cream—running the spoon across her mouth to get the bits.

Her last words to my father were: "Thank you, darling."

Love, to my mother, was—in the words of a Shakespeare sonnet she liked to quote—"an ever-fixed mark," an idea that "bears it out even to the edge of doom." It was single and indissoluble, the deepest truth of her tormented life. In death, against all odds, it was love that prevailed.

My mother died on January 2, 1999. Her corpse was carried out of the house in a black plastic bag. The undertakers carrying her wore dark suits. I thought they looked like murderers. As she was loaded into their van, the sky darkened. Inky clouds crowded across the sky. There was an explosive thunderclap—her soul, I thought, snapping loose. Lightning stabbed downward in a shard worthy of a Giorgione painting. Rain fell in torrents, the good rain. My father, a man of great self-control, was gripped by convulsive weeping.

"Go free now," my sister whispered.

At my father's request, I had made the mistake of trying to pry

June's wedding ring off her stiffening finger and struggled for minutes before completing a task that should have been left to others. My mother had always been slight but now seemed more bone than flesh. Her face was beaked like a small bird's, her arms as slender as those of Degas's dancers. Yet her finger was unyielding. I found myself whispering coaxing words—"Let it all go"—to the pinched mask of my mother, propped at a regal angle recalling the likeness of some undersize French monarch in a frosty medieval crypt.

The black van carrying her corpse disappeared into the deluge.

My father turned the ring in his long fingers, examining this evidence of his marriage as if it were a report on an unfathomable symptom. "You know," he said, trying unsuccessfully to stifle a sob, "I'm amazed how grief-stricken I am. This has been coming for so long. It's like falling in love again." Cathartic grief had drawn us, however fleetingly, into the togetherness June had always wanted.

Her funeral, a humanist service she and Sydney had chosen, was held at the Golders Green Crematorium, in the heart of Jewish London but without a Jewish reference. The chapel was packed with mourners. June's friends spoke movingly of her courage. I tried to say something of the light and the shadow:

> The air of the earth is sweeter, lighter, softer because your spirit now resides in it, whispering in the damp breezes of our winter. How gentle you were, gentle in thought and action, your hand in mine always so soft and searching. How kind you were. To the family you loved, to the "treasures" that are your six grandchildren, to your many friends and often to people you hardly knew. Kindness, you thought, was a much undervalued virtue. Another was humility. You understood the meek of this earth.
>
> Mama, you were strong in the end. It is said that people struggle against cancer. But you did not struggle. You defied the illness with your courage, mocked it with your dignity and overpowered it with your fearlessness. I cannot imagine that anyone ever went more graciously—more calm and open-eyed—into the light.
>
> I am sure that all of you here remember June's infectious laughter, full of the beloved sunshine of her native South Africa, bearing her away to the point where she had to wipe the tears from her eyes.

I know that you all recall the childlike brightness of that neat, trim, fragrant figure in the moments when the world smiled on her. I do not doubt that you noticed how at ease she was with children, how she sang along with them, and how they loved her. And I am certain that we were all disarmed, at one moment or another, by the silvery thrust of her self-deprecating intelligence, erudition and wit. Asked by her doctor the other day if she had been afraid during a moment of incoherence brought on by shortness of breath, she shot back: "No, I thoroughly enjoyed it." That, too, was my mother.

But there was, of course, a darker side, just as this day has been one of sun and shadow. As some of you here know, my mother suffered for most of the last two decades of her life from manic depression, a desperate, often incommunicable condition in which despair and agitation alternate. Each state, in its different way, could lead to misunderstanding and disaster.

The scraps of paper in her handbag—holidays untaken, courses untried, ideas unrealized—testified to an intermittent whirlwind of torment. But behind almost all these notions—however illusory, however desperate, however flawed—there lay some generous intention. To be happy together, all of us, as a family; to help somebody; to learn; to give. She was always, in her heart, on the side of the angels.

And I am certain that through her extraordinary stoicism, dignity, and patience, she wrestled down the demons—monsters we cannot even begin to imagine—and vanquished them in the end. That was her most painful and her greatest victory. In gaining it her spirit became so strong that this final passage was almost painless.

Her strength, as she often said, came in the end from love. Her life was about love. The love she felt for Sydney, her husband, father to Jenny and me. This love was uncompromising and greater than any suffering. However hard the world, she persisted. Of Sydney she felt, as Browning wrote, "I shall but love thee better after death."

My mother loved and gave with an immense heart and held fast to her truth. When the spring comes, as it will, I will feel her beside me in the brightness of the new leaves, leaves as delicate as the blessing of her memory.

Benaim, who knew more of the two facets of my mother than any-one present apart from my father, approached me afterward. "Thank you" was all he said. June, in death, had brought her psychiatrist to tears.

In the ensuing weeks, my father wrote to me a couple of times with an openness and generosity that had the consoling power, after the years of reserve, of a hand outstretched to a drowning man. In the first he said, "My beloved boy—I know with certainty that great achieve-ments and many triumphs lie ahead of you—but in my heart the four minutes of pain and passion during which you so perfectly encapsu-lated Mom's noble struggle and ultimate triumph, will always remain your finest hour."

And then, reaching into the core of his being, my father said this:

Now that Mom's life is spent, we are each of us left with the pain and turmoil of personal accounting. I agree with you that this should be a time of gentleness. For Mom there was always a need for tenderness and gentle compassion, and all of us are left with stark memories of our failure to satisfy this innocent, almost child-like requirement of her psyche. Your expanding memories of Mom have become infinitely precious and important; I share with you the vision of a light which is the obverse of her tormenting darkness and which in some miraculous way has become completely dominant since her death. I hope and pray that this vision of her will be an enduring source of strength and inspiration to you in all the years ahead, ever cherished and unsullied.

For myself, I did have a fleeting dream of a few tranquil years carrying me into the sunset. I still hope for that in a mental and bodily sense. But I know that my spirit will not soon be released from those cruel demons that tore so relentlessly at the entwining fabric of love between Mom and me. I did strive within the feeble limits of my human fallibility to preserve and cherish and sustain her. But alas—for Mama ultimately, death was the only angel that could shield her from despair.

My beloved boy—the matchless eloquence of your writing speaks vividly of how painfully you had to probe and what anguish heaped with torment you have suffered. I hope with all my heart that before too long the turbulence of your spirit will subside and you will reach to tranquility in your inner self.

We were too undone to ask for the urn with my mother's ashes. I do not know where it ended up. The girl from Human Street who married the boy from Honey Street left no trace of her anguished passage across the earth, from the Southern to the Northern Hemisphere. After her high school records from Barnato Park, after her medical records from the Holloway Sanatorium, her very physical remains vanished, too. In the end the only way I knew to recover her and quiet the turbulence she left was word by word. "Once you write it down," Hemingway noted, "it is all gone." From an early age, I had grown used to deploying my imagination as a defense. I told many other stories from many other datelines before I realized, returning to the place where I began, that the one story I had to tell was hers.

CHAPTER 10

The Lark Sings and Falls

Rena, I will call her, my cousin in the Holy Land. I had to find her, wherever she had gone. We shared the same great-grandfather, Isaac Michel, the founder of the OK Bazaars whose vast Johannesburg estate my mother roamed in her youth. We were both the descendants of uprooted South Africans who tried to reinvent themselves in strange lands, children of displacement.

In Hebrew *Rena* means "melody." The lark sings—and then falls.

The manic depression that tormented my mother, June, also afflicted Rena Levin, who knew the violent swings from light to dark and back again. She lived alone in a small studio on Shlomo Hamelech Street in Tel Aviv, a few blocks from the beach. She was tall and athletic, a good swimmer, with straight light brown hair, a half-shy smile, an infectious giggle, and irresistible rosy cheeks. Her features were fluid, shifting between beauty and plainness, as if prisoners of some prolonged adolescence. She would appear lovely or ungainly depending on the light or angle or her mood. Her sweet sincerity was constant, her eyes inconstant, brilliant or dull by turns even before the medication changed them. She lived at the cusp. Her voice was soft and low and calm. She was mystical. She looked for signs. Certain things were meant to happen.

In Tel Aviv, Rena felt freer than in the Jerusalem of her childhood, where the influence of the *haredim,* the "God-fearing" ultra-Orthodox, keeps growing. She liked to wander through her shabby neighborhood, listen to the breeze rustling in the palm fronds. The city was a mess. Cables from satellite dishes and telephone lines twisted into outsize tentacles. Washing hung on small balconies or pegged to lines in windows, as if on a Neapolitan backstreet. Plaster peeled off cracked facades. Leaves coated in a film of dust were gray-green.

Still, you could sit at Café Shine and order your avocado and mozzarella sandwich on pita and listen to the Jews debating their real estate deals and their dogs in a language that had been near-dead a century ago; and chat with the ex-Mossad agent now teaching Tibetan meditation and healing; and watch the long-legged Russian babes transposed to the Holy Land with their designer jeans and bejeweled sandals stride past a camp survivor in a wheelchair with her blue-tinted hair and tartan blanket and Romanian caregiver—and might find yourself considering that the place had a ramshackle charm, a blend of languor and zest that was satisfying.

Style, Flaubert suggested, was the "discharge from a deeper wound." Was this the secret of Tel Aviv's aura, a proud collective overcoming of Jewish injury? Ugliness is not an insurmountable obstacle for cities whose energy offsets it.

Down Gordon Street, past Café Marco, across Dizengoff and Ben Yehuda, over to Frishman and onto the beach: Rena always felt her heart lift at the sight of the sea and the feel of the cool currents of air coming off the water. She liked the *thwack-thwack* of the beach tennis games, one player as hitter, the other a wall. She loved the liquid chatter of children lifted on the breeze, as light as a white sail cutting across the bay. At dusk, the sun plunged into the sea after a moment of brilliant resistance on the westward horizon. The heat eased. The air in Independence Park was fragrant. Then, like a fingernail, the moon would rise over the Mediterranean.

Perhaps everything would be all right. Rena, in the presence of beauty, could convince herself at times. The conflict would find a resolution. Palestinians would stop blowing themselves, and anyone near them, to pieces. Buses would cease being metal containers liable to explode. Pieces of flesh would not hang from lampposts outside blasted cafés. The Second Intifada would not lead only to a sequel to the sequel. Dueling Israeli and Palestinian nationalisms would decouple themselves from the engine of myth, giving up some part of the past for the sake of the future. "Narratives" would be set aside. Her mind, which raced at night, would quiet itself, too. She would get off the awful medication, the pills she hated. She would see herself in her eyes again rather than some creature caught like a deer in headlights.

Her country, Israel, would set its borders at last; and she, in her own way, also, the frontiers within which she could balance herself and make her way. People, like nations, needed to know their limits. She was not a political animal, but she ached for an end to the conflict. By nature she was a peacemaker. Israel sometimes struck her as a borderline personality given to violent lurches that seemed incomprehensible in hindsight.

As she made her way back from the beach to Shlomo Hamelech, she watched the young women just out of military service with their sultry-sexy I'm-trained-to-shoot-you-dead air. The geraniums in window boxes were like little red torches. Was there a love so beautiful that she would be able to paint it purple?

Her eyes sometimes fixed on the spikes fitted near the top of lampposts. Beneath them was a sign: DANGER OF DEATH. Who, Rena wondered, would want to climb over these jagged protrusions into a tangle of wires, perhaps to steal somebody's cable service? The wires twisted into a tangle she found hypnotizing. They reminded her of Leonard Cohen's lines. She had tried, like his "bird on a wire," like his "drunk in a midnight choir," to be free.

She had gone to Canada in 2000 to do a two-year program for a master's in music therapy. But she lost control. Voices whispered to her. Her fingers were painfully sensitive. Shadows slithered in the dark. She became Argus-eyed. Details leaped out at her—a student's new glasses or shoes or gem-studded belt—and she could not stop staring. On a whim she decided to change her name to Renata, meaning "reborn." She liked that! It was more international; she would not have to spell her name out to the friendly Canadians in their placid country. A nation could have too much space as well as too little.

Her family was not sure what to think or what to call Rena-Renata. It irritated her that they did not respect her choice. She had a right to choose her identity.

She babysat in rainy, overcast Vancouver to make some extra cash. One day, holding the baby, she *knew* the child had been abused by his parents. Rena had no doubts. She telephoned her father, Meyer (not his real name), who was on a sabbatical in London; thoughtful Meyer, who had offered her contraceptives—*oral* contraceptives, as he put it—when she turned seventeen and took up with Aron, her high school sweetheart. Her relationship with Meyer had survived her parents' painful divorce a decade earlier. Meyer, a physician, wanted to know what evidence she had of child abuse.

"What can you see?"

"I'm observant, Dad. I just *know* it."

"How do you mean?"

"It's like when you see toys in the rubble after a village has been shelled."

"Huh?"

"The injury that has occurred is obvious."

"But, Reen darling, are there bruises, scratches, marks, something abnormal?"

"Dad, those are *external* signs. This is something I feel *inside*. I had a dream last night. I saw a collapsed pier in the sea. On each of the posts a white gull was perched. Then the baby called me. When I looked back, black crows had taken the place of the gulls."

Rena gave up her babysitting. She abandoned the course. Her family brought her home from Vancouver in 2001. Everyone seemed to agree she was delusional. She was twenty-six, two years younger than my mother when she broke down in London. She wanted to protect her family, be gentle with them. Meyer said something brave to his daughter: "Darling, listen to me, if ever you feel you want to kill yourself, you must tell me." Meyer-Dude, as she sometimes called her father to herself, was a thoughtful guy. But how could she burden her parents with her suicidal urges? When she arrived home, in her journal that was a mix of inspirational questions and her own thoughts, she wrote:

For a long time it had seemed to me that life was about to begin: real life. But there was always some obstacle in the way, something to be gotten through. Then life would begin.

At last it dawned on me that these obstacles were my life.

Trees have roots. Jews have legs. So it was with my family, always on the move. Our preferred toast, when the time came around for the South African sundowner, was: "Absent friends and relations!" There were plenty of those.

Rena was absent. I never met her. Now there is no alternative but to imagine her, inheritor through the family bloodlines of the condition that plagued my mother.

She was in Israel, I was not. It might easily have been the other way around. Rena's paternal great-grandfather—I will call him Max Levin—left the Lithuanian town of Panavezys (Ponevezh in Yiddish) in the early 1900s. Like Isaac Michel, our shared maternal great-grandfather, Levin sailed for Cape Town, one of the tens of thousands of Litvaks who headed from Lithuania to South Africa to escape the pogroms of the Pale of Settlement and seek opportunity.

At the time of Levin's birth in 1875, Lithuania was part of Russia. He fought in the Russian army during the Russo-Japanese War of 1904–05, only to witness the persecution of Jews on his return. By the time he emigrated, he was a convinced Zionist. No act of patriotism or sacrifice would secure Jewish acceptance in Europe. Levin settled in Queenstown in the Eastern Cape, where, with his brother, he established a small trading company and served for several years as president of the Zionist Society.

Among the papers I was given by my family in Israel is an obituary that appeared in the *Zionist Record* of South Africa in 1917. It describes Max Levin's last moments:

> The final scene was heartbreaking, when the deceased, having expressed his last wishes to his wife and children, bade farewell to his friends in touching words. "My dear friends," he said. "I beseech you after you have put around me the Talith, place over me the Zionist flag, and after my burial sing Hatikvah at my graveside and make a collection for the National Fund, and then I will rest in peace in my grave."

A tribute from a friend reads: "His sincerity of purpose, his Zionistic aspirations were so pure, honest and true that one only needed to know him to acknowledge him as a genius and a symbol of the

Jewish resurrection. . . . Truly was he called the Herzl of the Eastern Province."

Twenty-one years after the publication of Herzl's *The Jewish State,* in the year of the Balfour Declaration expressing Britain's favorable view of "the establishment in Palestine of a national home for the Jewish people" (with the pious caveat that "nothing shall be done which may prejudice the civil and religious rights of existing non-Jewish communities in Palestine"), and thirty years before the United Nations passed Resolution 181 calling for the establishment of two states—one Jewish, one Arab—in Mandate Palestine, a forty-two-year-old Jewish immigrant of Lithuanian descent dies in a remote corner of South Africa and has his coffin draped in the blue-and-white Star of David (Israel's future flag) and a prayer shawl of the same color. For this "Herzl of the Eastern Province," a Zionist forged in Russian pogroms, the song that would become the Israeli national anthem is sung. In these small ways was an unlikely nation forged.

Emerging from the static ghetto into the Sturm und Drang of the modern world, Jews saw three principal routes to emancipation. The first was assimilation, the second socialism, and the third Zionism. (There was also conversion, a different story.) Levin did not believe assimilation was possible because it demanded of Jews that they regard themselves not as a nation but, if anything, as a religion; and that they place their faith in the ability of enlightened democratic institutions to protect them. He was no socialist.

My family chose assimilation for the most part. They were lucky enough to do so in South Africa and Britain, places that eluded the century's horrors. Their wager on acceptance was not recompensed with slaughter as it was for the Jews of continental Europe. South Africa, with its vast black underclass, unfurled its opportunities for them before Britain enfolded them in a trading island's tolerance.

My father loathed nothing more than messianic religiosity and intolerance. People forged their destinies. They were not chosen; nor could they deem who did not make the cut. In our case, as for countless other Jews, the price of integration was the loss of millennia of

Jewish tradition. The Torah's instruction gave way to the moral void of modernity, a hectic dance over absence. Many who were taken to the Nazis' gassing facilities had no real idea what they were dying for. The place of Jewish identity had been taken by proud citizenship that, in Hitler's Europe, proved revocable.

One branch of the family, Rena's, descendants of Max Levin, made the Zionist choice for Israel. They went there from South Africa out of idealism, to be part of something bigger than themselves, beyond the solipsism of the modern world. They were convinced of the need for a Jewish state for the simple reason that that was the only state in which Jews without question belonged. They wanted to forge a noble thing. Hebrew scripture contains scant allusion to the afterlife. The society in God's image was to be built on earth. *Tikkun olam* was the Jewish watchword: "Repair the world, be a light unto nations." Understand the stranger, for was not Abraham himself one, and was not the insecurity of otherness the essence of Jewish experience?

The Founding Charter of 1948 declared that Israel would be based "on freedom, justice, and peace as envisaged by the prophets of Israel; it will ensure complete equality of social and political rights to all its inhabitants irrespective of religion, race, or sex; it will guarantee freedom of religion, conscience, language, education, and culture."

But Israel stiffened under attack. Annihilation angst devoured ecumenical velleity. Unable to resist the maximalist territorial temptation, Israel stumbled over time into controlling the lives of millions of Palestinians, a task that required administering a daily dose of the very humiliation that Jews had suffered as outsiders over centuries and that Max Levin's Zionism had sought to redress.

As Vikram Seth has observed, "The great advantage of being a chosen people is that one can choose to decide who is unchosen, and withdraw sympathy and equity from them." Palestinians became the *unchosen* of the Holy Land.

From Vancouver, shortly after the outbreak of the Second Intifada in 2000, Levin's great-granddaughter Rena sent her brother Yaakov (not his real name) a Halloween message: "I do not feel like going out and dressing up. If I did, I guess it would be as a peace dove. I wish things were calmer. I wish I could make things easier."

Like many Israelis, my cousin felt dueling emotions: anger at Palestinian violence and disquiet at her country's rule over the Arab "stranger" in the occupied West Bank, a place to which she never went.

Every year Rena's family would return to South Africa. Yaakov described a familiar scene in Johannesburg: "It felt like the garden in Houghton never ended. There was a tree house and a swimming pool. Ponies were brought in for our birthday parties. Nobody seemed to be working too hard. We always had chocolate cake with peanuts sprinkled on top. It was paradise. But there was a shadow. I never really felt comfortable with the black servants. I'd walk into the kitchen and want a frying pan to make an egg, and Johanna, the cook, would say *Quick quick quick,* be sure Granny does not see you!

"I couldn't believe how my South African cousins would scream at the nannies if the water in the baths they drew was not hot enough. I could see the servants' quarters behind the house, the little concrete-floored room, and every once in a while their children would visit, and I could sense this sadness of separated families. At dinner, Sam would dress up in his suit and white gloves. He would serve drinks beforehand on the red-tiled veranda. I can see him taking the gleaming glasses from their cabinets. Grandpa always had his White Horse whiskey on the rocks. We would sit down. Granny would ring the bell. Sam would appear. Coming from Israel, where I would come home from school at the age of seven and make myself lunch, it just did not seem quite right."

Yaakov's grandparents lived a few blocks from Isaac Michel's old Houghton mansion. This was my mother's pampered South African world. It was also that of Rena's mom. I will call her Pauline, a granddaughter, like my mother, of Michel, the *smous*-turned-patriarch. Pauline was a beauty. Chestnut hair framed her delicate pale features, and she had in abundance the bubbly Michel charm. She was quick and funny, and if you had asked her in Johannesburg if she would consider a future in Israel, she would have laughed. Zionism did not enter the picture.

Her pale brown eyes sparkled with life but could also smolder in anger, as if enveloped in a black cloud. Like my mother, Pauline went to Barnato Park School for girls—the last two years there were principally devoted to her first love affair—before going on to the University of Cape Town, where she studied art history and political science.

She sojourned in Europe. Men were always hovering. They included princes and swindlers, amusing men who whisked her off to palatial abodes where they made promises she seldom believed and they never kept.

Meyer Levin, when he came along in 1969, was the antithesis of such heady glamour. He was neither suave nor rich. He was a doctor—rational, steady, quiet, and introverted. A big man, attractive if not classically handsome, heavy-limbed, he moved and spoke with measured intent. He was intense, given to clenching his hands when he talked about the critical importance of control.

She was volcanic, he a rock: their temperaments could scarcely have been more different, a source of violent attraction and persistent tension. Meyer, like his grandfather, was also a convinced Zionist who wanted to whisk her off somewhere altogether different, to Jerusalem. He wanted, he told her, "to make a contribution, however modest, to the new state. I need a meaningful challenge." She admired his idealism, his sense of purpose; she was reassured by his devotion.

They had met on a blind date in South Africa, seen each other again in London, gone different ways with other partners, and come together once more. Pauline, turning thirty, sought my mother's advice: Should she go away to a strange land with a driven doctor? June, whose own immense difficulty in adapting to the strange land of England with another driven doctor was never aired, much less her breakdown, had no hesitation: Of course she should go!

They were married in London and left soon after, arriving in Israel on December 28, 1972, to make aliyah. Pauline was seven and a half months pregnant; Yaakov was born in Jerusalem on February 16, 1973. They settled in the upscale West Jerusalem district of Rehavia in a fourth-floor walk-up owned by the Hadassah hospital, where Meyer went to work. Within eight months the Yom Kippur War had broken out.

"I remember the sirens and the shutters coming down with a bang and the blackouts at night and buying stocks of food—there was less bread and less milk, and I had the baby, and Meyer had to be at the hospital a lot," Pauline tells me. "It was hard to understand the news. There was the initial shock, the Egyptian army rolling over the canal and the Syrians advancing across the Golan Heights into the Galilee, and all the terrible uncertainty before the tide turned. Yet I don't recall being afraid. I guess I have this ability to cope, somehow. I was living for the moment. The hospital had emptied with everyone going off to army units, and Meyer, as a recent arrival, was almost alone. Colleagues of his were killed—it was harrowing."

Pauline gazes out of her window. Geraniums bloom in abundance on her balcony. Her Jerusalem apartment is small in a country of limited space, unlike the African land of two-acre plots in which she was raised. The sun, a white glare, beats down on limestone. She smiles at me and sighs: "But from the beginning, it was easier than London in many ways. People were open and warm, and I felt more identified. I felt the vibrancy. It was good to be among Jews. In fact, for the first time in my life I could forget I was a Jew."

Explaining how life differed in Israel was not easy. That phrase of Meyer's in London—"a meaningful challenge"—came back to Pauline because it communicated the sense, absent elsewhere, of building something beyond oneself. A relative, a prominent member of the Cleveland Jewish community, visited from the United States and was shocked to see Yaakov running around without booties. What, he asked, can I get you? Pauline was unsure what to say—not booties, anyway. They went to South Africa in early 1974, a relief from the tension of war. The old country seemed unreal in its sunlit vastness, the harsh oppression of apartheid held at a distance. By the time she returned to Jerusalem, Pauline was pregnant again with Rena, her postwar baby.

The family needed more space. Friends told them of a new development on French Hill in annexed East Jerusalem. It was far from the center but cheaper for that reason. Still, Pauline felt uneasy. She was a liberal who could not help seeing the West Bank occupation in South African terms—one people dominating another, controlling them, disenfranchising them, and denying them their rights. Of course, it was not a perfect analogy, but the echoes were hard to ignore. Jews knew all about such exclusion. Israel, it seemed, had entered a permanent state of emergency. There was no rule of law in the occupied territories that she could discern. Certainly there was no consent of the governed.

Pauline would sit on the balcony gazing eastward. On a clear day, you could see all the way down to the Dead Sea. Everywhere there was construction, new cities, fortresses really it seemed to her, being built around Jerusalem—Gilo, Ramot, Pisgat Ze'ev. This, she thought, was *conquest*. It was not temporary. Official obfuscation overlaid relentless construction. Schoolchildren could not see on maps where the occupied territory began. The Green Line, the old border, was gone, swept away by religious-nationalist fever. Israeli intent was written in bricks and mortar. The mountains of the Land of Israel were beckoning the Jewish zealots of the State of Israel, summoning a tide of religious Zionism that would swamp the secular Zionism that had led to Israel's foundation. She listened to the haunting call to prayer of the muezzin drifting up from Palestinians villages. It was a reminder. Thoughts stirred of South Africa, where you could pretend the stranger was not there until you caught a glimpse of his ill-fitting shoes or the defiance in his eye.

Meyer had a different view. Israel was not the aggressor. It had been attacked by Arab armies in 1948 because they refused to accept the will of the United Nations—what Benny Morris has called "an international warrant for a small piece of earth." They had attacked again and again since. This was the consequence. *We won—get over it. They fought and lost. What nation ever handed back the spoils of war to an enemy bent on its destruction? The problem with liberals is their bleeding hearts. When you've got someone by the balls, hearts and minds will follow.*

Jerusalem was one and indivisible, the home of all Jews once again after the long dispersal. It would never be split again. French Hill would always be Israeli. The pre-1967 borders were indefensible. Had Abba Eban not called them the "Auschwitz borders"? What they gazed across was Jewish land, indeed the quintessence of Jewish land, the Judean Hills, birthplace of Patriarchs and of the millennial Jewish story, home of the eternal covenant between God and the Jewish people. Everything would shake out somehow if Israel stood its ground, did not bend. The new Jew of Zionist pedigree was through with the diaspora pliability that had proved a death trap.

Rena was born on November 10, 1974, in a house with a beautiful view over land with a disputed name. For much of the world—including her mother—and under international law, it was the occupied West Bank that receded into the shimmering haze beneath the balcony on French Hill. For many Israelis, including her father, it was Judea and Samaria, their dun-colored, inalienable biblical birthright, recovered after almost two millennia. She came into being in an Israel at the fulcrum of its shift from brave upstart to colonialist power, at the very moment when the messianic push to settle the West Bank shifted religious Zionism from a marginal phenomenon to the heart of Israel's internal struggle, and when the nation's culture began its steady journey from a communal to an individualistic culture. Down below French Hill, in the mountains leading to the river, the settlements began to grow, at first with official acquiescence, then with official support. The few thousand Jewish settlers at Rena's birth would grow to several hundred thousand.

Rena-Renata was born into a confusion of names, a land where the very choice of words betokened an ethos. Confusion would pursue her, the conundrum of who she was.

It was a wager on belonging that the Jews of continental Europe lost to Hitler. Michael Adler, the rabbi, had agonized over the acceptance of British Jews during World War I. They turned out to be the lucky ones. German Jews believed they were German citizens in the fullest sense. Had they not, in the service of the fatherland, won Iron Crosses, just as Levin had fought in the Russian army with distinction? They were to discover that they were in fact mere *Jews in Germany*. The same was true of French Jews, Dutch Jews, and all the rest. Near acceptance into Christian society turned out to be more treacherous than non-acceptance. The Jews, ascendant, became threatening, then disposable.

None had been more patriotic than German Jews. To the last, Jewish authorities, gathered in the Reichsvereinigung der Juden in Deutschland, cooperated with Hitler's Reich, much as Jewish Councils would in occupied Poland and Lithuania—deluded, like the Gens brothers in Šiauliai and Vilnius, into the belief that servility might save them. This Jewish cooperation in the Nazi organization of Jewish slaughter was the ultimate expression of diaspora submission.

Zionism, by contrast, placed no faith in others' goodwill. It sought, rather, to usher Jews to the full realization of their nationhood and so, in a sense, to normalize them—make them patriotic about something that was their own. It was anti-messianic in the sense that it demanded of Jews an act of political and physical will rather than the passive expectation of deliverance to the Promised Land through prayer, ritual, and contemplation of sacred texts. Scrawny scholars would become vigorous tillers of the soil in the Valley of Harod. Orange groves would blossom from the parched earth of Palestine.

My family story, like that of millions of other Jews, leads inexorably to Zionism. By the early twentieth century, no alternative offered a plausible chance of Jewish survival and belonging. As Joseph Roth once wrote, "If there is one nation that is justified in seeing the 'national question' as essential to its survival, then surely it is the Jews who are forced to become a 'nation' by the nationalism of others." Zionism was a necessary break with past, pogrom, and persecution. Yet Zionism sought the recovery of the Jews' historical homeland, terrain that overflowed with the past. It was a secular movement, initially scorned by the Talmudists, bent on the recovery of land steeped in religious symbolism. Moreover, it sought a state on land that was not empty. Zionist resolution of the Jewish question could only give birth to an Arab question. Inherent contradictions and inevitable tensions abounded.

As early as 1907, Yitzhak Epstein, a Zionist, wrote an article called "A Hidden Question" in which he observed: "We pay close attention to the affairs of our land, we discuss and debate everything, we praise and curse everything, but we forget one small detail: That there is in our beloved land an entire people that have been attached to it for hundreds of years and has never considered leaving it." The Arab, Epstein noted, "is, like any person, strongly attached to his homeland." Zionism, he predicted, would struggle with this core problem.

The warning was prescient. The Jews' "War of Liberation" in 1948 was also the Palestinians' *al-Nakba,* or catastrophe. Several hundred thousand Palestinians were driven from their homes in a war started by Arab states unwilling to accept UN Resolution 181 of 1947—that a Jewish state be constituted in the Holy Land. The first war fed the current of Zionist thought that had never been inclined to accept the UN-mandated division of the land into Jewish and Palestinian states, but for the first decades of Israel's existence such absolutism was contained.

After the lightning victory in the Six-Day War of 1967 and the trauma followed by triumph in the 1973 Yom Kippur War, messianic Jewish thinking made a vigorous comeback. If Israel now held all Jerusalem and the West Bank, how, in the minds of religious nationalists, could this recovery of Eretz Yisrael—a biblical term widely used to refer to the area between the Mediterranean Sea and the Jordan River—not be an expression of divine will?

Religious Zionism was the malignant offspring of secular Zionism, whose immense political achievement was to persuade the world, in the form of the United Nations, of the justice of a Jewish claim to about half of British Mandate Palestine. The cornerstone of Israel's UN-backed legality was territorial compromise. Rejected first by the Arabs, this division of the land was then progressively undermined from the 1970s onward by the settlers of Gush Emunim. They claimed Zionism's mantle. They mimicked its attachment to the soil. But they were not delivering the persecuted Jews of Europe to a new life. They were ushering Jews from within Israel to the West Bank, from the laws of Israeli democracy into lawless defiance of the very foundations of the state. God's covenant in the mountains of Judea and Samaria blinded the settlement movement to the Palestinians in their midst. Arabs in turn became disposable, and Israel, through overreach, placed itself in a morally indefensible noose.

Words were a sea of vagueness. Meyer and Pauline spoke only English together. The children, as their schooling progressed, spoke Hebrew. The result was domestic "Hebrish," a source of embarrassment to Yaakov and Rena when they brought friends home. They grew up between worlds, with what Yaakov called "a feeling of being neither here nor there."

Meyer and Pauline could not help with homework in Hebrew. The children cringed at their parents' inability to master the language. Pauline understood one advertisement to mean: *What are you doing with your free Arabs?* Which free Arabs would that be exactly? *Aravim,* in Hebrew, can mean "Arabs" or "evenings."

The children would go down into the wadi below the house. They played with the donkeys and collected fossils and picked succulent figs split by ripeness as stray dogs poked around in the dust. Stones and rocks lay everywhere, smooth on one surface, rough as nutmeg graters on the other. They fascinated Rena.

The situation had not yet hardened; mingling was possible in the absence of walls or barriers or fences. On weekends, the family might go on a trip to Jericho or Ramallah and eat hummus and lamb so tender you could cut it with a spoon. Rena loved these outings. She was an easy child, calm and friendly, good in school if not particularly scholarly, conscientious and warm, gentler and quieter than Yaakov, whose frustrations with language could lead to outbursts. Her quietness was not sadness, at most heaviness. Pauline thought of her as "my no-problem child."

The family lived in a small circle of friends of mainly South African Jewish descent. All English-speaking, they would gather for Shabbat. Pauline would light the candles, Meyer would say Kiddush, and someone would remind the children, "More than Israel keeping the Sabbath, it is the Sabbath that keeps Israel."

The family was traditional rather than religious. They did not keep kosher. They went to shul on High Holidays only. The children attended a conservative school where they said prayers every morning. That was the extent of religious observance. For Meyer, the important thing was to give them a strong sense of Jewish identity and of his family's Zionist heritage. Identity, he liked to say, is not forged through parental passivity.

Among the family friends were people who had participated with him in the South African branch of Betar, the right-wing Revisionist Jewish youth movement founded in Latvia in 1923 by Ze'ev Jabotinsky, who a decade later offered blunt advice to Jews: "It is important to build, it is important to speak Hebrew, but unfortunately, it is even more important to be able to shoot." Meyer, as a medical student in Cape Town, had been the camp doctor at Betar gatherings. It was natural that he would become a supporter of Likud. The party's leader, Menachem Begin, had himself been a Betar militant in Poland before becoming the leader of the Irgun, the Zionist paramilitary group that terrorized the British and embodied Jabotinsky's view that the key to attainment of a Jewish state lay in force and readiness to use it. Meyer's father had been a personal friend of Begin, who visited the family in the early 1950s when they were living in Bulawayo. The antisocialist platform of Likud appealed to him.

At election time, family tensions rose. Meyer was delighted by Begin's election as prime minister in 1977 at the head of a Likud-led government that ended the dominance by Mapai and the left since Israel's foundation.

"This is the day Israel became a democracy," he told Pauline. "No nation is a democracy until there is an alternation of power."

She retorted, "No nation can remain a democracy when it rules over people under occupation who do not have a vote—and Likud will do nothing to change that."

"*Occupation* is a loaded word."

"It is an accurate word."

"We fought for that land and won it."

"But it's not ours," Pauline said. "Another people live there."

"If we'd thought like that, there would never have been an Israel."

They argued a lot, and not just about politics. A third child, whom I will call Yonatan—curly-haired, doe-eyed Yonatan—was born in 1978. With three young children, pressure on Pauline mounted. Meyer was gone much of the time at the hospital or on overseas trips, and when he was home, it often seemed to her, he specialized in silence. They would go to a movie, and when they emerged, he said nothing, and she would ask: *Well, did you think anything of it? Anything at all you might care to pass along?* He was a black hole.

Meyer felt he was at his best when dealing with an exact, identifiable reality, but Pauline's moods remained an enigma. Their intensity overwhelmed him. Then the furies were gone, tropical storms that had passed through. He flapped around after them, like a sail when the wind drops.

She knew he expected an apology after their fights. He had to be vindicated. Remoteness was his fortress. He even called himself the Rock of Gibraltar! Silence is a master from Gibraltar. Pauline sometimes laughed at her fate. It was not that she wanted him to *gossip*, but he might lighten up, crack a joke, or even discover his inner frivolity. Was the sum of life's achievements really the ability never to raise one's voice?

Her feelings for him had always involved a thought process, which in itself said something. Did she love him? she wondered. In my family "love" was not a word thrown around. It had to be earned even when it was most craved.

Still, Pauline believed they should preserve their marriage. The children were beautiful. Divorce was always a disaster. Her parents had stuck it out through years of misunderstanding and resentment. Her mother, who was not physically affectionate, found the intimacy absent in her marriage with her bridge partner, a dashing polyglot. A few people muttered at the Houghton Golf Club; otherwise nobody seemed to notice. Time did not cure things but it did even them out. Meyer, who had loved Pauline with a passion but was not good at expressing feelings, burrowed deeper into his frustration, convinced that love was an abstraction to her, something she could not communicate with warmth or consistency, at least to him.

Meyer had been trained as a gastroenterologist but opted to stay in general medicine, before gradually migrating toward behavioral medicine. He specialized in stress and suffering. It was the large gray area between psychiatry and medicine that intrigued him. He called himself a "lumper," a doctor who enjoyed bringing disparate threads together. As a physician, he saw a lot of psychosomatic problems he felt psychiatrists were not giving him the tools to deal with. He knew, for example, that there was no such thing as recurrent or chronic pain without a psychological element. He began to work on theories of stress. Were the issues that threw somebody into stress as varied as each individual personality, or were there commonalities? He concluded that it is, above all, loss of control that defines stress. As he liked to put it, "There is a one-to-one relationship between feelings of control and the feelings of self-confidence an individual has."

When Rena was seven, a French psychiatrist friend came to visit Meyer in his office at Hadassah hospital. He had pinned up a couple of Rena's pictures. One was of a sparkling blue sky, sun, and butterflies. The other caught the psychiatrist's eye.

"Is your daughter depressed?" she asked.

"No. Why?"

"Look at that picture! All that black paint. In my experience this usually means depression."

"My daughter could not be sweeter or sunnier."

"Are you sure?"

Meyer shrugged off the conversation. But he would return to it many times and wonder—as any parent who survives a child must—what else he might have done.

That was about the time Pauline fell ill, in the aftermath of the 1982 Israeli invasion of Lebanon and the massacre by a rightist Christian militia of at least eight hundred civilians in two Palestinian camps. The slaughter at Sabra and Shatila, carried out with Israeli forces surrounding the camps and illuminating their narrow alleys with flares, would lead to the resignation of Ariel Sharon, then the defense minister.

Pauline was the sickest person Meyer ever saw recover. He had been convinced that it was the end, that the children were about to lose their mother. The illness began with a severe pain in her neck. By the time she was admitted to hospital, she was critically ill with an unbearable pain deep in her skull, an aggressive streptococcal infection. She went straight into intensive care. Meyer sat at her bedside. She was unconscious most of the time. Toxins had overcome her. In desperation, he suggested a total blood exchange. This was still an unusual treatment in infectious diseases. Meyer appealed to the head hematologist, who agreed it was worth the risk.

New plasma saved Pauline's life. She was in the hospital for months, enduring several major operations to treat the damage resulting from deep abscesses. Friends rallied to help Meyer with the children. Israel is good at support in a crisis. The children's visits to Pauline were traumatic. Her hospital room was down the corridor from a burn unit, where soldiers from the war in Lebanon were being treated. Terrible screams would issue from the ward as wounds were cleaned and dressed.

"It would probably have been better if we had never heard those screams," Yaakov tells me. "Mom being sick was bad enough."

The screams were intruders. Lives in Israel, however placid on the surface, cannot be cocooned from the "conflict." The Jewish national home is ever more comfortable, to the point where it is easy to forget that the foundations are uncertain. A window slams on a bus. A sleeping IDF soldier awakens with a start clutching his rifle, terror etched on his face, a vivid portrait of the hair-trigger, lock-and-load Israeli condition. A seven-year-old girl visiting her mother in hospital is traumatized by the sound of screaming.

On Rena's eighth birthday, her parents were at the hospital. A close family friend took her to the Israel Museum to see the movie *The Red Balloon*. She watched transfixed as the little boy hero, having lost his beloved red balloon to thugs, is lifted over the rooftops of Paris by a host of multicolored balloons that come to console him and carry him away over the zinc rooftops into a magical pure blue sky.

Rena always dreamed of a simpler, more harmonious life, an end to the "situation." Like my mother, she wanted things to be just right. In her journal she wrote:

It is all so hard, it's so hard. It's all so hard, it's so hard. I dream my dream. I'm sane, I'm insane. What is sacred? What embodies the soul? What is worth living for? What is worth dying for? Love.

CHAPTER 11

Death in the Holy Land

My cousin Yaakov Levin, a tall man with the soulful Michel eyes, lives in a small apartment on Zweifel Street in Tel Aviv. *Zweifel* means "doubt" in German. It is a quiet area of small houses and lush gardens far from the hum of the city center. A few years ago he and his wife, Maya, broke up. Yaakov lives alone, with weekly visits from his two children. He likes his wine—a taste developed during a year spent in France earning a business degree—and enjoys jazz.

One evening, his son and daughter asleep in their bunk bed, we sip an acceptable new Israeli cru, nibble more-than-acceptable cheese, and tell family stories. A scented breeze carries the wistful sounds of Yusef Lateef, an American jazz musician who, when he converted to Islam, changed his name. The great-grandchildren of the South African patriarch Isaac Michel, who was rich as Bavaria and sent money to Israel soon after its birth in 1948, we have met at last in the restless, wired city founded by Jews in Palestine just over a century ago.

Yaakov hands me something he wrote about his sister, Rena, who changed her name to Renata:

It has been a dark year without you, a year of un-living you. Birthdays, holidays and just plain old days, time slowly tearing the fabric of your life away. Memories of us all laughing our heads off around a Friday night table, with your sweet gentle giggle lingering in the air like a fading dream. I dreamt Maya and I gave birth to a baby girl. I am alone walking empty street drinking myself numb. I stop by a wall a man was painting portraits on. Every day he had made a different portrait. Returning home I find myself locking the front door in fear. The baby, the portraits, are you, my memories of you or me un-living you, Rena. If only I could hug the baby girl in my arms. If only I could stop the memories, the portraits from changing, from fading.

Yaakov calls the times when he is overwhelmed by memory "Rena moments." I am reminded of lines of W. G. Sebald: "Writing is the only way in which I am able to cope with the memories which overwhelm me. . . . Memories lie slumbering within us for months and years, quietly proliferating, until they are woken by some trifle and in some strange way blind us to life."

"When did you first notice Rena's depression?" I ask.

"Well, it's hard to say. I was her outspoken older brother, and I did not give her a lot of space, and at times I thought maybe she was a little sad. But around the time of the divorce, I guess something shifted."

"What shifted?"

"Divorce is insoluble to a child. There are more variables than you have equations."

Yaakov was eighteen at the time of Meyer and Pauline's divorce and away in the army. Rena was sixteen and took the brunt of it. She was very close to her father. She would listen to Pauline sobbing behind closed doors. Curly-haired Yonatan was thirteen.

"What happened?" I ask.

"It was pretty simple in the end. Dad didn't come home. Explanations and heart-to-hearts were not really his thing at the time."

It was a decision Meyer had been mulling for several years. In 1987 he had gone with Pauline and the children to Los Angeles for a one-year sabbatical at UCLA. He had begun to grasp the downside of his stability. Perhaps it prevented him from seeing and feeling things of which he should have been aware. He sought psychiatric help. At a group therapy session he talked for three minutes about his life. That was enough. A woman said, "Boy, you sound depressed." Meyer understood for the first time that his steady demeanor was a survival mechanism.

The patterns established by couples can be as destructive and immovable as the stereotypes of two nations at war. He and Pauline had struggled with incomprehension for so long, they no longer even tried to identify what it was they were missing about each other. After Los Angeles, he put off the moment only for the sake of the children. Finally, in 1991, while at a conference in the Washington area, he called Pauline to say he would not be returning. (The family had moved by now to a larger home in the Ramot area of Jerusalem.)

Pauline had been unhappy with Meyer for a long time, but that, she had always felt, was part of the marital condition. Marriage was a contract, an arrangement that bridled human instinct for the sake of societal stability. Love was all of life, yet it could not be more than a fleeting escape from self. In bridge, her mother's consolation in marital misery, you played even a bad hand to the very end.

Yaakov delivered a stark verdict: "You fucked up, Dad." Rena did not show her anger. She was quieter than usual. When she met with a cousin visiting from Denver, she cried inconsolably before gathering her strength to tell him: "I just want them both to be happy. It is time each of them found their happiness." That was Rena, the peacemaker.

In 1991 Yaakov was spending most of his time in the West Bank. He had wanted to do his military service as a pilot and had gone through a battery of tests for admission to the air force. He passed every exam, but just before his service was to begin, he suffered a tiny puncture of a lung. Instead of joining an elite unit, he was drafted into the civil administration in Hebron, overseeing the lives of Palestinians under occupation. It was a painful experience.

"You are put in an impossible situation," he says. "You realize the way things are run—you see the occupation up close. You are treating families in a way you would not want your own family to be treated. It is as simple as that. There's this sense of injustice. You have control of their lives—births, deaths, taxes, property, movement, everything. I remember going into Palestinian homes in the middle of the night to arrest people, the screams and the chaos. I found it hard to take."

He would travel by bus every morning from the base to his office, through the central market, a sea of hostile Palestinian faces. He could never get used to it. The First Intifada was dying down, but not its impact on Israeli and Palestinian alike. Once he saw a Jewish boy, no more than ten years old, running through the maze of Arab market stalls and wondered if the child felt his fear. In sweaty palms he clutched his rifle to his thumping heart.

The army had placed Yaakov at the epicenter of the conflict. Hebron, revered by Jews and Muslims alike, is a sacred battleground where, as in Jerusalem, interwoven religious passions and a long trail of violence banish reason. If history enlightens, it is equally true that too much history can blind.

Abraham is buried in Hebron alongside his wife, Sarah. He is the first Patriarch to the Jews; a prophet called Ibrahim and a model for mankind to Muslims; and a forefather who battled idolatry for all three ancient monotheistic religions. To the eight thousand Jewish settlers in the town itself and in the adjacent settlement of Kiryat Arba, this is the first Jewish city in the heart of the biblical hills of Judea and Samaria. How, they ask, in such a place, can they be "occupiers"? To the Palestinian majority, who number some 175,000, this is their centuries-old home under an Israeli military occupation dedicated to the protection of a small number of Jewish fanatics.

The town, a commercial center, snakes over hills. The situation has not improved since my cousin ended his service in 1994. In some parts, the homes of Palestinians and Israeli settlers are perhaps sixty feet apart. Yet there is no contact between them. Bullet holes in the walls of their respective homes are shown off to prove the irremediable violence of the other. The past is pored over, an immense repository of spilled blood that justifies more bloodletting. The features of feared neighbors are blotted out.

Slaughter is the hook on which each side hitches its identity: the killing of twelve Israelis by Palestinian snipers in 2002 as settlers returned from Friday-night prayers; the 1994 murder of twenty-nine Muslims at prayer by Baruch Goldstein, a Brooklyn-raised doctor from Kiryat Arba; the killing, also on the Sabbath, of six Jews in 1980; the massacre of dozens of Hebron Jews by Arab residents in 1929, their bodies mutilated, limbs hacked off, faces smudged by blows. Ever backward the cycle goes, all the way to Abraham's decision, several thousand years ago, to acquire a cave here for his family's burial.

Violence turns most intense when inflicted on one's likeness. The mirror image must be bludgeoned out. Today in Hebron, the descendants of Abraham and the descendants of Ibrahim—the same man— are locked in hatred. Some roads are known as *tzir sterili,* or "sterile roads," by the Israel Defense Forces, because no Palestinian is allowed to travel on them whether in a car or on foot. Jews and Arabs enter Abraham's tomb through separate entrances. Religion becomes a claim to real estate. The conflict's creeping diktat is separation. The mingling in the wadi of Yaakov's childhood has drained away. In the end, the question before the two peoples is whether winning an argument is worth more than a child's life. Competitive victimhood produces nothing. When the dead hold sway over the living, the future is blotted out. Words like *destiny* and *divine right* brook no contradiction. The Holy Land needs prosaic words.

The West Bank occupation was almost a quarter century old when my cousin was put to work in its service. It is now close to a half century old. At its outset, the philosopher Yeshayahu Leibowitz warned that if Israel tried to rule another people, "the corruption characteristic of every colonial regime will also prevail in the State of Israel." No democracy can be immune to running an undemocratic system of oppression in territory under its control. To have citizens on one side of an invisible line and subjects without rights on the other side of that line does not work. A democracy needs borders. Since 1967 Israel's has slithered into military rule for Palestinians in occupied areas where state-subsidized Jewish settlers have the right to vote as if within Israel. The problem is evident.

The nationalist-religious credo that the West Bank was land promised to Abraham's descendants has intensified over the past half century. Settlers see their work as the culmination of the Zionist idea of settlement. The opposite is true. Israel has undermined its Zionist founders' commitment to a democratic state governed by laws. Gershom Gorenberg puts the issue with great clarity in *The Unmaking of Israel:* "If Israel really believed that the territorial division created by the 1949 armistice was null and void, it could have asserted its sovereignty in all of former Palestine—and granted the vote and other democratic rights to all inhabitants." It chose not to. The reason was evident: the size of the Palestinian population—1.1 million in the West Bank and Gaza in 1967, 4.4 million today—would have meant the end of the Jewish state. And so Israel "behaved as if the territories were part of Israel for the purpose of settlement, and under military occupation for the purpose of ruling the Palestinians."

Humiliation of the occupied becomes a way of life. In Hebron, I once crossed the lines, after talking to settlers who described every Palestinian as a murderer, and found myself in conversation with Feryal Abu Haikal, the headmistress of a girls' school. Israeli soldiers had burst into her home twice the previous year, shot up the refrigerator, shot up the bathroom, destroyed a fax machine. Her husband, a contractor, was having difficulty maintaining his business because the barriers to travel across the West Bank had become so intricate. As we talked, her cell phone rang; her daughter was calling from China, where she was on a business trip. Other local children were studying at colleges in Turkey and Cairo. Palestinians, like Jews, put a high value on their children's education; incitement is not the whole story.

"If there is hope or no hope, we are here," the headmistress told me. "Not to make anyone happy. Not to make anyone angry. But we are here. Can you imagine that you would leave your home for any reason?"

The temptation to exclude, subjugate, and exploit "the other" is always there—whether the shtetl Jew, the black "kaffir," or the oppressed Palestinian—and justifications will be found. The family journey from Lithuania to South Africa and beyond had demonstrated that. But no people has more ethical reason to resist the inebriation of domination than the Jews, most of whose history has involved exclusion imposed by the powerful.

The Talmud portrays humanity as beginning from a single person and declares on this basis: "Whoever destroys one life, it is as if he destroyed an entire world, and whoever sustains one life, it is as if he sustained an entire world." The Talmud also says: "Hold too much, and you will hold nothing."

Israel, surrounded by Arab hostility, facing movements like Hamas that call for its destruction, in thrall to fears that no amount of power allays, has succumbed to the very temptation of unrestrained rule over others that the Jewish experience most decries. Such dominion can endure only at an unacceptable price. Israel cannot be a Jewish democratic state and at the same time control the lives of millions of Palestinians. It was this conviction—that the cost to Israel of policing another people was unbearable over time—that persuaded Prime Minister Yitzhak Rabin to seek a land-for-peace deal with his enemy, Yasser Arafat, the Palestinian leader.

Rabin's assassin, Yigal Amir, was an admirer of Baruch Goldstein, the mass killer of Hebron. Like Gandhi, assassinated by a fanatical Hindu convinced the mahatma was giving too much away to India's Muslims, Rabin was murdered by one of his own, a fellow Jew convinced the Israeli prime minister and war hero was ceding too much to Palestinians. Jew killed Jew over the political issue that divided Meyer and Pauline: whether the modern state of Israel, born out of a UN resolution that divided the territory of Mandate Palestine, had a right to all the biblical Land of Israel or should seek territorial compromise in the quest for peace.

The entitlement view was put forth with eminent straightforwardness by Israel's former prime minister Yitzhak Shamir: "Eretz Yisrael is ours. Why? Because, without any justification or explanations, it is."

Few assassinations have proved as effective as Rabin's. Gandhi's put a brake on India's communal slaughter, but Rabin's accelerated Israeli-Palestinian estrangement. The ascendancy of religious-nationalist ideology was assured. The painful concessions needed from both sides for peace were shelved. Yet the loss of Rabin and the continued expansion of settlements only accentuated Israel's dilemma. The country prospered, becoming a miracle of rapid development. It was perched still on the brittle foundation of coercion of another people.

"The aggression in Israel is a reflection of the corrupting force of the occupation," Yaakov tells me. "Generations of kids, myself included, served in the West Bank and treated the Palestinians the way we did. I had to get out of Hebron. I had to tell my commanders the situation was driving me crazy, I could not take it. You lord it over these people, and then you come back home, and you bring these attitudes with you. We know where the border of Israel is. There is even a wall now to give us a general idea. So we have to look at our consciences and act.

Do we want to remain a Jewish state? Do we want to remain a decent people?"

Rena began her military service in 1992. In some ways, it was a relief. After her parents' separation, she broke up with Aron, her high school sweetheart. Meyer was often busy at the hospital; Pauline had developed a career as an English teacher and a guide at the Israel Museum. Rena felt a void inside. "In order to have self-expression," she wrote, "we must first have a self to express."

Who was she? Rena wanted to give to people but was not sure how. She was gentle. Perhaps she needed to be more assertive. She felt spiritual, not religious, in need of some framework now that the family was shattered. She believed in God. No, she believed in *a* God. No, she believed in the existence of the divine. But that did not help her. It was not an organizing principle for her life. She noted a line of Dostoyevsky's: "Taking a new step, uttering a new word is what people fear most." To overcome fear, that was her issue, and to gain self-esteem. Her mother had been so glamorous, so beautiful, and so cosmopolitan journeying around Europe. She felt she was none of these things.

After high school, after the First Intifada, she fantasized about escape, reinventing herself, perhaps in France or the United States or even India. In one moment of particular anguish, while Pauline was away in Cairo at a conference, she ran a sharp knife across her wrist and called a family friend. It was a cry for help.

In the army, after basic training, she did social work, traveling to the homes of conscripts from difficult backgrounds. The assignment took her all over Israel for the first time—to Haifa, Ashdod, Beersheba, Petah Tikva, Eilat. She was moved by the diversity of the country. The stoicism of its women struck her—widows whose only sons were serving in the West Bank or in Gaza, mothers who had already lost a child. To carry on in the knowledge that your life could never be whole again after the loss of a child seemed the most remarkable form of courage.

Her military service ended in 1994. She enrolled in Hebrew University to do a degree in art history and education. Seeking to continue her social work, she took a job in a home for people with mild forms of mental illness, lost souls who would have ended up in the streets. She had a series of photographs taken of her with the residents, her arm around them, smiling. Meyer was struck by how she had chosen to sit with them rather than photograph them herself.

The Oslo peace accords and Rabin's handshake with Arafat on the White House lawn raised for the first time in Rena's life the possibility of an end to the conflict. Approaching her twenty-first birthday, she allowed herself to believe for a moment that Israel could resolve its existential dilemma and find its place in an angry neighborhood. It would be good for her country to settle on its contours.

She traveled to Europe, as her mother had at the same age, and sent her a photograph from Italy similar to one she had seen of Pauline in her youth. Rena is seated at a window, in profile against a backdrop of the Mediterranean coast with her hand on her chin, a faraway look in her eyes. She is wearing a black shirt and earrings with a black pendant. Despite the beauty of her surroundings, my cousin appears to be looking in rather than out, consumed like my mother by her inner demons, my mother who in Italy had stayed at the Gritti Palace in Venice and thought only of death by drowning in the Grand Canal.

"It was such a strange thing," Pauline says. "I sometimes asked myself: Is she trying to relive my life?"

Rena wanted to reconcile the beings in her. When Rabin was killed, she thought her country had gone mad. She twice traveled to India looking for peace and truth, doing Vipassana meditation to pacify her mind. In a journal she wrote, "The guru teaches you about your own strength, capacity, power, love—and draws out your goodness." She urged herself on: "It is a matter of being determined and having the spirit to break right through to the other side." She quoted a Chinese proverb: "Life moves in a positive direction. Get out of the way." She wanted to paint, she wanted to write, to be creative and to give—but that only brought her back to the elusive quest for an identifiable "self."

Rena took up with a fellow college student called Andrei, a recent immigrant from Russia. He was kind and sensitive. He grappled still with Hebrew as her parents had. His funny accent made her laugh. They had different political views—the Russian mind could not begin to grasp the notion of voluntarily giving up conquered land. (Had Russia given up the Kuril Islands?) But that did not seem to matter as they hiked in the Galilee or strolled along the Tel Aviv seafront. It was good to feel less alone even if the relationship was, she felt, not quite serious.

Everyone gathered for Yaakov's wedding in 1999. Already deep in therapy and trying to fathom what had happened in her parents' marriage, Rena felt distant. She had little sympathy for her brother's wife, Maya, whom he had met during his military service. Not for the first time, Rena felt she had to get away. She was drawn to the idea of practicing as an art therapist, putting her creative impulse to use to understand and help people, as she already had in her social work. When the University of Vancouver offered a place to do a master's, she did not hesitate.

She was lonely. The city was beautiful but left her cold. Canada left her cold. Fellow students had opinions on Israel, often critical ones, but it seemed to Rena they had no feeling for it, no sympathy with it, no gift of empathy that might open a path to understanding a fundamental Israeli condition—fear; the fear, however irrational, of the country's annihilation that was part of the national condition. What did they know of the widows and bereaved mothers of Ashdod? What did they know of the miracle of Hebrew apiaries and dairies rising from the barren land?

Zionism had succeeded against the odds. But it had not overcome Jewish fear after all. It had recast it in a different guise.

Rena could not sleep, racked by intractable thoughts swirling in circles. Intense bursts of energy during which she painted all night—large, colorful abstract paintings with great splashes of purple—alternated with spells of inertia. She lay in the bath and let the water run out. She gazed at the gossamer moon at first light. Days succeeded each other like tour groups filing into a museum, gloomy and hangdog. Nobody understood her. Nobody understood Israel.

She was lonely. Fulfillment with men had often eluded her. They pursued their own pleasure, they failed to understand hers, she could not feel them, and sometimes she was left with a dim anger. She wondered about her sexuality. She wondered about everything. She was unsettled. She did not want to cause a commotion.

At last it dawned on me that these obstacles were my life.

Israel was convulsed on Rena's return from Canada in the fall of 2001. Buses went up in balls of fire. Nights pivoted on the dull blast of an explosion. There was always a silence, an absolute stillness, afterward. Then the sirens and yelling and screaming started. Sometimes a second explosion was timed to hit the people converging to help. Nobody wanted to go near a bus or into a shopping mall. TV images were of one horror after another: the Ben Yehuda Street bombing (11 dead) on December 1, 2001; the Haifa bus bombing (15 dead) on December 2, 2001; the Yeshivat Beit Yisrael bombing (11 dead) on March 2, 2002; the Café Moment bombing (11 dead) on March 9, 2002; the Passover massacre (30 dead) on March 27, 2002; the Matza Restaurant bombing (16 dead) on March 31, 2002; the Rishon LeZion bombing (16 dead) on May 7, 2002. Rena tried to avert her gaze. She moved from confusion to ephemeral conviction and back again to confusion.

The Oslo peace process was in tatters, and President Bill Clinton's last-gasp efforts to reach an agreement were buried in a welter of mutual recrimination. Rabin's conviction—that quiet in the absence of peace could only be temporary and that therefore a compromise with the Palestinians had to be made—was vindicated. Suicide bombs became the Palestinian weapon of choice, martyrdom the brutal refuge of the weak as the Second Intifada raged. Palestinian recognition of Israel had not stopped relentless incitement to destroy it or violence toward that end. Israel's engagement in a peace process had not stopped the steady settlement construction that undercut a Palestinian state and underwrote the Jewish claim to all the land that had been evident in its acts and half-hidden by its words since 1967. Humiliating domination met murderous resistance. Victimhood fed victimhood. Violence was always the stranger knocking at the door of Israel's unfinished house.

Rena was diagnosed as bipolar and put on medication. She felt dulled by it. Her life energy drained out of her. She felt lost, unsure about what work to pursue. Pauline disliked her daughter's psychiatrist, a colleague of Meyer's in Jerusalem. He had a good reputation but lacked empathy. The medication did not seem right. Under the pressure of violence, everyone's nerves frayed.

At the National Lottery, Rena found a job in marketing, but she hated the cold calls and sales pitches. It was not in her to be false, and it took a lot out of her to generate enthusiasm. She rented the apartment on Shlomo Hamelech in Tel Aviv, beginning her daily meanders through the neighborhood. She sat at Shine Café (the cafés were emptier now) and watched the rain. Popular wisdom had it that when the rain fell straight down rather than at an angle, it was the last of the year.

Afterward the blue of the sky was more perfect and luminous than she could bear. Hagar, her closest friend, would sit with her at Shine. In a soft, calm voice, Rena would describe her troubles, her quest for the spiritual, for a connection beyond the material, and she spoke of her feelings of weakness, and Hagar would insist on her amazing courage in being able to smile in the face of agony and confusion. (Later Hagar would reflect on the café's name and Rena's smile that *shone* from the inside.)

At the corner of Spinoza and Gordon, there was a wooden bench with a canopy. Rena liked to sit there. She imagined herself under a chuppah. Would she ever stand under one to be wed? Could happiness ever be simple or shared? Aron had loved her. Andrei, too, in his way; they had seen each other for a while after her return, but like all the moving parts in her life, she and he did not quite mesh.

In her journal she wrote:

Yesterday was a very important day. Andrei and I said goodbye to each other. It was sad then but today with the sadness I feel relief and a certain sense of freedom. We reached a stage where it could either be all or nothing. He started mentioning things like marriage and family and how he thinks I am ready for that because it is such a noble thing—to raise kids, have a family and all. It is the hardest thing there is, he says, and he is not able to handle it, he thinks poorly of himself in this regard. I told him I'm not ready now. I still need some time. Not that he proposed to me or anything. He is very precious and unique. I had no expectations of him in Vancouver but when I got back we got close again and expectations follow like a tail to make things tricky. This is a responsible decision and I am thankful that he is doing his best to make it less hard for both of us. I trust him completely as a friend but former lovers cannot be friends. It is simply impossible.

Depending on the day, she could be quiet or feverish. When Yaakov was with Pauline at her Jerusalem apartment, Rena arrived carrying a chair she had bought at the flea market. It was heavy, but she was so manic, she did not know how far she had walked with it. She picked up the one-year-old Uri. A shadow fell across her face. "I can feel he's suffering," she said. "I can feel he's unquiet."

Yaakov was spooked. Rena's illness was frightening. She had no boundaries. The suffering of others, real or imagined, compounded hers. It was hard to talk about it or confront her. He did not want to make her uncomfortable. At the same time he felt he should do something. She was alone in a dark place peopled by demons. On January 5, 2003, two Palestinian suicide bombers blew themselves up outside the Tel Aviv bus station, killing twenty-three people. The city was nervy, on edge all the time. A little over a month later, on February 16, it was Yaakov's birthday. "Rena was so low," he recalled. "She came with my dad. It was like she was dragging herself on the floor. She was slumped on the couch. There was this tension between us. I can't help feeling we could have been there for her in a different way. We wanted to do the right thing but all we came up with was awkwardness."

Later that month, on the eve of the Iraq War, Rena went to South Africa with Pauline. Her mother had been offered a "repatriation" ticket by her employer to get her out of harm's way during George W. Bush's war. Throughout the trip Rena was depressed. Reunions with cousins and the beauty of what they still called the "old country" could not shake her mood. Once, near the end, Rena told a close friend she wanted to know more about Judaism. What Renata the reborn was saying was that she wanted to get closer to God.

Sometimes she would meet with Yaakov at a neighborhood café. Often he was late, blaming work. She wanted to get close to him again. His marriage to Maya had created a distance—and now they had little Uri. She had begun therapy and urged her brother to do the same.

"Thanks, really. But I'm all right," Yaakov said. "Everything is fine. And besides it's terribly expensive, and we do not have enough now with the baby, and the usual spending, you know."

"I'll help you, if that's the problem," Rena said. "I'll clean houses, find another job, anything to help you, help us. It will work out, you'll see."

"But I'm all right, all right, really."

"I need you to help me fill in the picture," Rena insisted gently.

"Which picture?"

"The whole picture—Mom, Dad, the divorce, our life here in Israel, our Jewish identity, South Africa, the past. I am trying to understand how I got to this point, discover who I really am. You know, sometimes I feel like a transplant that did not take."

"Rena, I don't think I can go over that again now."

"Okay. But one day."

She smiled, before adding: "And, you know, I'm Renata now!"

Later, after his sister's death, Yaakov began sessions with a therapist he had seen years earlier. He found himself going back to childhood days in Israel, to Pauline's illness, to the California sabbatical, to the divorce, and as he did so, more and more pain and anger surfaced, and he found himself cursing the fact that all he had was his single account, and Rena, who had been there with him, who had been through everything with him, was gone; and throat choking, sobs welling up, he sees how alone she had been with her memories and how, in her anguish, she had wanted to sift through them with him because she thought it might help; and he remembers how she had told him, with a laugh, that he had often bitten her when they were children; and in his dreams he runs back to the same café, where he had been late, hurrying, hurrying to find Rena and ask for forgiveness, forgiveness for being late, forgiveness for everything, and hug her and hold her and go over their lost, shared memories together.

Rena would ride the bus down Dizengoff Street out to Bar-Ilan University in Ramat Gan. She gazed at the shoppers pouring into the stores and malls—this modern capitalist state of Israel that had taken form around her, almost overnight it sometimes seemed. She had been born into a raw country where the communal spirit of the kibbutz lingered still. Now she lived in a rich one of high-tech start-ups and high-priced brands and material obsessions, and if you allowed yourself to dream a little, you might imagine you were in California.

Not for long: her journey was punctuated with cries of *"Rega! Rega!"*—"Wait!"—as the gum-chewing, unshaven drivers tried to hurry the doors shut against some struggling grandmother or straggling child, and passengers eyed one another, making instant inspections of suspect packages or bags, rapid threat assessments of potential Palestinian suicide bombers. Suicide to kill others—it was a strange idea, and it seemed to be everywhere. Or perhaps it was not so strange, given the aggression in suicide. She could not think straight. The idea of it haunted her. On into Tel Aviv's eastern sprawl she went, leaving the Mediterranean behind, crossing the eight lanes of the Ayalon, or ring road, past the Azrieli Center towers, which had gone up a few years earlier at the former location of the city's garbage truck parking garage. She felt her gaze tugged toward the skyscrapers. Rectangular and circular, male and female, they loomed over the ramshackle sprawl of Tel Aviv, their glint greenish and magnetic and sickly in the sunlight.

It was a relief to get off the bus. Bar-Ilan was a haven, a large campus of lovely trees and unlovely buildings, as much an architectural hodgepodge as Tel Aviv itself. It had been founded in 1955 with the aim of blending the teaching of Talmud and secular academic studies. It sought to synthesize the ancient and modern, the sacred and the material, the spiritual and the scientific.

Through an old friend of the family, Naomi Becker (not her real name), Rena had secured a job helping out in the music school at the university's Yehuda Amir Institute for the Advancement of Social Integration. Becker, another South African drawn to Israel by the desire to make a personal contribution to the building of a Jewish state, had done her doctorate on children's musical understanding, with a focus on a Zulu song. Her department created teaching programs in music: material for kindergarten and schools, exercises for teachers, courses in music therapy. Rena was particularly active in a project developed for the Jaffa Institute, a center for Jewish and Arab children from underprivileged backgrounds who would go there after school, get a hot meal, and attend a variety of classes. Rena made a video chronicling the children's progress.

Everyone liked Rena. She was quiet, cooperative, and responsible. She was natural, a young woman without airs. Her soft, low voice was soothing, her smile gentle. Nobody could know the courage it took sometimes to produce that sweet smile. If you happened to mention you had not had anything to eat, she would be back with a sandwich. When somebody left the department, she arranged the gift. She felt they were a great team and let that be known. She played the piano. She had a strong social conscience. She combined the qualities needed to get ahead. But when Becker suggested she could go further, perhaps move into the administration, she demurred. She still did not know what to do with her life.

Becker knew through Rena's parents of her mental difficulties, but they were not apparent. Nobody else in the department seems to have been aware of them. "Some days she would say she could not concentrate," Becker said. "I'd say, Take a break and come back later. There were times she was more bubbly, and others when she was very quiet, but not, it seemed to me, beyond normal mood swings."

Rena's uncertainty about her future was a regular subject of conversation. "We had long talks about that. She started a course in communications. She talked about pursuing art therapy. She took yoga classes. One day she arrived very low. We were going to install a stand with our music materials for a conference at a sports center, and it was very hot. She had to load and unload and set up all the stuff, and you know, by the end of the day, she was elated! There was someone there teaching capoeira. She'd decided to do a course."

That was Rena, always questioning, tripping, and getting up again.

On Wednesday, April 30, 2003, Rena and her mother have breakfast on Gordon Street. It is a beautiful day. The pomegranate juice is sweet. They head for the beach. On the way they pass a young army recruit in her olive-green uniform, chewing gum, rifle at her side. Rena notices her pearl earrings and the reddish-brown-and-gold Shulamith hair cascading out from under her orange beret. Her black boots are polished. Perhaps she is going to an IDF rehearsal for Yom Hazikaron, Remembrance Day, which will begin in a week. Rena likes the solemnity and silence of that day as the fallen for Israel are recalled, and the way it flows into the celebrations and picnics marking Independence Day, when flags and pennants are everywhere and pride in the achievements of the young nation is irrepressible and air force jets streak across the blue sky in formation.

At the corner of Ben Yehuda and Gordon, there is a store selling T-shirts. She notices one that says, "America don't worry, Israel is behind you," and manages a half-smile. Someone behind her, talking real estate, says, "If you miss it, you miss it—you know how life is." The story of Israel and Palestine, she thinks, is a story of missed opportunities. But then perhaps there is no room for both, just as there seems to be no place where Rena belongs, precisely. Oh, sometimes, she just wants to stop her brain, decouple it from whatever current keeps prodding it in different directions. Life is just one snake-oil salesman after another, hustling to make a buck. Not even Zionism could resist that. The kibbutzim seem quaint these days, renouncing possessions, sharing their passion. Even the generals have brokers. Oh, the heat. Life is molten, like gold. She wants to be in a place so quiet that all she can hear is her breathing. She wants to live in a place that is not a "situation." She wants to swim out two hundred meters into the ocean and dispose of all her pills, the pills that steal her energy, the pills that muffle and cover up and falsify. The pills she hates. No, more than hates—hate is like love—it is more implacable than that. It is loathing. She wants a life within defined borders.

Rena shuts her eyes. She can still taste the cardamom in the coffee. It fades slowly like the sound she loves of the ram's horn. You have to be perfect in a new country, almost armor-plated, in order to adapt and belong and survive transplantation. Dad worked so hard. He helped, day after day, to build Israel, a noble undertaking after all. This beautiful Hebrew language had been as good as dead a century ago! Mom learned Israel through its archaeology and guided tourists through the Israel Museum. That was also noble. They were good people. They were decent people. Meyer-Dude with his data! They did their best and fucked up like all parents do. An unhappy marriage is unhappier in an adopted land. Our longings are merciless. It had not been simple for Pauline to remake her life. When Rena was nine, she had prayed at the Western Wall for her ears to be pierced. Her cousin from Cleveland prayed for a Pontiac Firebird Trans-Am. Or was it a Mustang? The city hums. The children chatter. The malls murmur, *Buy me, buy me, buy me.* What's that cosmetic where body meets soul? Why is life always glimpsed as if through the slats of a blind? All the dogs here in upscale Tel Aviv are groomed, unlike the stray dogs down in the wadi of her childhood, where the figs broke their skins in their ripeness and she tossed pebbles into the brook. Before the aggression came and took over, the shouting and the shoving, the high-tech miracle with all its intoxicating millions, cars nosing in front of each other, never giving way at intersections. Intersections, dreams of surgeons cutting into her, getting sectioned, admitted to hospital whether you liked it or not, her scarred ovary with its emptied follicles, cesarean sections. She would wake up in a cold sweat.

Rena does not know what she can say to her mother to convey the raging in her mind. They stroll up and down the beach beside the sea where the sand is firm. Police are everywhere; there has been another suicide bombing early that morning, at Mike's Place on the beach. Three Israelis have been killed. It would have been much worse if the security guard had not stopped the bombers from getting inside. You can be dead with scarcely a scratch depending on how the shrapnel sprays.

Rena tells Pauline about her sleep issue, about her job issue, about her indecision issue, about her medication issue, about her intifada issue, about her Iraq War issue, about her fatigue issue, about her psychiatrist-in-Jerusalem issue. She does not talk about the madness issue. That might be awkward. She was brushed with madness like a truffle brushed with cocoa dust! *Mom, I'm crazy!* Would that work? Nor about the fear issue, which comes and goes. *Mom, I'm scared shitless I'm going to kill myself!* Oy, life can be heavy. We have learned, here in the home of the Jews, how not to say things clearly, how not to talk about the Palestinian villages that were emptied, how not to talk about the nuclear missiles at Dimona, how not to talk about the occupation, how not to talk about where Israel's borders lie. I've been scared all my life, Rena thinks. *Yiush,* she whispers, so lovely in Hebrew: despair. *Yiush-yiush-yiush,* like the sea receding.

"What would you like to do? What do you feel like doing?" Pauline says.

"I would like to go somewhere else."

The words hang there in their vapor of ambiguity.

"Somewhere else?"

"Yes, Mom, somewhere else."

"You mean, like abroad?"

"No, Mom, not abroad. Israel is my home. I've tried that. Maybe a moshav, a village community. Somewhere very quiet. I have to leave my job. Naomi is so good to me, and I love the kids in Jaffa, but it just isn't working for me."

"At least it's a job."

"But I'm tired. I don't want to take the medication anymore. I'm flat."

Pauline is silent. She feels helpless. Perhaps if Rena comes up to Jerusalem over the weekend, they can talk to the psychiatrist, see what Meyer thinks, and plan some new course. That would be a good first step. The medication cannot be right if it makes Rena feel awful. But then, would she feel worse without it? They stroll back up Gordon. A shutter is slammed shut. Everyone is jumpy. At a café a man is seated with a notebook. The city is full of journalists covering the intifada. To be paid to observe life—that would not be bad. Rena thinks she might be able to tell stories even if she is not sure she could order the facts. Or decide what the facts are—because, ha-ha, here everyone has a different set of "facts." She might be able to describe painful situations, but she is not sure she could walk away from them afterward. Yes, life is molten, like gold. She is not sure she could separate one strand from another, deploy inadequate words and package life into stories.

Rena goes to work, and that afternoon Pauline returns to Jerusalem. Dusk falls. Rena wanders the streets of a rattled Tel Aviv. She cannot think straight. Her footsteps cloy as if in mud. She feels she may fall. She will go to Jerusalem Thursday and talk to the doctor.

That night she scarcely sleeps. When she lies on her left side, she feels her heart thumping. Her mouth is dry, she feels hot, close to panic.

Thursday morning is May 1. It is a time of rebirth. No more bombs had exploded the night before. What was that song they played at work whose first line was "Even on a heavy, hot day"? Rena crawls out of bed. May! Trees are budding. She forces herself to dress and go board the bus out past the Azrieli towers with their sickly greenish glint. She gazes at them, as usual. The serried ranks of the high-rises are dense as organ pipes. They have never looked so hideous. She is late for work. She hates being late. She believes in serious, committed work. She believes in her Israel, a place at last where Jews belong, if only she could *feel* her belonging.

That morning, in a drawer, she has stumbled on a passage she had written down in Canada: "It is an individual choice how long you want to hold on to the tree of life, how long before you feel that you have shown your true colors and lived your life. If you have lived your life and had your moment then it will be much easier to let go. You will know and your loved ones will know your unique beauty and it will be something they remember and live with. Then you truly achieve immortality."

Yiush-yiush-yiush: the whisperer-reaper who will not go away. It is death that turns time into a living thing.

She will go on. She will persevere. The trees offer welcome shade on the Bar-Ilan campus. There is Naomi Becker with her big smile—such a good, kind woman. Rena thinks of the children in Jaffa covering their faces with their hands in shyness, singing scales, learning how to measure time through rhythm, learning that there is a time for self-expression, and a time for another's expression, and a time for joint expression. Music demanded mutual respect. It was a valuable lesson for children.

And now, in the way time skips for her these days, Rena is in Naomi's cramped little office telling her that things are not good and that, for the first time, she will have to leave early. She is suffering *intermittences.* "I'm so sorry, I feel so low. I'm very upset about my medication." She will go to Jerusalem for the weekend, see Mom and Dad and the psychiatrist. She will somehow pry the demons from her throat. Naomi tells her not to worry. Of course it is no problem to leave early. She is uneasy, however, and calls Meyer in Jerusalem.

Rena walks to the bus stop. In the distance a siren wails. The bus driver wears reflector shades. She closes her eyes. The city hums. A soldier's beret is tucked into her epaulet. Blue-and-white Israeli flags flutter here and there, the bunting of happy-uneasy Israel. Forgive me, forgive me. Kids with smiley cartoon figures on their T-shirts. *Stay gold, stay gold. This is life—it is not a situation. The only life you have, for all its obstacles.* The bus lurches and sways toward the city. What do the suicide bombers think before they detonate themselves? I am going somewhere else. The moon is like a fingernail.

At the Ayalon, Rena gets out. The Azrieli towers, magnetlike, attract her. It will be cool and fragrant and purring in the past-erasing mall. It will be the obverse of the Israel of the kibbutzniks who got their hands dirty to change the land and change Jews at the same time. On the escalator into the tower, she notices surveillance cameras. So there will be film of her. The store names and brand names and advertising slogans come at her in a gaudy torrent: SEXY SALE, CALL IT SPRING, TURN IT ON, KISS ME, IT'S A MAN'S WORLD, INTIMA LINGERIE, TAKE A DEEP BREATH, ONE LIFE LIVE IT WELL, BASIC IS BEAUTIFUL, IT'S A MAN'S WORLD, FOX BABY, MAGNOLIA, ZIP, REPLAY, CRAZY LINE, LIFE AIN'T JUST BLACK 'N' WHITE, IMPRESS, ELECTRIC SUMMER. This Israel of luxury articles and antidepressants is a stranger to her, perhaps a stranger to itself. Rena's head spins. She looks up at the sun slanting through the glass roof.

Mom and Dad will understand. It has been a long story and in the end an unbearable one. They will be better off without her burden. *I only tried to love you with the full wingspan of my heart. I'm sorry for causing such a commotion.* She must go elsewhere in order not to create any further disturbances. Her cell phone rings. It is Meyer calling from Jerusalem. She hesitates but does not pick up.

Now she stands on the second-floor terrace. The warm wind is in her face. Children dart about squealing, pursued by anxious parents. Two hundred feet below, people move on their set paths, disembodied little shapes. They are very busy going nowhere, like a cloud of gnats. Stop! On the far side of the broad ring road, a massive Israeli flag is draped down the side of a building. She presses her palms to those rosy cheeks. Independence Day is coming, picnics and gatherings and laughter. Israel will be fifty-five years old! And she will tumble, a lovely cousin with an old family curse, down the length of the flag she loves, the blue and white in which her Zionist great-grandfather's coffin was draped.

It will be quick. It will be better. It will be over. The lark sings—and then falls. Rena-Renata Levin jumps.

When Yaakov, later that afternoon, identifies his sister's broken body at the Abu Kabir morgue, he finds a note in her bag: "Dad, I love you. Mom, I love you. Yaakov, I love you. Yonatan, I love you. Uri, I love you. Stay gold."

That is all.

CHAPTER 12

The Ghosts of Repetition

Almost two years after my mother died, we brought her spirit home. At the West Park Jewish cemetery in Johannesburg, where her family is buried, we gathered to honor her. It was a day of blinding sunlight on the high reef. A fragrant storm-washed breeze coursed over the graves, the kind that used to ruffle June's curls on the prickly grass of Houghton. Beneath our feet, gravel crunched.

We walked to the back of the cemetery. There was the grave of the patriarch, Isaac Michel—"so dearly loved, so sorely missed by his wife, children and relatives." An urn stood beside it, donated by his "loving grandchildren," among them my mother. Jennie Michel, Isaac's long-suffering wife, died on January 15, 1955, six months before I was born. She had survived her beloved tormentor by just eighteen months. Only when she could no longer fight with him did she begin to miss him.

A plaque in a wall was unveiled to my mother's memory. Absent her ashes, that's all we could do. Her bravery made me weep. Once again, now in the Southern Hemisphere, I tried to capture some essence of her. "For most people, death succeeds life," I said. "But for my mother, I believe, life and death coexisted—she could feel and taste one in the other. As she knew death in life, so she now knows life in death."

Her mental illness, I recalled, would toss my mother this way and that—one minute she was a brisk, assertive, bustling bundle of energy, the next an inert creature crushed by mental pain. These states, each a distorted image of the true June, could provoke bewilderment and anguish in friends and family. In a soul as fragile as hers, it induced torment. She held in contempt the cancer that took her life, for she had known suffering of a far more potent kind.

My mother was home at last, almost half a century after she emigrated. To the land where she fell in love with my father, to her sanctuary, to her sunlight; and the exile that was also an inner exile was over. I thought of the chaos after her death, the scribbled notes discovered in coat pockets, the jewelry hidden here and there, the bequests not bequeathed, the copy of *The Joy of Sex* found at the bottom of a laundry basket (a cry for help from the bottom of a well), the disarray and black bile of despair. I thought of her cooing with laughter and her small acts of kindness and her tobacco-tinged scent and her delicate hand on the green tasseled rope banister of the last house in Hampstead and the way she wiped the tears from her eyes when she giggled and the confident way she knitted and the postcards she used to send from South Africa of straight-backed black women with jugs on their heads.

I thought of my father, remarried and absent now, and how he had tried to stand by my mother through everything, and the way she had thanked him with her last words, and his shattering grief when she died; and how, as sure as a law of physics, the survival arrangement he had made (and that had now surfaced in the form of his marriage) had held everyone at a distance because there was only so much intimacy such an arrangement could withstand. My parents' love had been twisted by the manic-depressive scourge, and yet it had persisted. My father was the fixed point of my mother's life, her one man, her only and forever man. This was not a fashionable idea but it was a powerful idea.

I cast my mind over all the confusion, how June's brother, Sydney, standing now beside me in the cemetery, short and stout in the Adler mold, had been obliged to intervene discreetly when June in one of her hyper states was caught pilfering lipstick and cosmetics from the Checkers department store in Killarney, and how she had given him hell for the thoughtfulness that got her out of trouble. It was not easy to help June. It could be bruising. Perhaps, since it was Checkers that acquired her grandfather's OK Bazaars for a single rand, June thought she was entitled to the lipstick—an insult repaid in kind. More likely she did not know what she was doing. I saw my mother in all her turbulence, in all her states, the multiple states whose depths I had to plumb to live.

Whenever June was in the United States, she would visit a cousin in Cleveland, Peta Moskowitz, who had emigrated from South Africa. She and Peta would go to the Cleveland Museum of Art. June had a particular favorite painting there, Van Gogh's portrait of Adeline Ravoux, finished in June 1890, a month before his death. Adeline is caught in profile, set against the infinite blue night, her gaze inward-looking, consumed by dark thoughts. It is a disturbing work in blacks, yellow, blues, and vibrant citrines. Van Gogh wrote to his sister Wille-mien, "I would like to do portraits which would look like apparitions to people a century later." The painting had the force of an apparition for June. She was transfixed before it. She would tell Peta, "I feel her angst"—and then, "Enough! It's time for a cup of tea." That was my mother, anguished but stoic.

The day we gathered, June's mother, Flossie, turned one hundred. My no-nonsense grandmother, with her cash hidden in the hems of curtains and in balls of wool and her belief in De Beers stock and a good broker, had lived the twentieth century from first to last. Her husband, Laurie, the *bon viveur* in his tank corps black beret with a cognac and a cigar, had died two years earlier at the age of ninety-eight, water never having passed his lips. They never fully grasped their daughter's illness. Few did.

South Africa was good to them. They never had to boil an egg.

The family is still here, postapartheid, diminished by departures to Australia and the United States and Britain and Israel, but hanging on. South Africa has looked after its Jews. Letting them live through the twentieth century was in itself a considerable gift. They rose steadily. The definition of chutzpah was a Jew who moved from the misery of Doornfontein to Houghton without passing through Highlands North. A cousin recalls his grandmother's familiar phrase: "Thank God for the blacks. If not for them it would be us, the Jews."

Now a few affluent blacks have moved into Houghton, as have many affluent Indians. The Michel mansion, where my parents met, has been subdivided. Gated communities with names like The Sky's the Limit are the rage. Security is the white community's obsession, not without reason. There is plenty of grumbling among them about the new order, about violent crime and gross inefficiency and rampant corruption in the governing African National Congress, as if they have forgotten the miracle of forgiveness and reconciliation that allowed them to stay on and prosper in this bountiful land of boundless black misery. You shouldn't complain of the cold on a lifeboat. Zimbabwe demonstrated how easily all might have been lost. I hear the familiar phrases—"You like it here, hey?" "Shame" "He's a brainbox" "Let me just go and put on my face" "I stopped at the robot"—and realize how deep in me South Africa resides, how necessary to me it is, the sunlit part of my youth even with its shadows. That also I inherited from my mother. Against all logic, it feels deeper in me than England.

At a gathering of the clan over Shabbat dinner, a cousin, Myron Pollack, says, "I feel like a visitor here. The future is for the blacks." Perhaps that is only right, I suggest. After all, for decades black South Africans were noncitizens barred even from work as bricklayers.

"I feel really angry that they couldn't lay bricks," Myron's wife, Jan, says.

Their son, Brett, a gifted and idealistic young attorney with fierce patriotic feelings about the new rainbow-nation South Africa, shoots back: "Why are you angry now, Mom, when you weren't thirty years ago?"

"I just am," Jan says.

"Your anger's useless now, Mom. Just drop it. When it would have been useful, you didn't have it."

Tension ripples over the chicken soup. Brett says, "I was just a Jewish kid who knew nothing. Now I'm starting to have a brain."

"I preferred you without one," Myron says, laughing.

"What is freedom to the blacks?" Brett asks. "It's just a word. They want sewage systems, houses, and schools. They want *justice*."

"Maybe," Myron says. "All I know is that before things worked."

"For whom?"

"Okay, for the whites, but they worked."

Myron and Jan have been tied up at gunpoint and robbed, but they are sticking with South Africa, for all its problems and all their gripes. Conversation turns to how the Parkview and Royal Johannesburg golf clubs are now accepting Jews ("They accepted blacks, so they had to let the Jews in, too") and how awful the swanky redesign of the

Houghton golf course and clubhouse is, and how being a landlord in Yeoville (where my father had his bar mitzvah in 1933) has become impossible; the only thing to do, Myron says, is sell to wealthy black entrepreneurs who know how to deal with the black tenants who have taken over the neighborhood.

The next day I stroll up through Houghton across the rugby ground where my father and uncle spent hours as adolescents attempting drop goals or taking a seven iron and hitting a golf ball between the goal-posts (an unorthodox conversion). I reach Second Avenue, where my grandfather Morris, when he sold the Honey Street house, built the family home opposite the golf course. It is gone now. The adjacent school acquired the land and demolished the house. But the three jaca-randas planted by my grandmother Polly are still there. I reach over the fence and run my hand down the ridges of the trunks. I feel her presence, the soft touch of her hands, the woods of Žagarė. These lines that come out of the past trace the elusive path to belonging.

A friend takes me one Friday evening to the Great Park Synagogue in Houghton, a short walk from Château Michel. Jews moved north as they grew wealthier, and so in time did their synagogue. The pews here, a century old now, are the originals from the Great Synagogue on Wolmarans Street, where my great-grandfather Sidney Adler was married and where South Africa's former chief rabbi, Louis Rabino-witz, once called apartheid "an abomination." The bimah, the ark, and the pulpit are also from the old synagogue, as is the chandelier that hangs from a central dome. The original silverware decorating the Torah scrolls still shines and sparkles, and the synagogue officials still wear top hats and frock coats in the old tradition. The atmosphere is relaxed, familiar, and warm—people chatting among themselves at times, and joining in responses and communal prayers as the spirit moves them. When the time for the sermon comes, in line with the practice at the Great Synagogue, the congregation stands until the rabbi has passed on his way to the pulpit. It is only when the rabbi speaks that there is complete silence among the congregants.

I find myself seated next to Michael Jeffrey Maisels, a physician who lives in Bloomfield Hills, Michigan. He is the son of Issy Maisels, the legendary attorney who led the defense team at the 1956 treason trial in which Nelson Mandela was among the accused. The trial lasted five years; it ended in acquittal. Another member of the defense team at the trial was Sydney Kentridge, my father's classmate at King Edward VII School, one of the Jews who had to stand around with him in the courtyard during prayers. Kentridge was deputed to gather information from Mandela ("Accused Number Six") before the trial. He has told me that "Mandela's answers were always logical and even under horrible cross-examination in court he was always courteous and dignified, just as he was with me. It was something innate." This experience would lead Kentridge to the conviction that "both sides would realize that neither could win."

Maisels says that whenever he returns to South Africa, he likes to come to shul because of the links he feels there with his forebears and the past. I say, yes, I can understand that. It turns out—of course—that his parents were friendly with my grandparents Laurie and Flossie. Community is close and easy among those gathered on the pews of South Africa's Jewish pioneers in the soft glow of the chandelier and the murmur of prayer. This is what my family, and so many other families like them, left behind, a life of habits in a confined setting where everyone knew each other.

Down in the Cape, at Muizenberg, I find my grandfather's house, Duxbury, empty, a FOR SALE sign outside. I clamber over the gate and stand for a moment on the patio looking out across the railway line to the ocean and the Cape of Good Hope. Some things do not change. They are the most reassuring things. There are the rock pools where I would dangle a little net, there is Simon's Town across the water ready to illuminate its necklace of lights at night, and there is the parapet where a black nanny perched me as an infant and told me she was sure I would not want to fall. The fathomless precipice of memory turns out to be a drop of a couple of meters.

Between the railway line and the sea, accessible through a tunnel, is a seawater swimming pool fashioned in the rocks. It was much loved by my great-uncle Willie, the gentle soul and bird-watcher who suffered from manic depression and went through electroshock treatment. He would go out early every morning to swim there. A sign now points to WOOLEY'S POOL. How strange that he should be immortalized in this way, even if the spelling is not quite right. The tidal pool is the most perfect place, never still, washed by tides and winds from the bottom of the world. It is everything and nothing, as true destinations should be. If I am so happy here at Duxbury, in Willie's Pool, so unreasonably happy, it is also because this is where I remember my beautiful mother laughing.

The other side of the world, the journey in reverse, time's arrow going backward: I return to Lithuania in the summer of 2012, not quite two years after my first visit. I drive through my grandfather's drab hometown of Šiauliai, with its tiny Jewish cemetery, and on to Joniškis, where the handsome white and red synagogues (built in 1823 and 1865, respectively) are being restored. On their lunch hour, construction workers sprawl on the floor beside discarded bread crusts. I cannot imagine how a minyan will ever be constituted in these once-crowded places of Jewish worship.

From Joniškis it is a short distance to my grandmother's Žagarė,

A plaque in the main square in Žagarė commemorating the more than 2,200 Jews killed by Nazis and their Lithuanian collaborators on October 2, 1941, was unveiled in 2012. It is the first to occupy such a prominent place in a Lithuanian provincial town. VALDAS BALČIŪNAS

where she wandered on the banks of the River Švėtė and ran her fingers along the ridges in the willow trunks and came to love the cranberries. The small town in which thousands of Jews were annihilated on October 2, 1941, retains its otherworldly aura beneath a canopy of trees. The town is full of storks now. They have returned from winter migration to South Africa.

A few Jews, stranger birds in these parts, have returned with them to attend a ceremony in the main square. The Jewish past has been stirring in Žagarė more than seven decades after Jewish presence died. The square, dilapidated and dismal when I first saw it, is in the midst of repaving and a cleanup (delayed by the discovery during excavation of coins, shoes, and other items from former Jewish stores) in preparation for the unveiling of a memorial.

A plaque inscribed in English, Lithuanian, and Yiddish is to commemorate the slaughter of the town's Jews. It is something almost unique in Lithuania; a memorial acknowledging Lithuanian collaboration in the destruction of the country's Jewish community placed in

On lurching gravestones in one of Žagarė's two disused Jewish cemeteries, Hebrew inscriptions crumble or fade into mildewed illegibility. ROD FREEDMAN

the middle of a small town, rather than deep in the forests where the ditches were dug that collected the heaped bodies of murdered Jews from more than 250 vanished communities.

Rose Zwi, the South African–born author whose *Last Walk in Naryshkin Park* played an important role in summoning her parents' lost Jewish Žagarė from the shadows of denial, is here from Australia. Rod Freedman, the director of the movie *Uncle Chatzkel*—about his great-uncle Chatzkel Lemchen, a renowned philologist who survived the war after losing his parents in the Žagarė massacre of 1941—is also here. He has traveled from Australia, too. To our astonishment, we discover that our mothers were both born in little Krugersdorp, on the South African gold reef.

A small crowd gathers on the square. Žagarė, with the help of the Internet, is reeling in its diaspora children, a far-flung bunch. It is a day of rain and sun, black clouds and bright shafts of light, heat and cool, thunder and quiet. A day like that of my mother's death, when a blue sky suddenly boiled up in darkness and lightning struck as her body was carried out of our London home.

More than one hundred people are seated on rows of chairs. I have already seen the plaque, lying in the back of the car of Valdas Balčiūnas, a young local entrepreneur appalled by the suppression of Žagarė's Jewish past. He was the energetic chief instigator and planner of the memorial project. He has picked up the plaque from stonemasons in Šiauliai. Balčiūnas had described his motivation to Freedman in a letter: "My initiative to unveil the plaque is a small step forward to explain to the locals the truth. I do not want my children to grow up in the world of lies. I do not want the future of the town to be built on a curved foundation."

Now the plaque stands veiled in a just-paved section of the square. The first to speak is Zwi, whose grandparents and other close relatives lie in the mass grave:

> More than three thousand Jewish men, women, and children were massacred by the Nazi invaders and their Lithuanian helpers. . . . To this day there are those who seek to obliterate the memory of this catastrophe. . . . However, a younger generation has become aware that historical facts cannot be distorted. . . . With the setting-up of

this memorial, on the very place where the massacre began, the first step has been taken toward propitiating the unquiet spirits of the innocent victims and salving the conscience of the perpetrators and bystanders. Perhaps, at last, genuine repentance and reconciliation will be achieved. . . . My forebears lived in Žagarė for hundreds of years. . . . It was the place they called Der Heim.

The facts assert themselves. They push through silence, resist denial, undercut manufactured truths, and set curved foundations to right. It can take a long time. As Czesław Miłosz, the Lithuanian-born Nobel laureate, put it, addressing brutal killers of ordinary people in the poem "You Who Wronged":

> Do not feel safe. The poet remembers.
> You can kill one, but another is born.
> The words are written down, the deed, the date.

Rain falls. People cover up, hoist umbrellas. The good rain is on my lips. I think of the late Isaac Mendelson, the last Jew in Žagarė. His son Vidmantas is in the square. Zwi ends her speech with eloquence: "As I stand before this plaque, I am overwhelmed by the thought that my parents and I might also have lain in the mass grave together with my father's family had they not left Žagarė in the 1920s. I never knew them, only saw faded photos many years later, but I mourn them to this day. 'Remember us,' their unquiet spirits seem to call from the grave, as though anyone could ever forget. They do not ask for vengeance, only remembrance. They will always be remembered. And in the language we would have had in common, I say: *Mir zeinen doh!* We are here!"

The plaque is unveiled. Freedman reads the English text: "For hundreds of years Zhager [the Yiddish form of Žagarė] had been home to a vibrant Jewish community. Zhager had many Jewish shops and was a center of commerce for merchants from here and a range of other towns. Many of their shops surrounded this square. Zhager was also famous for its many Hebrew scholars, the 'Learned of Zhager.' German military occupiers and some Lithuanian collaborators brought the region's Jewish men, women, and children to this square on October 2, 1941. Shooting and killing of the entire Jewish community of Zhager began here and continued in the forests nearby. About three thousand Jewish citizens were killed."

These few declarative sentences took seventy-one years to be engraved in stone. Vidmantas Mendelson recalls how his father never spoke of what happened. He says, "I wish everyone peace in your hearts, smiles on your faces, and remember, to see the future you must look into the past."

We are here, reclaiming our story. Cliff Marks, an American urban planner from Washington State who edits a website called Zhager, has made the long journey. Joy Hall, the founder of Lithuania Link, a nongovernmental organization that works closely with the people of Žagarė, has come from Britain. Her Israeli cousin Sara Manobla, who worked as head of the English-language section of Israeli Public Radio, presides at the ceremony. Both are descended from the Towb family of Žagarė. Manobla recounts how the family that saved George Gordimer, the child survivor of the Šiauliai ghetto who now lives in New Jersey and suffers from depression, also rescued two other Jews, Batya Trusfus and her granddaughter Ruth. Each of us, somehow, battles deracination, amnesia, and the knowledge that this continent had decided its Jews must die.

Balčiūnas reads the Lithuanian version. Finally, the Yiddish text is read by Dovid Katz, an American scholar resident in Lithuania who has been passionate in his quest to uncover Jewish history and denounce Lithuanian denial. As Katz later points out in an article, the Yiddish version speaks of "German military occupiers and their Lithuanian collaborators," whereas the English refers to "*some* Lithuanian collaborators." This small difference suggests how ideological battles rage on.

The Museum of Genocide Victims in Vilnius, the Lithuanian capital, still devotes almost all its space to Soviet crimes against a valiant Lithuanian resistance, rather than to the Holocaust in which many Lithuanians were perpetrators. "Double genocide" debates pit Stalin's crimes against Hitler's in what Antony Polonsky of Brandeis University has called "the suffering Olympics." The Lithuanian foreign minister has recently declared through a spokesman that the only difference between Hitler and Stalin was the length of their moustaches. So when a message of sympathy from the minister is read out in Žagarė at the ceremony, it rings false.

The plaque restores meaning to words. It constitutes a small miracle here in my grandmother's *heim*. Žagarė is coming fitfully to life. Its old timber houses, which once struck me as stage flats for some shtetl play, are acquiring volume. The annual cherry festival has been revived. Some of the gravestones in the two Jewish cemeteries are being cleaned up, their Hebrew inscriptions returned to legibility. Schoolchildren are learning about the town's Jewish past. There is even a rumor that a Jewish woman named Sarah has come to live in Žagarė. (She is Sarah Mitrike, a Londoner of Italian descent who came here in 2004 to do social work and ended up marrying the local policeman.) I recall the nameless Jews of my first visit and how the plaque next to a bridge on the River Švėtė commemorating the death on June 29, 1941, of Jonas Baranauskas, who was killed defending "his homeland," seemed offensive through omission. There are no Jewish names on the new plaque in the main square. But it is a start.

The sky clears. Žagarė is filled suddenly with light. A davening Dovid Katz intones the Mourner's Kaddish in Aramaic, and it carries across the square where my family might have met its end and on into the woods where the death trench was dug and out over the Baltic nations now safely ensconced, after long banishment, in the European Union; and the ancient sound restores to me a Europe that vanished and a chain that was severed and a young girl in the woods in all her innocence whose loving embrace I would know.

Mir zeinen doh.

CHAPTER 13

A Single Chain

Anyone who journeys to Jerusalem gazes at rocks and gravestones on the looping ascent into the city. It is a place where the dead carry as much weight as the living. Amos Elon, the Israeli writer, called Jerusalem a "necrocracy," because it is "the only city where the vote is given to the dead." There is no escaping the past. In the dimpled walls and smoothed alleys of the Old City, its impression is written. The restless, entangled memories of Jews, Christians, and Muslims find in Jerusalem their most contentious battleground. Reason here finishes a poor second best to revelation.

On the southwestern slopes of the city, where cats slither over sharp shadows on the grave-packed terraces, my cousin Rena was buried. From her grave, you look down on an ancient landscape dotted with cypress groves, broken up by highways, and crossed by rail tracks tunneled into hills. Her younger brother, curly-haired Yonatan, the most spiritual of the children, found that the experience of mourning cemented a growing identification with Judaism. Rena's suicide was unfathomable. Therefore, Yonatan concluded, you have to let go of the need to understand everything. There is more to this world than you can know.

Jewish ritual struck him suddenly as condensed wisdom—the mourner barred for three days from standing up to welcome anyone, the interdiction on speaking to a mourner until he or she turns to you. "My parents just wanted us to have a little taste, Kiddush on Friday nights," Yonatan says. "But I began to understand how essential Shabbat is. A human doing is not a human being." After the funeral, his distraught mother said, "Maybe we are going to become religious." Yonatan replied, "I think I am already religious."

Yonatan listens carefully and moves deliberately. He is big-limbed like his father. His heavy-eyed smile is radiant. A *kippa* is pinned to his curls. He has gone back, in the revived Jewish homeland, to the books, the rituals, and the prayer that shaped life in the shtetl before the onward-rushing family exodus and emancipation began a little over a century ago. Three generations on from our shared Lithuanian forebears, my cousin has come full circle. He has turned his back on modern ambivalence. Religious belief sets the contours and rhythms of his life. He is a man who has defined his borders. From diet to davening, from synagogue to bedroom, he follows habits observed by my great-grandparents before they headed for South Africa, the uprooting that saved us all from the ditches and the gas of what had been considered European civilization.

His conversion to Orthodoxy was gradual. In the army Yonatan served in a Nachal unit, seeing combat and doing community service. He worked with drug addicts outside Beersheva. He spent time in Lebanon and Gaza. ("In Lebanon at least we knew where the border was and what we were defending. In Gaza, everything seemed gray, borderless, we were trying to defuse tensions between settlers and the local population, it was terrible.") When he emerged after four years, he began to find prayer more meaningful. During a half year teaching English in South Korea, he encountered many Koreans who spoke of the wisdom of the Talmud and wondered how he might approach it and how he, an Israeli, knew less of it than they did. He felt he might learn more from going to yeshiva than from a professor at Hebrew University. Then, in 2003, Rena took her life.

Manic depression lacerates a family, in Jerusalem as in London. The girl from Human Street, my mother, and the girl from French Hill, my cousin, left unanswerable questions. Bipolarity is a violent thing, yet Rena was a creature of peace. She and Yaakov had been very close in age, older siblings Yonatan adored but whose intimacy he could not quite share. A relationship of equals was just beginning between them when she vanished. He had felt in Rena his own yearning for something spiritual at a distance from the new hypermaterialistic Israel. Now Yonatan seeks his sister's essence through the holy books. His starting point is the first major formulation of the Oral Torah, dating from 220 CE. Hillel said: "Be among the disciples of Aaron loving peace and pursuing peace, loving people and drawing them close to the Torah." Aaron haCohen, forefather of all Cohenim, was characterized by the sages as one who pursues peace.

But how is that calling to be fulfilled? Yonatan cites Leviticus, chapter 19, and the dense, difficult mitzvah, or divine commandment, at the heart of it: "Do not hate your brother in your heart. You must surely admonish your neighbor and not bear sin because of him. Do not take revenge or bear a grudge against the children of your people. Love your neighbor as yourself."

Interpretation of the holy texts is the transmission belt of Jewish life as Yonatan now sees it. He tussles with the words. Maimonides interpreted the mitzvah's reference to sin as expressing failed responsibility toward society if someone who has given offense is not rebuked. Other sages have taken a more psychological approach to the mitzvah, arguing that if an offender is not admonished, resentment will fester, leading to hatred in the heart and inability to "love your neighbor as yourself." It is therefore vital to admonish through love.

In observing the mitzvah, a grudge may be removed from the heart, Yonatan argues, and at the same time an enemy or sinner offered an avenue to self-improvement through contrition. "A prerequisite for this is sensitivity. We must first be aware of the other's needs and feelings if we are to pursue peace effectively and fulfill the mitzvah of rebuking through love," he says. "One thing that stood out about Rena, of blessed memory, was her deep sensitivity, to such a degree that I find it hard to describe. This central, deep, and beautiful quality of hers is one everyone in the family can take with them in elevating her soul."

The journals are written in Hebrew just as Zionism is beginning to revive it, page after page penned on the porch of a modest South African house on Honey Street in the Berea district of Johannesburg in the early years of the twentieth century, almost two millennia after the language's hibernation began. They are the work of my great-grandfather Shmuel Cohen, born in Lithuania, founder of the wholesale grocery Cohen & Sons at 103 Pritchard Street in downtown Johannesburg. My uncle Bert, who would go out on the mule-pulled wagons that delivered goods imported from England to Shmuel's South African clients, has treasured the journals without ever understanding them. One day he hands me the frayed soft-covered books and asks if I might find a way to bring them to life.

For a long time I wonder what to do with these reflections of a man transplanted from the shtetl into the emergent South Africa. Late in life Shmuel had a leg amputated as a result of complications from diabetes. Writing then became his consolation. It seems to me that Yonatan, who has returned to something my family spent a century shedding, is the natural translator. The act will draw together the paternal and maternal sides of my family. I have traveled a long way to find both men—a forgotten great-grandfather distilling wisdom acquired over a life in Europe and South Africa, a lost Israeli cousin whose sister suffered as my mother did: patterns within patterns reaching backward as if to mock the inadequacy of the forward-looking gaze.

As Ecclesiastes has it: "That which hath been is that which shall be, and that which hath been done is that which shall be done; and there is nothing new under the sun."

My great-grandfather's journals constitute the framework of a book entitled *The Mindful Being*. Shmuel's Hebrew is eloquent and refined, Yonatan says. The book ranges far and wide, from prehistory to modern times, from evolution to faith. At its core lies an individual quest to structure a life of fulfillment and happiness through acute observation of human behavior and purposeful exercise of the will. It is the work of a free man of faith, writing at the dawn of the isolating modern world in the years between the Enlightenment and the Holocaust—a man who is rigorous in his appraisal of actions and their consequences and seeks to situate God in the theater of rational debate. His idea of religion is inclusive rather than exclusionary. It is arrived at not through revelation but through inquiry about nature and humanity. Its raison d'être is reconciliation—of the ancient and the modern, humankind and nature, the personal and the universal. It makes no territorial or material claims; nor does it promise any reward other than the serenity of mindfulness. It provides a moral and ethical framework for the linked fates of all mankind, with God as the expression of this unity.

Shmuel writes:

> To begin living a life based on the mind, one is to observe oneself first, one's own tendencies. For the more one is aware and refrains from that which triggers one's acting according to a certain tendency the easier it will be to resist. If we observe the world, and realize that one who acted toward us in an evil manner, for example, was forced to do so because of circumstances and perhaps was not able to overcome his inclinations, our anger will soften. For one naturally tends to come to terms more easily with that which is a necessity.
>
> Moreover, if one is aware of one's personal tendencies and whatever prompts acting in a certain way, it is wise to strive to balance them through acting in the inverse way: clinging to subservience to overcome pride, to compassion to overcome anger. One who recognizes the tendencies of his personal character shall be able to weaken the negative ones by awakening positive counter-tendencies.
>
> A man engaged in a mindful life, seeking his own benefit, seeks for true benefit, not for something false or virtual. This benefit must increase his vitality. It shall be increased by his inner happiness, decreased by inner sadness. Love shall increase happiness; hate sadness. Therefore he who lives according to his mind accustoms himself to love all humans. The more the love expands in his heart so does the circle of life. His world expands and extends and he lives with all of creation entirely. . . . He fears not death. He knows that real life is eternal. He fears not annihilation knowing well that in nature annihilation does not exist, but rather only change and transformation.

As I write out my great-grandfather's words, I become part of something I was not, something larger. Belonging is this chain of connection. Over the millennia, ever since Moses received the Torah, words have been passed down, the intergenerational Judaic links. The flimsy exercise books from my father's first home on Honey Street are the familial iteration of all the scrolls and tablets, codices and parchment, that have been the means by which a dispersed Jewish people bore with them an inner homeland.

I am an atheist. Yet I can relate to Shmuel's conception of a God reasoned toward, who is the ultimate expression of the unity of man and nature, a linchpin of the mindfulness for which his life has been preparation. It is a God representing what he calls "the eternal ideals of Judaism in their purest form: absolute justice, absolute peace, and absolute love."

This is not the cruel God of revealed truths invoked in the Holy Land to claim all Eretz Yisrael, a God used to stoke the fires of conflict between two peoples and two national movements with a claim to the same land. This is not the unforgiving God who, from Gaza to Gujarat, is invoked by believers to justify zealotry and violence and discrimination. This is not the God of dangerous certainties endemic to fundamentalism. No, this is God as reconciling idea. It is the God of a man who accepts his own fallibility and the limits of his self-knowledge. It is the God of "whoever saves one soul, it counts as if he saved the whole world." It is the God to whom Israel and those Palestinians who would annihilate it should return, if it is a God they seek. Alternatively they could just deploy reason.

For Shmuel, self-knowledge and sensitivity to others are the basis of a mindful life. He struggles in pursuit of this quest. In another passage he writes:

> Every man is a book worth reading. The "Book of Man" includes many chapters. Those speaking of others I have learned well. The first, speaking of my own character traits, I have learned but do not know. I have sought but not found. Many chapters transcend my wisdom.

The difficulties are redoubled when trauma occurs. My mother, pulled out of her community and set down on a faraway shore, fell apart in the English chill. Manic depression took her from me. Trauma locks in a pattern of defensive behavior that erects a barrier to self-knowledge. It is, in the Lacanian definition, "a missed encounter with the real." And so we repeat the trauma to control its reality, but, as

Zadie Smith puts it, "in doing so reproduce, obliquely, some element of the trauma."

The trauma was my mother's disappearance in 1958 into a redbrick Victorian sanatorium. The trauma was the electricity through her brain three days before my third birthday and again the day before it and again, I know not how many times, in the weeks after it. The trauma was the ensuing silence. Punishing her for that has involved my own disappearances from loved ones, an insatiable quest for consoling vitality (seen as insurance against death-depression and abandonment), and the periodic reenactment of the internal division with which I first protected myself and sought the physical love I had lost.

The only way back to mindfulness and wholeness has been writing down the world as I see it. Words alone bring me to a single voice, a unified being, and an inner peace. Voiceless at the time of the trauma, I have been terrified of the power of words even as I was drawn to them. Words, and through them understanding, were what I did not have as an infant. What was left was repetitive enactment.

I always wanted to tell stories, which involves giving yourself to the moment. Time must weigh on you, its lulls, accelerations, and silences, as I first experienced them in South Africa's Kruger Park. The life within, the deeper story, does not yield itself with ease. War zones give you time. Most of war is sitting around. In Beirut, I watched children on the sidewalks, facades of buildings blown away behind them, constructing elaborate castles of cigarette cartons, flimsy creations that defied shelling as the spirit defies measurement. In Sarajevo, besieged for more than three years, I watched women burn books to heat stoves to cook the rabbits they raised in cages in their bedrooms. Always the smash of a shell, the flat boom of rending and fracture in that narrow valley, took my breath away. Exhaustion followed.

At the Central Bank, in Beirut, I met a young woman. I was waiting. Her name was Sana. Later she took me to her family's shuttered apartment. All but she had fled to Europe. There were heavy drapes over the ornate furniture, and the airless, opulent rooms spoke of a rich life eclipsed. That abandoned apartment taught me something essential about Beirut's cosmopolitan soul, a truth deeper than all the labels of the war's militias, Christian, Shia, Druze, and the rest. Sana taught me about the proud defiance of loss. I felt like a trespasser on family secrets, gazing at formal portraits. Storytellers are trespassers. There can be something indecent about what we do, plunderers of others' lives. The faster we move on, the more indecent it is. I've been the chronicler of too many tears. In the end, I came to my own.

My great-grandfather's struggle is of a different kind, yet it resonates. In the face of injustice and enigma, he pursues an ordering principle:

From the very first day that man is old enough to think for himself he starts collecting materials and building blocks to establish his fort on strong foundations, to be able to rest in it securely in days to come. Working himself continuously, eventually he falls under the burden—just as stones piled incorrectly may tumble down.

While assured in himself, declares he thus: "I am supreme above all creatures," imposing himself over others. Similarly, nations boast, "You have chosen us from all others," only leading to acts of hostility against their fellow nations.

Oh, if only awareness came unto man and he truly knew that all of creation—from the sand granule to the shining star—is connected like one chain. That all are equal and summoned to fulfill their role; that the force of life springs from one source, that it is He who sustains all the children of life. All are intertwined.

All are intertwined in a single chain: over the century since my great-grandfather wrote, the connections linking humanity have increased exponentially, and a conflagration on the scale of World War I, which Shmuel experienced from afar, seems almost impossible. The world is networked. In virtual space, borders have vanished. At the same time, personal isolation has grown. Physical community has weakened as virtual community has spread. More families are scattered or split. Western societies are full of device-absorbed lonely people whose dark secret is the antidepressants they take. They fail to see the single chain.

You can live somewhere for decades, and still in your heart it is no more than an encampment, a place for the night, detached from community. Across the world today millions are bivouacked, dreaming of return, beset by twinges of longing. The inverse is also true: home can sink its roots in little time. But that is rarer than lingering exile.

One day, banking over New York City on the approach to LaGuardia, watching the serried towers of midtown, a single word welled up from deep inside me: *home*. I had left England a quarter century earlier, not through a conscious decision to emigrate but because the life of a foreign correspondent beckoned. I had written about what I saw, what I found below the surface. Often the stories were about lives swept away in the gale of history: the children of Beirut in 1983 who could not sleep without the familiar and so reassuring sound of gunfire; a Polish priest who discovered in middle age he was a Jew, entrusted by his Nazi-murdered parents to a Catholic family; mixed families broken asunder by the Bosnian war as boozy killers injected the virus of sectarian hatred into multiethnic cities like Sarajevo; a German woman unable to contemplate her beautiful blue eyes because they reminded her of a former Nazi concentration camp commander, her father; the difficult mental journey of a prominent Israeli politician from her family's hard-line dismissal of Palestinians to belief in territorial compromise. Often I was drawn to stories of repressed memory and buried truths and Jewish identity. I wandered far and wide, privileged to be the outsider looking in but unsure where I belonged, until I reached New York. There I belonged in a city of "incomers," like my grandparents' nascent Johannesburg; and there I realized I had, after all, left Britain for a reason. I had to put a distance between myself and the locus of the trauma.

The city embraced me. As Robert Frost put it, "Home is the place where, when you have to go there, they have to take you in." It is "Something you somehow haven't to deserve." My mother's unconscious whisper in talking about Jews as she cut her spaghetti was replaced by full-throated bawdiness about the Jewish condition. American citizenship—the miraculous, ever-renewed gathering-in of strangers made equal before the law—conjured away strains of contrived identity. The difference between those who came first and those who came last in the United States seemed negligible beside the intricate matter of British ancestry.

The awkwardness, neither awful nor negligible, was gone: what the poet and author James Lasdun called "that throttling knot of annulled speech gathering in my throat." Lasdun, another English Jew grappling with the murmuring disquiet of that condition, wrote in the same poem of his family in England as "anglophone Russian-German apostate Jews mouthing Anglican hymns at church till we renounced that too." As for self-knowledge, it was "knowledge of not being this or this or this."

Lasdun was a contemporary of mine at Westminster. He moved to New York in 1986 and experienced the same immediate sense of homecoming. Before Westminster, he had been sent to an Anglican boarding school. His Jewish parents had joined the Church of England. They then lapsed into a state of "being not quite English without being unimpeachably Jewish either." At the school, as he relates in *Give Me Everything You Have,* a memoir woven around the trauma of being stalked, he joined the choir and wore a "white surplice with modest pride." Lasdun signed up for confirmation classes, but unease gripped him, intensifying into dread a few weeks before the Bishop of Chichester was to perform the ceremony. The feeling was similar to that of Jonathan Katz, the future head of College at Westminster, before his confirmation. Unlike Katz, Lasdun pulled out. He writes, "Sometimes, looking back, I have been tempted to see this episode as the sign of some authentic core of Jewishness in my soul, recoiling from the act of apostasy." But he sees the decision more "as a kind of surging veto, unaccompanied by any more positive sense of who or what I might be if I was not this." Overall, his feeling throughout his English schooling in the late 1960s and early 1970s was that being Jewish was a form of "mild disability."

I meet Lasdun, whom I have not seen since school days, at a restaurant in Stockbridge, Massachusetts. We go through the long-time-no-see adjustment of linking the physiognomy of adolescence to that of the graying man, a fast-forward detection of unchanging patterns in a changed surface. Lasdun's father, Denys, was an eminent architect whose buildings—from the Royal College of Physicians in Regent's Park to the National Theatre on the South Bank—form part of the texture of London. Yet Lasdun now feels only thinly connected to England. When he was growing up, his father would tell him they were Jewish and not English. They were Jewish by race and Christian by faith and British (perhaps)—until the Christianity lapsed, as Katz's had at Oxford. Assimilation and conversion produced a strange hybrid.

In Sussex, where the family had a weekend house, Lasdun felt his otherness most keenly. Villagers would ask his mother what her "background" was. They would wonder what a woman so olive-skinned was doing in their little church. The message was subtle, a not-quite-anti-Semitic thing that put you not quite at ease. "And so that feeling for me in America of being comfortable in the Jewish part of my identity was novel and unexpected," Lasdun says. "I just felt more at home, that creaturely sense of being among people for whom it is not an embarrassing, awkward, or negative thing."

Our American discovery, or deliverance, is a shared thing. It came late. A sense of home is typically absorbed in childhood. It is the landscape of unfiltered experience, of things felt rather than thought through, of the world in its beauty absorbed before it is understood, of patterns and sounds that lodge themselves in some indelible place in the psyche and call out across the years. My mother's illness came between me and that place.

And what of Israel, offering its open invitation to any Jew? The Jewish question, far from settled by Israel's establishment and success, keeps morphing into new puzzles. I admire and love the country but, South Africa inside me, cannot live with the knowledge of its trampling on "the stranger," the Palestinian whose right to the land and love of the land is equal to the Jews'.

Over many journeys through Israel, Gaza, and the West Bank, I have grown into a liberal Zionist, that dwindling breed. I am critical of the West Bank occupation, convinced that it is incompatible with a Jewish and democratic Israel, and supportive of a two-state outcome. Such criticism is anathema to major American Jewish organizations, particularly the American Israel Public Affairs Committee (AIPAC), whose policy is one of unconditional support for the Jewish state. Unbridled debate about Israel in the United States, in the Congress, and beyond has been curtailed for too long by the orchestrated opprobrium that any public critic of Israel incurs. The president's room for maneuver has also been limited. Support for Israel, it often seems, is not enough unless it is blanket support, however self-defeating the occupation of the West Bank is for the Jewish state.

Across the Atlantic, it is a different story. I am a Zionist because of what I learned of Jewish history on the ground in Lithuania, Germany, Poland, Hungary, France, and other countries. It's not that I fail to see the injury and loss Zionism caused in its triumph; it's that I see no alternative for the Jews, and a Jew is what I am, and there are six million reasons why Jews must mean it when they say "Never Again." Millennia of persecution demonstrated the need for a Jewish liberation movement and a homeland where nobody could tell the Jews they do not belong. Such feelings are visceral more than logical; they are also powerful.

This conviction brings the wrath of the many European intellectuals, Jews among them, who now equate Zionism with occupation, the West Bank with Algeria, and Israel with imperialist expansionism. Tom Paulin, an Oxford professor and poet, writes of the "Zionist SS," a calumny that passes muster among some of Europe's *bien-pensants*. The apartheid analogy, inexact as it is, spreads, not without reason. It gains purchase because the "apartheid wall," "apartheid roads," house demolitions, and land confiscation in the West Bank—as well as the relentless expansion there of the settlements—tell an irrefutable story of the oppression and humiliation of one people by another.

I knew apartheid. I saw how its implacable persecution was applied and codified. Israel's oppression of the Palestinians does not constitute apartheid reborn in the Holy Land. Israel's Arab citizens, 20 percent of the population, enjoy rights unthinkable in apartheid South Africa (and rare for minorities in the Middle East), even if discrimination, both blunt and subtle, exists. Disappearances and judicial hangings were commonplace under apartheid. They are not the stuff of the West Bank treatment of the Palestinians. But as my cousin Pauline discovered long ago as she watched the relentless construction around Jerusalem from French Hill, the apartheid echoes are there for anyone with South African roots. Jews, having suffered for most of their history as a minority, cannot, as a majority now in their homeland, keep their boots on the heads of the Palestinians in the occupied territories.

It would be gratifying if there were perfect justice, if Israelis and Palestinians could learn overnight to live together as equal citizens in some United States of the Holy Land, a binational and democratic secular state that resolves their differences and assures their intertwined futures. But it is an illusion to think this could ever happen. The one-state idea is a pipe dream. The fault lines are too deep. A single state cannot mark its Day of Independence and Day of Catastrophe on the same date. Even where sectarian divisions are less combustible, the regional example of multiethnic states is conclusive: they do not function.

Two states, as set out by the original United Nations Security Council Resolution of 1947, are needed, living side by side in peace and security: the nation-states of the Jewish and Palestinian peoples. The compromises required will be painful for both sides, but the alternative is conflict without end. The messianic idea of Greater Israel, occupying all the land between the Mediterranean and the Jordan River, must die. Palestinians can overcome the crippling divisions within their national movement and accept the permanence of the State of Israel. Competitive victimhood can cede to collaborative viability. The South African truth that my father's classmate Sydney Kentridge intuited long ago, at Nelson Mandela's 1956 treason trial, is also an Israeli-Palestinian truth: neither side can win, neither is going away.

One state, however conceived, equals the end of Israel as a Jewish state, the core of the Zionist idea. Jews will not allow this to happen. They have tried trusting their neighbors and discovered the trust was misplaced. The so-called right of return of the hundreds of thousands of Palestinians driven out in the 1948 war (whose descendants now number in the millions) cannot be exercised, any more than the Jews of Baghdad and Cairo, the Greeks of Asia Minor, the Turks of Greece, or the ethnic Germans of Poland and Hungary have deeds to return home. There can, and should be, agreed compensation for the dispossessed, but there cannot be a reversal of history. The "right" is in fact a claim. As the Israeli novelist Amos Oz once told me, "The right of return is a euphemism for the liquidation of Israel. If exercised there will be two Palestinian states, and not one for Jews." When Oz's father was a young man in Lithuania, walls in Europe said, "Jews go home to Palestine." Now the graffiti screams, "Jews get out of Palestine." Enough said.

One problem is that anti-Zionism easily becomes an alibi for anti-Semitism. The effect of the growing Palestinian-led Boycott, Divestment, and Sanctions (BDS) movement is to put pressure on Israel to end the occupation and settlement construction. This, in theory, is positive. When the largest Dutch pension fund and the largest Danish bank withdraw investments from, or cease business with, Israeli banks because of their operations in the settlements, they send a signal Israel cannot ignore.

Yet these developments make me uneasy because I do not trust the BDS movement. Its stated aims are to end the occupation, to recognize the rights of Arab-Palestinian citizens of Israel to full equality, and to fight for the right of return of all Palestinian refugees. The first objective is essential to Israel's future. The second is laudable. The third, combined with the second, equals the end of Israel as a Jewish state. This is the hidden agenda of BDS, its unacceptable subterfuge. The anti-apartheid movement did not have to deal with any such ambiguity. Those who urged divestment from South Africa had no agenda other than the liberation and enfranchisement of an oppressed black majority. BDS can too easily be commandeered by anti-Semites posing as anti-Zionists who channel the quest for peace in a direction that ultimately dooms Israel as a national home for Jews. As Lasdun has written, "There is something uncannily adaptive about anti-Semitism: the way it can hide, unsuspected, in the most progressive minds."

The Jewish national home is needed. It must now be reinvented. For that, the corrosive occupation has to end, and with it the settlement industry. Israel can be a state of laws again only when the lawless enterprise beyond the Green Line ends. As my cousin Rena knew, Israel requires borders. My great-grandfather Shmuel wrote:

> Were nature to outline borders for humans, as if to say "no trespassing," we would be able to enjoy every delight in the world. But as it is, without borders, we move from one delight to another, finding ourselves, overdoing it, finally in a murky valley.

I have followed the chain back. The search began at the Punta Spartivento in Bellagio, where World War II ended for my uncle, Capt. Bert Cohen of the Sixth South African Armored Division. Now, more than two years later, I find myself paging once more through his war diary.

It is April 9, 1944. Bert is sleeping in a tent in Helwan, Egypt, drinking Egyptian whiskey that "smells like a drain," gazing at the dim, distant lights of Alexandria. He is worried that his Rome family—my grandmother's sisters, the Žagarė-born revolutionaries Assja and Zera and their families—have been murdered by the Jew-hunting Nazis who have occupied Italy. He writes: "My hopes are largely centered upon the thought that I will find Auntie Assja in Italy. That would be a shining hour. Hell, if only I can."

On April 15, 1944, Bert boards the 11,500-ton HMS *Circassia* for the crossing from Egypt to Italy. Searchlights, he writes, "deftly flick their swift fingers across the face of the sky." Five days later he catches his first sight of Europe, "a tongue of brown and green land stretching into the Ionian Sea." For a couple of weeks, as his unit gets organized and awaits orders, he remains in southern Italy among meadows of poppies and fruit trees. He writes a short story called "Forbidden Fruit," about a friend killed picking cherries from a booby-trapped tree. The entry for May 4, 1944, reads: "I could not help wondering at the chain of circumstances that should bring me—plain-routine, rut-living Bertie Cohen of Johannesburg—to be driving in a cumbersome truck through a rural part of southern Italy."

Bert skirts the carnage of the battle for Monte Cassino, abandoned by the Germans in mid-May after repeated Allied assaults. He gets there on July 21, 1944, as he heads north toward Rome, and notes:

Poor Cassino, horror, wreck and desolation unbelievable, roads smashed and pitted, mines, booby traps and graves everywhere. Huge shell holes, craters filled with stagnant slime, smashed buildings, hardly outlines remaining, a silent sight of ghosts and shadows, and the notorious Continental Hotel guarding the long approach of Highway 6 to destruction and havoc beyond belief. Pictures should be taken of this monument to mankind's worst moments and circulated through every schoolroom in the world.

He has taken a brief detour to Capri, to try to find the family there, and reaches Casa Julmira, built by Zera's artist husband. It is a beautiful house hewn into the hill, looking out on the Faraglioni, the island's iconic spurs of rock. Nobody is there. Nobody knows where the family is or if they are alive.

In late July, Bert reaches Rome, liberated a few weeks earlier. He and a friend leave their vehicle in an army parking lot and walk a mile to the Colosseum. It is a hot summer's day. Bert is carrying a huge kit bag crammed with food he plans to offer to the family—if he still has one. Bert has an address for Assja and her husband, Felix Tannenbaum, and their two children, Elena and Mya: Via del Parco Pepoli. Outside number five stands a short, haunted-looking man with startling blue eyes, a bald pate, and a bush of gray hair on either side of it.

"Is this the house of Mrs. Tannenbaum?"

"Bert, are you Bert?"

He and Felix rush into the house. The diary continues: "Bertila! Bertila! Assja sat up in the bed with wild staring brown eyes and shuddered with wide arms. She hugged me and hugged me, weeping and sobbing. I was moved acutely. It was difficult to soothe her. She recovered slightly and begged eager questions about the family."

Bert is struck by young Mya (who would become a concert pianist and later music critic at *Corriere della Sera*), with her "wonderful eyes and lovely mouth and red dress." He calls her "Mee." Dinner is served at eleven p.m.

Platters of macaroni followed by tongue which I had brought, a gay and jolly meal. We went down to the "piano flat," which Elena and Mee share, quite the most beautiful room I know with big deep brown chairs, a dim diffusing light, fat candlesticks. Little Mee played the piano for us very beautifully. She does not seem to strike the keys; rather she strokes the keys and so conjures from them a rapture of melody with the light caresses of her hands. We talked about more happiness and sorrow. We heard of the indomitable courage of these two frail women, Assja and Zera, who preferred to

The Italian branch (left to right): Elena, Assja, Felix, and Mya

hide like lions and not like rabbits when the Nazi Germans bestrode Rome, and they lived in a world of underground intrigue.

I know the Rome apartment, that "dim diffusing light." As a Rome correspondent in the 1980s, I spent many happy hours in it, unaware, then, of shared roots in Žagarė and my uncle's desperate wartime search for his Jewish family in Europe. Mya the pianist married a Polish Jew, Riccardo Landau, and had a daughter, whom they named Assja.

When the younger Assja and I meet in Rome almost seven decades after the wartime meeting of her mother and my uncle, she gives me a box of photographs found discarded in the attic of the Via del Parco Pepoli (now renamed Via di Villa Pepoli). One catches my eye. It is of four children sitting on a rock on a beach in the sun. Two girls sit

*A photo I found in Rome of my father, Uncle Bert, with his hand
on my father's shoulder, and their sisters, Selma and Ann*

on either side of two boys, one of whom is seated, the other kneel-ing above him. Who are they? What is this photograph discovered by chance in a house on Rome's Aventine Hill?

I know the faces of those young boys and the girls also seem famil-iar. It takes me some minutes to realize that the kneeling boy is my uncle Bert, with his hands on the shoulders of my father, Sydney, flanked by their sisters, Selma and Ann. So much has been effaced. The photograph, stumbled upon by chance in Italy, is evidence of life before the scattering, obstinate proof of a story almost forgotten because it seemed better that way.

Three months after reaching Rome, my uncle was in Florence. Toward the end of his long life, he wrote a brief account of how, on

October 14, 1944, the small brown bird that became known as Ishbel settled on his shoulder there and stayed for five days. He recounts how the bird remained as, near Castiglione dei Pepoli, "artillery fire toward the German lines punctuated the night sky and throughout the night the intermittent roar of an American Long Tom, with an echo like rolling thunder, was heard"; and how old Florentine women thrust grandchildren toward him to be blessed; and how an American soldier took a photograph of him with the bird near the Ponte Vecchio. He writes:

> Not five minutes after the photograph had been taken my bird took off and flew across the river that, as the photograph shows, is at least as wide as the Thames at Westminster. I watched it as it flew southward, without so much as a backward glance, and in less than a minute it was out of sight. I stood, dumbfounded, and waited for several minutes before resuming a lonely walk along the right bank of the Arno. I felt bereft. Some fifteen minutes later, as I approached the Lucchesi, I was looking out over the river when I saw a bird flying in my direction. Unbelievably it alighted on my left shoulder. "Where on earth have you been?" I asked angrily, but without being able to suppress my elation. To this day the question remains unanswered.

Like Noah's dove, Ishbel returned to my uncle. In Bellagio, I told the poet Mary Szybist the story of Bert and the bird. Later she wrote a poem called "Another True Story" about the incident, part of her collection *Incarnadine*. The poem concludes:

> Saint Good Luck. Saint Young Man who lived through the war. Saint Enough of darkness. Saint Ground for the bird. Saint Say there is promise here. Saint Infuse the fallen world. Saint How shall this be. Saint Shoulder, Saint Apostrophe, Saint Momentary Days. Saint Captain. Saint Covenant of what we cannot say.

I pass through the Damascus Gate into Jerusalem's Old City. Here Jews and Palestinians rub shoulders still, between the market stalls piled high with oranges and dates and pomegranates and almonds. Palestinians emerging from the Al Aqsa Mosque move toward me on El-Wad Road in a vast throng. They run straight into a group of ultra-Orthodox Jews headed toward the Western Wall, and at that moment, out of the Via Dolorosa, a crowd of Philippine Christians emerges, carrying a heavy wooden crucifix and pausing outside the Armenian-Catholic Church of Our Lady of the Spasm.

It is an impossible scene, funny even: the three great monotheistic religions jostling, maneuvering around the crucifix in the packed alley. The act of mingling seems natural enough. Yet these convergent religious passions can boil up as suddenly as overheated milk.

Resentment seethes beneath the harum-scarum surface. Israel annexed East Jerusalem after the Six-Day War of 1967 but concluded, conveniently, that international law forbade imposing one country's citizenship on another. So Arabs in the annexed territory were granted the status of permanent residents of Israel but not citizenship. The Palestinians of Jerusalem, consigned to limbo by Israel, know the score.

I make my way down to the Western Wall, the only remnant of the Second Temple, destroyed in 70 CE by the Romans. Davening Jews wedge prayers scrawled on slips of paper between the massive stones. The wall buttresses the Temple Mount, where King Solomon built the First Temple of the Jews in about 950 BCE, and King Herod expanded the Second. After conquest by Arabs in 638, the Temple Mount became the site of the Al Aqsa Mosque. The exquisite Dome of the Rock was also built there by a caliph over the Rock of Foundation, believed by Jews to be the spiritual junction of heaven and earth and later identified by Muslims as the place from which Muhammad ascended to heaven to receive the Koran from the Angel Gabriel.

As in Hebron's Cave of the Patriarchs, the two faiths, Judaism and Islam, are interwoven, their holiest places braided together. Nearby, for the third great monotheistic faith, Jesus Christ, the son of God, was crucified. The three religions can no more be disentangled here than the historical argument of Jew and Arab over claims to the Holy Land can be won. What matters is not victory in argument but the victory of coexistence.

In South Africa, thanks to Mandela and de Klerk, the long and hard road of coexistence has been embarked upon. The two leaders heeded, decades after they were uttered, the words of Bobby Kennedy in Cape Town in 1966, addressing all the people of South Africa:

> But the help and the leadership of South Africa or the United States cannot be accepted if we—within our own countries or in our relations with others—deny individual integrity, human dignity, and the common humanity of man. If we would lead outside our borders, if we would help those who need our assistance, if we would meet our responsibilities to mankind, we must first, all of us, demolish the borders which history has erected between men within our own nations—barriers of race and religion, social class and ignorance.

Here barriers harden still. At one corner of the plaza in front of the Wall is the entrance to the Dome of the Rock. Hangdog tour groups gather. A sign says, VISITORS WITH PEACE-MAKERS [*sic*] SHOULD CONSULT SECURITY. Another sign from the Chief Rabbinate says, ACCORDING TO TORAH LAW ENTERING THE TEMPLE MOUNT AREA IS STRICTLY FORBIDDEN DUE TO THE HOLINESS OF THE SITE. The prohibition on Israeli Jews entering the Temple Mount is partly political. Ariel Sharon's visit in 2000 ignited the Second Intifada. It also relates to the religious requirement that entry to the area where the First Temple once stood is permissible only in a state of purity.

I stand in line, pay a fee, and get a ticket. As a Jew of the diaspora, I am permitted entrance. I climb the rigged causeway up onto the wide expanse of sacred ground. The air feels washed, clear, and bright. Winds out of the desert bluster here and there, whistling over the ancient stones. There is Al Aqsa against its cypresses. There is the Dome of the Rock, an octagon within an octagon. At its entrance a Palestinian official bars my entrance as a non-Muslim. I find a wall to lean against, feel the warm sun on my face, the cleansing wind.

I shut my eyes. Once again, as in Cape Town, my mother comes to me and a conversation ensues:

"You know, I have empathy for people who are suffering or in pain. They are familiar. When I found myself in war zones, in Lebanon or Bosnia, it was easy

to write about the wounds of people, physical and psychic. I understood loss with a great facility, and the agitation of memory. All wars become wars to go home. I had a sixth sense about the intersection of wider events and personal plight. In the same way as I began to understand that Jewish displacement across the twentieth century—the story that was ours even if we pushed it away—had a connection to our suffering."

"Do you think so, darling? Well, I suppose we did just try to put all that behind us. It was the past, Jewish or not. I did often feel like a fish out of water. The English have a way of letting you know you are from elsewhere. I got tired of all the throat-clearing and lowered voices. I ached for something that was so hard to articulate. But in the main, we were blessed. I always thought life was a gift. We must be stoic. We must look forward and make the best of things."

"I have found that if you dig at all into people who are depressed, you find that their distress at some level is linked to a sense of not fitting in, an anxiety about where they belong. Freud got the sex, but he did not get the belonging issue."

"I don't know about that, darling."

"You loved Dad very much, didn't you?"

"Oh, I did. I would have done anything for him."

"He was distraught when he lost you, inconsolable."

"I know that through everything he loved me. Everyone's vices are intrinsic to their virtues. Your dad was no exception. Even when his patience ran out, even when he was cruel, he loved me because I had touched the most sensitive point of his nature. That love endures somewhere. It was very pure."

She waved toward the hills and roofs of Jerusalem and turned a smile full of love toward me.

"Sometimes still I can feel what it was, the love you and Dad had for each other."

"You know, darling, if you dislike existence, then death is your release. That is how I feel. Without death there is no resolution. Life becomes a mirror with no back to it. In the moment of passing, I had this light-headed feeling. Somebody was asking me: Who are you? I laughed—I could not remember. That was such liberation. I was free of the flesh that holds you captive."

"Often I have tried to imagine how you suffered. Your suffering appears to me as a featureless expanse. The difference between sadness and depression is the difference between feeling and unfeeling. And I want to make a cocoon of comfort for you."

"It's over, darling, all over now. And look at the beauty around us—the

heedless children, the human circle of hope. Do not underestimate the power of hope. Remember the silver ripples on black water, and remember that even falling leaves dance. Remember the brightness of the waves cresting! Look at the kite, how it swoops through the light!"

I open my eyes. My mother is gone, my reverie over, and all I know is the pleasure of the moment, the "covenant of what we cannot say." I feel whole, not a thought in my head, part of a single chain. I watch an Italian tourist wandering around with a purple sarong over his shorts. I watch boys and girls, the messengers of a new order, kicking a football among the ancient graves. Acceptance—it comes down to that, for acceptance may be bountiful. Epiphanies are overrated. They tend to fade; better the lucid pursuit, in full knowledge, of a full life. This is how I came to this point, and to this place, by this looping road, from such anguish, and I am still alive and full of hope, filled with love. The children's insouciance, their use of the ruins as goalposts, makes me think of the poet Yehuda Amichai's lines about redemption coming for all the peoples of the Holy Land only when a Jerusalem guide tells his tour group:

"You see that arch from the Roman period? It's not important: but next to it, left and down a bit, there sits a man who's bought fruit and vegetables for his family."

The youthful voices rise and eddy, carried by the undivided wind. Peace is theirs to imagine and to will. I skirt the game, take in the shimmering city, and descend step by step toward the covered market—garlanded with delicacies, alive with the chatter of human exchange—in search of sustenance.

Acknowledgments

The writing of this book involved the excavation of memory. Many helped me in my endeavor to restore the past. I met with great kindness and generosity from family, friend, and stranger alike. I cannot thank them all by name. Some who gave profoundly of themselves prefer to remain anonymous.

I began work on the book during a month spent in Italy at the Rockefeller Foundation's Bellagio Center. Thanks to Stephen Heintz and Rob Garris for making this delightful interlude possible. Thanks also to Nick Burns of Harvard University for offering me a Fisher Family Fellowship at Harvard's Belfer Center, and to Cathryn Cluver for her help there. To write a twice-weekly column for *The New York Times* is a demanding privilege. For my liberation to write this book, I thank Arthur Sulzberger and Andy Rosenthal. Serge Schmemann and Stephen Dunbar-Johnson gave me remarkable support throughout, for which I am deeply grateful.

In Lithuania, my thanks go to Paulius Ambrazevičius, Sarah Mitrike, Rod Freedman, Valdas Balčiūnas, Sara Manobla, Rose Zwi, Dovid Katz, Cliff Marks, Joy Hall, Christine Beresniova, Saulius Sužiedėlis, Antony Polonsky, Mejeris Mendelson, Vidmantas Mendelson, Simon Gurevicius, Jonathan Berger, and Zofija Kalendraitė. Special thanks, for their patience and understanding, to George Gordimer and his wife, Dorothy, encountered in New Jersey through our Lithuanian connection.

In South Africa, Trevor Sussman, of blessed memory, his wife, Bernice, and their children were extraordinarily hospitable. Thanks to Sydney Adler, Lynn Adler, Robbie and Di Lachman, Mark Lachman,

Myron and Jan Pollack, Brett Pollack, Greg Mills, Terry McNamee, Joe and Isa Teeger, James Teeger, Susan Teeger, and the late Nadine Gordimer. I am grateful to the staff of the S. A. Rochlin Archives (formerly the South African Board of Deputies Library and Archives), particularly Naomi Musiker. Sebabatso Manoeli was a remarkable and resourceful assistant in my research in South Africa. Andrew Levy, with whom I exchanged ideas before I began writing, ushered me deep into the mysteries of South Africa and my family's existence there.

In Israel, I am grateful to Alex Levac, Sherry Anski, Salam Fayyad, Shlomo Avineri, Amos Oz, Jodi Rudoren, and the staff of the *New York Times* bureau.

Thanks to Jonathan Katz, Marion Underhill, Ed Vulliamy, David Bernstein, Constantine Phipps, Mary Szybist, Richard Bernstein, Assja Landau, Christopher de Bellaigue, James Lasdun, John Field, Peta and Rollie Moskowitz, Kara Moskowitz, Daniel Wolf, Maya Lin, Jose and Amalia Baranek, Charlie Competello, Kati Marton, Erroll Jacobson-Sive, Jane Danziger, Mary Warshaw, Eve Polecoff, Tessa Weber, Noreen Webber, George Packer, Robert Worth, and Dexter Filkins for support, sustenance, and, in some cases, critical counsel on the manuscript. Freya Berry helped my research in London in important ways. Lark Turner did remarkable work over many months to help me uncover, organize, verify, and chronicle the events related here.

I am lucky to have in Amanda Urban an extraordinary agent whose creative support for my work now extends over more than two decades. Sonny Mehta has always encouraged me to write books. At Knopf, I also wish to thank Meghan Houser and Ellen Feldman for their superb professionalism. My particular gratitude goes to my editor, Jonathan Segal, who helped me conceive this idea, prodded me in moments of difficulty, brought his discerning eye to every phrase, and made whatever I did better. It goes without saying that responsibility for any errors is mine alone.

Rebecca Ring made an immense contribution to this book through her insight and intuition. She saw me through.

This is the story of a family over several generations. Without my family's support I could not have reached understanding. I wish to thank my sister, Jenny Walden, who shared more intensely than anyone several of the experiences related here. Francesca Gardiner was a very sensitive reader. Barbara Brown took notes that made a difference. Frida Baranek always urged me to forge pain into expression. The last act of my uncle Bert Cohen, an immense figure in my life, was to read the manuscript with his customary illuminating meticulousness. My father, Sydney Cohen, challenged me to understand.

My children, Jessica, Daniel, Blaise, and Adele, know too much by now of the demands book writing makes on their father. They were a constant inspiration. With this knowledge, on this foundation, may they and their children love, prosper, and be happy.

Notes

CHAPTER 1 *Circle of Disquiet*

4   "If there is any substitute": Joseph Brodsky, *Less Than One: Selected Essays* (New York: Farrar, Straus and Giroux, 1987), p. 150.

9   About eight thousand Jews were still there: In my discussions of the Šiauliai or Shavel Jews in this and subsequent chapters, I relied upon the work of Ellen Cassedy, who details their plight in *We Are Here: Memories of the Lithuanian Holocaust* (Lincoln: University of Nebraska Press, 2012), p. 253. See also *The Šiauliai Ghetto: Lists of Prisoners* (Vilnius: Vilna Gaon Jewish State Museum, 2002), pp. 202–54, and Christoph Dieckmann and Saulius Sužiedėlis, *The Persecution and Mass Murder of Lithuanian Jews* (Vilnius: Margi raštai, 2006). See also Nancy Schoenburg and Stuart Schoenburg, *Lithuanian Jewish Communities* (Northvale, NJ: Jason Aronson, 1996), pp. 271–77 and 389–93.

9   A massacre of at least 2,250 Jews: On the Žagarė massacre, see Rose Zwi, *Last Walk in Naryshkin Park* (Melbourne: Spinifex Press, 1997), an invaluable source for the story of the town and the massacre of its Jews in 1941. See also the chapter on the Žagarė ghetto in *The Šiauliai Ghetto*, pp. 254–58.

14   "sense of personal contamination": Saul Bellow, "A Jewish Writer in America—II," *New York Review of Books,* November 10, 2011.

14   "No one loves victims": Joseph Roth, *The Wandering Jews* (London: Granta Books, 2001), p. 124.

27   "You really had brought": Kafka quoted in Yosef Hayim Yerushalmi, *Zakhor: Jewish History and Jewish Memory* (Seattle: University of Washington Press, 1982), p. 79.

27   "Previous generations *knew* much less": Meyerhoff quoted ibid.

CHAPTER 2 *Bones in the Forest*

31   Seldom did he talk about the catastrophe: Interviews with Mendelson's sons Mejeris and Vidmantas, Vilnius, November 2011.

31   "Asiatic Bolshevik slavery": Quoted in Rose Zwi, *Last Walk in Naryshkin Park* (Melbourne: Spinifex Press, 1997), p. 130.

31   "long-standing Jewish yoke": Ibid., p. 233.

32   "I should like to call you": *Anna Akhmatova: Everyman's Library Pocket Poets* (New York: Alfred A. Knopf/Everyman's Library, 2006), p. 193.

32   The Naryshkins: Zwi, *Last Walk in Naryshkin Park,* p. 245.

33   That year Cossacks swept: Ibid., p. 14.

34   "When my mother evoked": Mya Tannenbaum, *Fuga dalla Polonia* (Novara: Interlinia Edizioni, 2010), p. 104.

35   When Soviet forces: *The Šiauliai Ghetto: Lists of Prisoners* (Vilnius: Vilna Gaon Jewish State Museum, 2002), p. 257.

36   "I can confirm": Jäger quoted in Christoph Dieckmann and Saulius Sužiedėlis, *The Persecution and Mass Murder of Lithuanian Jews* (Vilnius: Margi raštai, 2006), p. 229.

37   "The murder of the Jews": Timothy Snyder, *Bloodlands: Europe Between Hitler and Stalin* (London: Vintage, 2011), p. 345.

37   "rootless cosmopolitans": Ibid., p. 348.

39   He worked for a time: Details on the lives of soldiers in the Sixteenth Lithuanian Division of the Red Army are documented in *Road to Victory: Jewish Soldiers in the 16th Lithuanian Division,* ed. Dorothy Leivers (Bergenfield, NJ: Avotaynu, 2009).

41   On the morning of October 2, 1941: *The Šiauliai Ghetto: Lists of Prisoners,* p. 256.

41   "As these Jews were being led away": Dieckmann and Sužiedėlis, *Persecution and Mass Murder,* p. 226.

42   "The murderers laid her down": Peretzman quoted in Zwi, *Last Walk in Naryshkin Park,* p. 106.

CHAPTER 3   *Gin and Two*

48   "You coolies are not allowed": Bruce K. Murray, *Wits: The Open Years* (Johannesburg: Witwatersrand University Press, 1997), p. 56.

52   With conspicuous exceptions: That Jews disproportionately opposed apartheid is discussed in Gideon Shimoni, *Community and Conscience: The Jews in Apartheid South Africa* (Hanover, NH: University Press of New England, 2003).

54   "foreign": *Jewish Migration to South Africa: Passenger Lists from the UK 1890–1905,* consulted at the South African Jewish Museum, Cape Town.

55   escorted to the Shelter: Aubrey N. Newman, Nicholas J. Evans, J. Graham Smith, and Saul W. Issroff, *The Poor Jews' Temporary Shelter and Migration to South Africa, 1885–1914* (Cape Town: Jewish Publications South Africa, 2006).

57   A few Jews: The history of some of South Africa's most successful businessmen is vividly chronicled in Geoffrey Wheatcroft, *The Randlords: The Men Who Made South Africa* (London: Weidenfeld & Nicolson, 1993). See also Milton Shain, *The Roots of Antisemitism in South Africa* (Johannesburg: Witwatersrand University Press, 2001).

59   "Jewburg": Richard Mendelsohn and Milton Shain, *The Jews in South Africa: An Illustrated History* (Johannesburg: Jonathan Ball, 2008), p. 42.

59   "To the ordinary member of the public": Ibid., p. 45.

59 "sixty-eight Cohens": Ibid., p. 42.

60 "the Jews who had come to South Africa": Milton Shain, *Jewry and Cape Society* (Johannesburg: Historical Publication Society, 1983), p. 12.

64 "My rational mind is nonetheless unable": W. G. Sebald, *The Rings of Saturn* (New York: New Directions, 1999), p. 187.

65 large enough to host a minyan: Ralph Cohen, "Krugersdorp Jewish Community Celebrating Diamond Jubilee on Sunday," *Zionist Record,* April 9, 1954.

65 In 1902 the town's first synagogue: Arthur Tannenbaum, "The Early Days of Krugersdorp's Jewish Community," *Jewish Affairs,* October 1962, pp. 8–11.

69 "This abbreviated form of the Prayer Book": Michael Adler, *Prayer Book for Jewish Soldiers and Sailors* (London: Eyre and Spottiswoode, 1914).

71 "History will ask": Rev. Michael Adler, War Diaries, January 1915–November 1918, University of Southampton Archives, Samuel Krauss Collection; and Michael Adler, ed., *The British Jewry Book of Honour* (London: Caxton, 1922).

CHAPTER 4 *In the Barrel*

73 Sylvia Plath had the same treatment: Sylvia Plath, *The Bell Jar* (London: William Heinemann, 1966), p. 138.

74 I tracked down George Gordimer: This chapter is based largely on a series of interviews I conducted with Gordimer and his wife, Dorothy, in 2012 and 2013.

83 "Germans brought fox and wild boar skins": *The Šiauliai Ghetto: Lists of Prisoners* (Vilnius: Vilna Gaon Jewish State Museum, 2002), p. 210.

83 "the gray zone": Primo Levi, *The Drowned and the Saved,* trans. Raymond Rosenthal (New York: Vintage, 1989), p. 58.

83 "When they ask me for a thousand Jews": Jacob Gens quoted in Paul Johnson, *A History of the Jews* (New York: HarperPerennial, 1988).

84 "The day that our representatives": Miriam Offer, "Medicine in the Shavli Ghetto in Light of the Diary of Dr. Aaron Pik," YIVO Institute for Jewish Research, International Conference, November 3–5, 1996, p. 4.

85 "The only place": Ibid., p. 3.

85 "Injections of potent poisonous drugs": Ibid., p. 5.

87 "Both ghetto gates were besieged": Ellen Cassedy, *We Are Here: Memories of the Lithuanian Holocaust* (Lincoln: University of Nebraska Press, 2012), pp. 248–49; emphasis added.

87 "The SS wants me to kill children": Israel Gutman, *Resistance: The Warsaw Ghetto Uprising* (New York: Mariner, 1998), p. 136.

87 "Though the responsibility for the crime": Quoted in Timothy Snyder, *Bloodlands: Europe Between Hitler and Stalin* (London: Vintage, 2011) , p. 292.

88 "Under conditions of terror": Hannah Arendt, "A Reporter at Large: V—Eichmann in Jerusalem," *New Yorker,* March 16, 1963, p. 58.

88 "The question was to be or not to be": Cassedy, *We Are Here,* pp. 216–17.

89 "The morning after my brother was transported": Declaration given to me by George Gordimer.

94   "In the summer of 1998": A copy of this account for MIT was given to me by George Gordimer.

CHAPTER 5 *Château Michel*

98   An inventory of Isaac's furniture: Found in the National Archives and Record Services in Pretoria, which houses documents of the South African government, institutions, and individuals.

103 Len Miller wrote to me: The history here of the OK Bazaars was informed by conversations and e-mail exchanges with Len Miller, before his death in 2013, and by pages from his father's unpublished memoir.

103 "I normally tell people": Quoted in *City Press,* June 1, 2012.

109 Operation Matateh: Benny Morris, *1948: A History of the First Arab-Israeli War* (New Haven, CT: Yale University Press, 2008).

111 "orchestrated to transmit": Yosef Hayim Yerushalmi, *Zakhor: Jewish History and Jewish Memory* (Seattle: University of Washington Press, 1982), p. 44.

112 "The political misfortune": Freud quoted ibid., p. 111.

115 Barnato was born Barnett Isaacs: This account of his life is drawn chiefly from Geoffrey Wheatcroft, *The Randlords: The Men Who Made South Africa* (London: Weidenfeld & Nicolson, 1993).

116 by then more than five million had been gassed: Cited in Timothy Snyder, *Bloodlands: Europe Between Hitler and Stalin* (London: Vintage, 2011), p. 343.

116 "Jewish resistance in Warsaw": Ibid., p. 292.

CHAPTER 6 *Picnic in a Cemetery*

124 "sufficient defense to any charge": This is from the Immorality Act of 1957, before it was amended and renamed the Sexual Offences Act.

125 "There was a sense of déjà-vu": This section is based on André Ungar, interview by author.

125 "Any person who willfully enters": From the Reservation of Separate Amenities Act, 1953.

126 "I have been reproached": Quoted in Gideon Shimoni, *Community and Conscience: The Jews in Apartheid South Africa* (Hanover, NH: University Press of New England, 2003), pp. 13–14.

127 "The non-intervention of the Board": Arthur Suzman quoted in *Jewish Affairs,* June 1974, pp. 28–29.

128 "There is no occasion": Quoted in Shimoni, *Community and Conscience,* p. 39.

128 South Africa's brave chief rabbi: Shimoni, *Community and Conscience,* provided important details about Rabinowitz.

128 "There are some Jews in the community": Ibid., p. 42.

130 "No form of oppression": Ronald Segal quoted in Richard Mendelsohn and Milton

Shain, *The Jews in South Africa: An Illustrated History* (Johannesburg: Jonathan Ball, 2008), p. 138.

130 "As a result of their upbringing": Cited ibid., p. 139.

130 "a picnic in a beautiful cemetery": Nadine Gordimer, *The Lying Days* (London: Bloomsbury, 2002), p. 366.

131 "commitment to justice": Quoted in Shimoni, *Community and Conscience,* p. 138.

134 Tensions rose: Information on the Sharpeville massacre and aftermath ibid., pp. 64–66.

CHAPTER 7 *Patient Number 9413*

140 "We are in a mental hospital": This section is based on Joy Whitfield, interview by author, August 5, 2012, and a tour of what was the Holloway Sanatorium.

152 "Young children are": Anthony Storr, *Human Aggression* (London: Allen Lane, 1968), p. 80.

CHAPTER 8 *Jews in a Whisper*

158 "In England, whenever I'm in a public place": Philip Roth, *Novels and Other Narratives 1986–1991* (New York: Library of America, 2008), p. 506.

158 "the intergenerational quizzing": Amos Oz and Fania Oz-Salzberger, *Jews and Words* (New Haven, CT: Yale University Press, 2014), p. 35.

159 "I have discovered in myself": Howard Jacobson, *The Finkler Question* (New York: Bloomsbury USA, 2010), pp. 213–15.

160 A year later a young headmaster: Information on John Rae's tenure is drawn largely from his autobiography, *Delusions of Grandeur: A Headmaster's Life, 1966–1986* (New York: HarperCollins, 1994). Further information on John Rae was drawn from his posthumously published book, *The Old Boys' Network: John Rae's Diaries, 1970–1986* (London: Short Books Ltd., 2009).

162 "worked out that half": Quoted in Rae, *Delusions of Grandeur,* p. 76.

163 "Another deterrent": Ibid., p. 87.

164 "No boy who is not a British subject": Interview and e-mail exchange with Elizabeth Wells.

164 "The demography of London": John Field, interview by author, November 2009.

164 "I thought her an unattractive parent": Quoted in Rae, *Delusions of Grandeur,* pp. 87–88.

165 "we needed all the bright boys": Ibid., pp. 88–89.

168 "The European Jew was always a visitor": Karl Shapiro, *Creative Glut: Selected Essays of Karl Shapiro* (Chicago: Ivan R. Dee, 2004), p. 303.

168 "We wanted to shake off the fears": Irving Howe, *A Margin of Hope: An Intellectual Biography* (New York: Harvest/Harcourt Brace Jovanovich, 1984), p. 137.

168 "a self-sufficient people": Ben-Gurion quoted in Karen Armstrong, *Holy War: The Crusades and Their Impact on Today's World* (New York: Anchor, 2001), p. 85.

169 Fifteen years after I left Westminster: This section is based on a series of interviews I conducted with Jonathan Katz in 2013 and 2014.

171 "Wherever they burn books": A widely accepted translation of the original German. Heinrich Heine, *Almansor: A Tragedy* (1823).

CHAPTER 9 *Madness in the Brain*

183 "Everything has gone from me": A suicide note by Virginia Woolf, quoted in Herbert Marder, *The Measure of Life: Virginia Woolf's Last Years* (Ithaca, NY: Cornell University Press, 2001), p. 342.

185 "What is important for a painter": Orhan Pamuk, *Istanbul: Memories of a City* (London: Faber and Faber, 2011), p. 378.

188 "As an experience": Virginia Woolf, *The Letters of Virginia Woolf: Volume IV, 1929–1931* (New York: Harcourt Brace, 1978), p. 180.

189 "The adjective endogenous": Anthony Storr, *Human Aggression* (London: Allen Lane, 1968), p. 74.

190 "At this point in my existence": Kay Redfield Jamison, *An Unquiet Mind: A Memoir of Moods and Madness* (New York: Alfred A. Knopf, 2009), pp. 88–89.

CHAPTER 10 *The Lark Sings and Falls*

204 Rena, I will call her: The account, in this and the next chapter, of my cousin's life and suicide is based on multiple interviews conducted over many months with all her closest family members in Israel, as well as with friends, family, and acquaintances in South Africa and the United States. Because of the painful nature of her story, and its difficult legacy, her family requested that names be changed; I have respected that wish here. I have taken liberties in rendering my cousin's thoughts and doubts. While nobody can be certain of what precisely was in her head at what moment, as her moods careened and her life moved toward its tragic end, the story told here reflects the observations and descriptions of those who knew her best, as well as the often anguished reflections contained in her own journals.

205 "discharge from a deeper wound": Gustave Flaubert quoted in Adam Thirlwell, *The Delighted States* (London: Picador, 2010), p. 21.

210 "The great advantage of being a chosen people": Vikram Seth, *Two Lives* (New York: Penguin, 2008), p. 343.

214 "an international warrant": Benny Morris, *1948: A History of the First Arab-Israeli War* (New Haven, CT: Yale University Press, 2008), p. 65.

216 "If there is one nation": Joseph Roth, *The Wandering Jews* (New York: W. W. Norton, 2001), p. 52.

216 "We pay close attention": Yitzhak Epstein's "The Hidden Question," quoted in Alan Dowty, "'A Question That Outweighs All Others': Yitzhak Epstein and Zionist Recognition of the Arab Issue," *Israel Studies* 6, no. 1 (Spring 2001), p. 40.

218 "It is important to build": Vladimir Jabotinsky quoted in Karen Armstrong, *Holy War: The Crusades and Their Impact on Today's World* (New York: Random House, 2001), p. 103.

CHAPTER 11 *Death in the Holy Land*

224 "Writing is the only way": W. G. Sebald, *The Rings of Saturn* (New York: New Directions, 1999), p. 255.

227 *tzir sterili:* Jonathan Freedland, "An Exclusive Corner of Hebron," *New York Review of Books,* February 23, 2012.

227 "the corruption characteristic": Yeshayahu Liebowitz quoted in Gershom Gorenberg, *The Unmaking of Israel* (New York: HarperPerennial, 2012), p. 66.

227 "If Israel really believed": Ibid., p. 77.

229 "Eretz Yisrael is ours": Yitzhak Shamir quoted in Ian Lustick, *Unsettled States, Disputed Lands* (Ithaca, NY: Cornell University Press, 1995), p. 358.

CHAPTER 12 *The Ghosts of Repetition*

247 "I would like to do portraits": Vincent van Gogh quoted in William H. Robinson, Marcia Steele, and Galina K. Olmsted, *"Adeline Ravoux,* the Innkeeper's Daughter," in *Van Gogh: New Research and Perspectives* (Cleveland: Cleveland Museum of Art, 2014); http://www.clevelandart.org/events/exhibitions/van-gogh-repetitions/supplement/adeline-ravoux.

254 "Do not feel safe": Czesław Miłosz, "You Who Wronged," in *Collected Poems, 1931–2001* (London: Allen Lane, 2001), p. 103.

255 "German military occupiers": Dovid Katz, "Trilingual Memorial Plaque Unveiled on Zhager Town Square," DefendingHistory.com, July 13, 2012.

CHAPTER 13 *A Single Chain*

257 "the only city where the vote": Yehuda Amichai quoted in Amos Elon, *Jerusalem: Battlegrounds of Memory* (New York: Kodansha International, 1995), p. 182.

263 "in doing so reproduce": Zadie Smith, "Man vs. Corpse," *New York Review of Books,* December 5, 2013.

265 "Home is the place where": Robert Frost, *The Poetry of Robert Frost: The Collected Poems, Complete and Unabridged* (New York: Henry Holt, 1969), p. 34.

266 "that throttling knot": James Lasdun, "American Mountain," in *Landscape with Chainsaw: Poems* (New York: W. W. Norton, 2003); James Lasdun, *Give Me Everything You Have: On Being Stalked* (New York: Farrar, Straus and Giroux, 2013).

268 "Zionist SS": Tom Paulin, "Killed in Crossfire," *The Observer,* February 17, 2001.

269 "The right of return is a euphemism": Amos Oz, interview by author, Tel Aviv, January 27, 2013.

270 "There is something uncannily adaptive": Lasdun, *Give Me Everything You Have,* p. 196.

275 "Saint Good Luck": Mary Szybist, *Incarnadine: Poems* (New York: Macmillan, 2013), p. 31.

279 "You see that arch": Yehuda Amichai, "Tourists," in *Poems of Jerusalem and Love Poems* (Rhinebeck, NY: Sheep Meadow Press, 1992), p. 135.

Index

Page numbers in *italics* refer to illustrations.

Printed in the United States
by Baker & Taylor Publisher Services